KANSAS

CURIOSITIES

Help Us Keep This Guide Up to Date

The author and editors have made every effort to make this guide as accurate and useful as possible; however, many things can change after a guide is published—regulations change, facilities come under new management, and so forth.

We would love to hear from you concerning your experiences with this guide and how you feel it could be improved and kept up to date. While we may not be able to respond to all comments and suggestions, we'll take them to heart, and we'll also make certain to share them with the author. Please send your comments and suggestions to 64 S. Main St., Essex, CT 06426.

Thanks for your input!

KANSAS

CURIOSITIES

QUIRKY CHARACTERS,
ROADSIDE ODDITIES
& OTHER OFFBEAT STUFF

FOURTH EDITION

PAM GROUT

**REVISED BY
DEBORAH BOUZIDEN**

Globe
Pequot

ESSEX, CONNECTICUT

To my grandson, Jordan, an adventurer, who has rambled through Kansas many a time, and all the Kansans who opened their hearts and businesses to me as I worked my way through the state revising this book.

Globe
Pequot

An imprint of The Globe Pequot Publishing Group, Inc.
64 South Main Street
Essex, CT 06426
www.globepequot.com

Copyright © 2026 by The Globe Pequot Publishing Group, Inc.

Photos by Pam Grout unless otherwise noted
Maps by The Globe Pequot Publishing Group, Inc.

British Library Cataloguing in Publication Information available

Library of Congress Cataloging-in-Publication Data available

978-1-4930-9299-4 (paper)
978-1-4930-9300-7 (electronic)

The prices, rates, and hours listed in this guidebook were confirmed at press time. We recommend, however, that you call establishments to obtain current information before traveling.

Contents

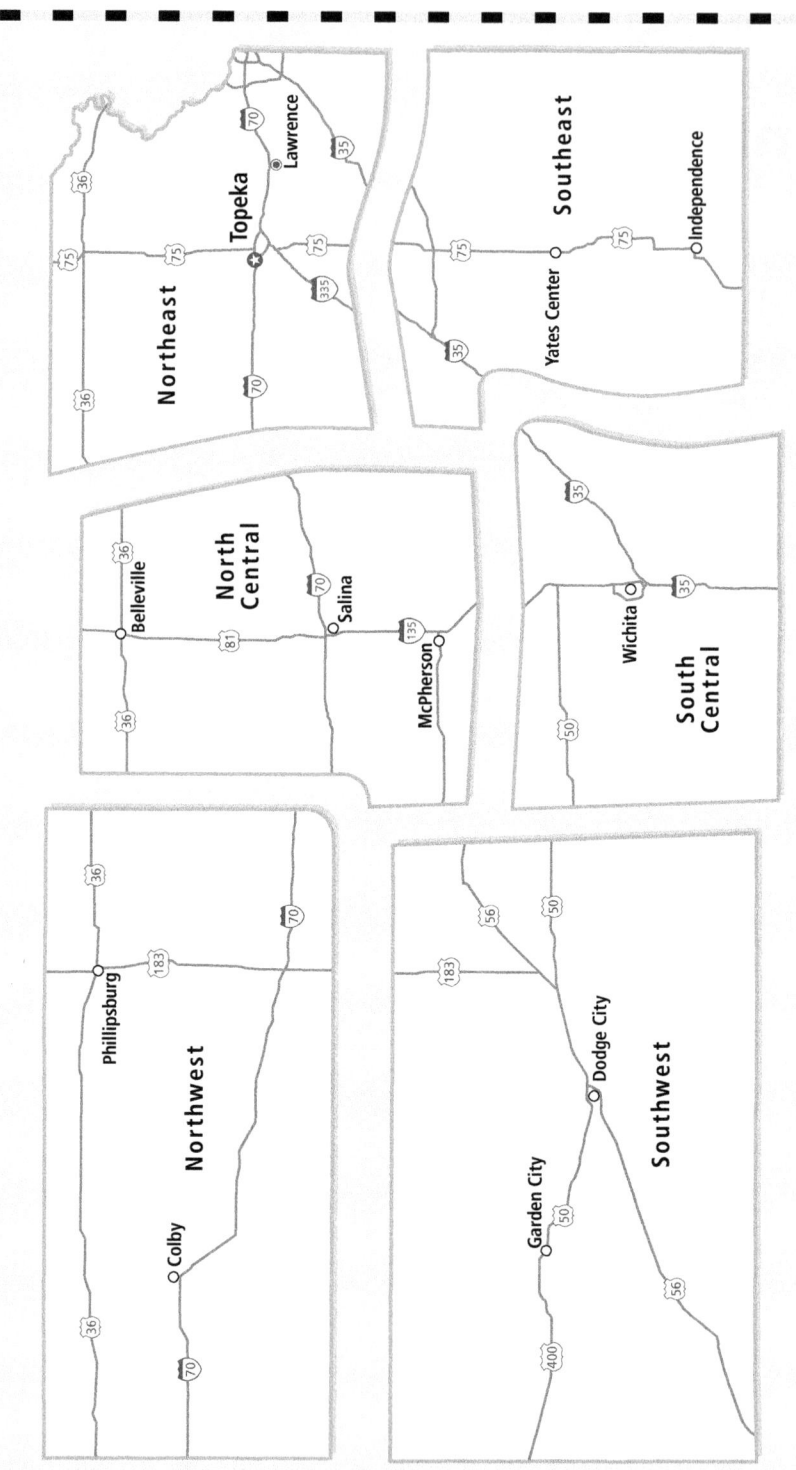

Kansas

Preface to the Fourth Edition

Being as this book is about Kansas, it is fitting I think that I was immediately reminded of the first hay bale maze I went through as a kid. I don't remember where, except that it was in Kansas, probably on the ranch where my uncle Danny worked. I have since graduated to cornfield mazes, and more than once I have felt like I've been in one of those mazes while working on this book.

Imagine a nice, sunny fall day in Kansas. I was excited to see the entrance of the maze. I also knew there was an exit, but getting from in to out would be a challenge. In the beginning, I was thrilled to be on an adventure, but once inside, things changed. It became hot and stuffy, almost smothering at times. I could not see out the top and, looking down the long corridors, everything looked the same. At turns in the maze, I'd take the wrong path, end up at a dead end, have to turn around and go back to the beginning of the directional split; that is, everything looked like where I just came from. I questioned, do I go right or left? After many wrong turns and some claustrophobic moments, I was relieved to finally spot the exit with light pouring in. When I stepped out into the cool breeze, I was glad I went through, but glad to not have to make any more decisions about which way to go.

It was a similar feeling with this book. I knew where to start, where I was going to end, but in the middle of it, I have to admit there were panic attacks and some intense, stressful moments. Having a full-time job only allowed me to work on the book on Friday and the weekends. With each entry I deleted, I had to add an entry and find a picture. I would speak to people, get a good Kansas lead, only to find it led to a dead end, sometimes literally. When I started my third pass through the book, I started to feel a little better, like I could breathe when Sunday night arrived.

Finally, the end was in sight. Every time I finish a book, like going through mazes, I question if I should have done this or that. Sometimes I think I should have zigged when I zagged. Knowing I have good editors helped me not to hyperventilate. When all is said and done, looking at the accomplishment, like making it through one of Kansas's cornfield mazes, makes it all worth it.

I hope you enjoy this literary Kansas cornfield maze. I think you'll enjoy the twists and turns, the places like Belvue and Coldwater, and people you'll meet along the way as much as I did. It was a challenge, but Kansas is worth it. I think you'll think so too.

Introduction

When I was asked to update this book, I have to be honest, I was a little surprised. Globe likes to choose authors based on their being native to the state they write about. After giving it some thought though, I decided to take the assignment. Even though I wasn't born in Kansas, I have spent a lot of time there. And after all, it is the sister state to the state (Oklahoma) I was born and raised in.

My first experience in Kansas is driving through Medicine Lodge on the way to visit my grandparents and aunts and uncles in Wilmore. My uncle worked on a ranch outside Wilmore, which is located in the southwestern part of the state, and my grandparents lived in the town proper right off Main Street. My grandmother's sister and her husband lived across the street, which was actually just a little shared driveway where they would park their car on one side and my grandparents would use the other side.

We'd walk down to the post office to get the mail, and if we were lucky and the only restaurant in town was open, we'd grab a soda before driving out to the ranch where my uncle worked. I remembered him either repairing saddles or loading us in the truck to go find the badger that was harassing the livestock.

Anyone who has been to Wilmore knows it's in the middle of nowhere Kansas. When my parents and another uncle and aunt moved there, I asked why here? Why Wilmore? My uncle told me he used to go to school here and in fact, it was quite a bustling town at one time. As population was only about 60, I didn't believe him until he went and showed me the school's brick foundation. But I'll let you read more about Wilmore in one of the book entries.

I will have to add that Wilmore had one gas station—sort of. It's two pumps that you have to have a key to turn them on. Since everybody in town has a key anyway, I asked my grandfather why they just didn't leave the pumps unlocked. "We don't want riffraff coming in, stealing our gas," he said.

A trip to town meant going to Coldwater, which is about 20 miles away, for maybe ice cream or getting a pizza at Dave's for dinner if it was a weekday. For groceries or any kind of "big" shopping, Dodge City was the destination, and it would be an all-day affair. Most people had gardens; ranchers in the area supplied meat or a planned "huntin'" trip bought in squirrel or rabbit. A trip to the local lake or pond would also supply some fish for the table.

I once heard Kansas described as the "land God forgot" because trees are sparse, and it doesn't have mountains like Colorado. But a drive down I-70, then a turn on any of the county roads, which most call "side roads," and Kansas comes alive. The vineyards, sunflower and wheat fields, cows, and antelope along the way give plenty of personality to the flat land—and that's just for starters. Sure, a tractor or wheat baler may slow you down a bit, but western Kansas people enjoy a slower lifestyle and that's fine by them.

As you go farther east, if you want fast-paced areas with chain restaurants and stores, you can find them in Lawrence, Saline, Kansas City,

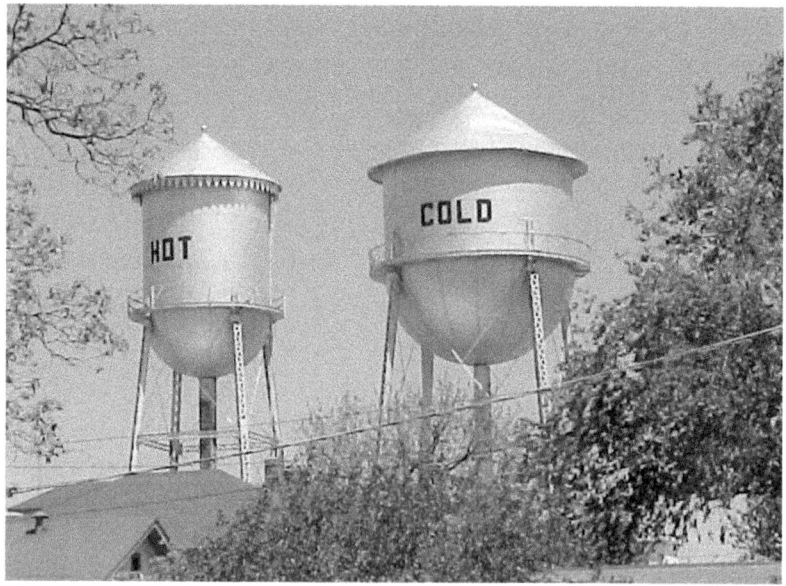

Perchance the only state with two towns with hot and cold water towers?

and Wichita. But there's also Troy, Kansas—home to a taste of Louisiana at Cajun Food Coma—and some other places of interest like the Etzanoa archeological dig and the town of Lincoln, where the Kansas state flag was born.

As far as land diversity goes, in the east you've got your hills and valleys where glaciers once carved the landscape in the north, while rolling hills and oak trees sit predominantly in the southeast. To the west, the terrain shifts to grasslands with rocky soil. The western and central part of Kansas is mostly flat, let's face it, but there are those beautiful red-soiled canyons down by Medicine Lodge that make up for some pretty up-and-down roads. And the drive down I-70 and 25? Where else can you go and see operational trains, antelope, oil, sunflower and wheat fields, a chimney sweep, and acres of windmills? Those two highways are as familiar to me as my own reflection. I drive them at least four times a year and always look forward to stopping at the Braum's in Salina and seeing that chimney sweep up the road from McPherson.

You can get lost on the back roads of Kansas, but that just allows you to find some gems. I once ran across a little antique store just outside Sun City, where I discovered a set of old playing cards that I used for an art project.

No, I don't see Kansas as a state God forgot, I see it as a state God decided to give to ranchers, farmers, and anyone else who wants a different lifestyle. Kansas holds a special place in my heart. My parents, grandparents, aunts, and uncles loved the state so much, they wanted to be buried in its soil. And they are, just outside of Coldwater in the Crown Heights Cemetery. Kansas and all of its people are what makes America who she is. Kansas is truly a state in the heartland with people who make the state what it is.

While writing this book I learned a lot about the state, its people, its places, and the pride the citizens who live here have in their home. Even though I wasn't born here, Kansas too has won a place in my heart. I hope I have done right by the people and places I have introduced you to here, and as you travel around the state you'll find those little oases like Troy, Wilmore, and Sun City. I hope the next time you find yourself in Kansas or just thinking about it, you smile and think that Kansas is perfect and know in your heart it is; its location and its people make it so. It is truly a wonderful place to live and if you are ever fortunate enough to visit, don't hesitate. I bet you'll fall in love with Kansas too.

More Powerful Than a Locomotive, More Liberal Than California

Before we go any further, we need to burst some bubbles, a couple of myths that need dispelling.

About the tornadoes, I can't dismiss the fact that we've had a few over the years. In fact, there used to be a town called Irving, up in northeastern Kansas, that was hit by two tornadoes in one day, something weather forecasters claim is a statistical impossibility.

On May 30, 1879, a little after 4 p.m., the first tornado hit, killing six at the Gale residence (none, as far as I know, was named Dorothy), breaking every bone in the bodies of tethered livestock, and picking up a wagon carrying 1,000 board feet of lumber, which was never seen again. Hardly had the folks of Irving recovered from the first shock when the second tornado blew in from a different direction, flattening what was left.

Did somebody say something about flat? CHARLIE REIDEL

In another incident, in what used to be Codell in Reno County, a twister struck on May 20, 1916, May 20, 1917, and May 20, 1918. May 20, 1919, I'm happy to report, was a beautiful spring day. Then there was the Greensburg tornado on May 4, 2007. It tracked 28.8 miles, killed 12 people, injured 63, and was the first to be rated EF5 on the new Enhanced Fujita Scale.

But despite these anomalies, the fact remains that Kansas is not even remotely close to being the state with the most tornadoes per year. In fact, it's fourth, behind Texas, Oklahoma, and Florida. And if you're keeping tabs on killer tornadoes, it doesn't even make the top 10.

And then there's the issue of being backward. All I can say is, Kansas women have been voting, holding office, and passing bills for almost two centuries. In 1888 an all-woman town council led by a female mayor was elected in Oskaloosa. This was 32 years before women in the rest of the country could even vote. And Oskaloosa's wasn't the first female mayor. Argonia elected Susanna Salter a year earlier.

Kansas was also the first state to ratify the 15th Amendment, giving Black people the right to vote. It was the first to advocate a 40-hour work-week, and the first to push for the 1906 pure food and drug laws.

When Kansas was first settled, it was a place of daring social experimentation. Whole communities were established on such progressive concepts as racial equality, vegetarianism, socialism, and open marriage. In the 1890s, an Irish promoter even convinced English dukes and lords to send their lazy sons to Kansas to train in the art of farming. Runnymede, one of dozens of communities started in Kansas, had a racetrack, a polo field, a steeplechase course, and an official purpose: to dispense agrarian knowledge to the frivolous rich. Hundreds of reform newspapers were published in Kansas, including *Lucifer the Light-Bringer*, a Valley Falls weekly vehement in its quest for equal marriage rights.

Some of the bold experiments failed. Others prospered and led the way in social, religious, and political freedoms for the entire nation.

As journalist William Allen White once said, "Things start in Kansas that finish in history."

Northeast

Northeast

If it weren't for the northeast corner, the state of Kansas would resemble a perfect rectangle, 400 miles long and 200 miles high. Luckily, that end of Kansas looks like a ravenous mastodon came along and gnawed off a big chunk. To my mind, that gives our asymmetrical state a little personality. A tad bit of geographic charisma.

The northeast, of course, claims Kansas City, the state's eponymous and most well-known city, but truth be told, most of what people associate with Kansas City—the Chiefs, the jazz, the barbecue—is situated in the other Kansas City, the one a stone's throw across the river in that wannabe—Missouri.

The one with all the flair—Strawberry Hill and the Ag Hall of Fame—is on our side. Again, Kansans are kinda too busy to spend much time bragging about it.

The northeast also has lots of little towns with fascinating graveyards, motorcycles built out of pull tabs and bones (both chicken legs and cow mandibles), and architecture you won't find in any Frank Lloyd Wright museum. Or at least last we checked, the famous architect wasn't setting old pickups in concrete.

And They Said the Moon Had No Trees
Atchison

I've heard of some pretty crazy gardening techniques—mixing beer with apple juice and ammonia, using Juicy Fruit gum to ward off moles—but the International Forest of Friendship on the slopes of Lake Warnock outside of Atchison might just take the cake. Tree planters there sent a sycamore seed all the way to the moon and back before sticking it in the ground. The Moon Tree, as it's called, was planted from a seed that Command Pilot Stuart Roosa took with him on Apollo 14.

The forest was planted in 1976 when the Ninety-Nines, the International Organization of Women Pilots, decided to uphold the wish of their

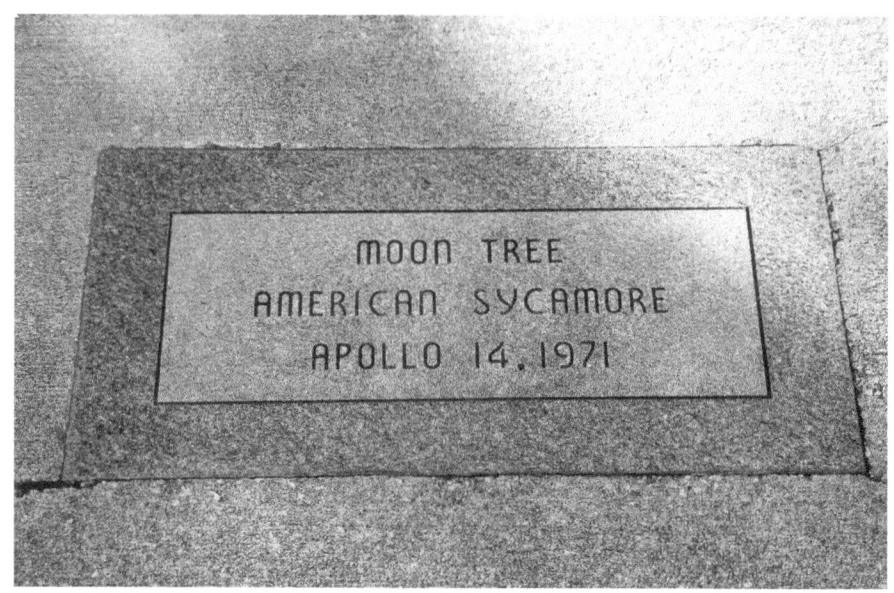

To infinity and beyond! MARY BETH HOWE-BERNHARDT

One giant sycamore for mankind
MARY BETH HOWE-BERNHARDT

first president, Amelia Earhart, who dreamed of world peace through flying. They sent out a plea to members the world over: "Send your native saplings to Amelia's hometown of Atchison."

The saplings, now more than 49 years old, grew into a forest. Joining the Moon Tree are trees from all 50 states and more than 40 countries, a cherry tree from George Washington's Mount Vernon estate, and a redbud from President Eisenhower's home. In addition to a bronze statue of Amelia, there's a walkway called Memory Lane that has more than 750 plaques commemorating aviation and notable pilots the world over.

On the second weekend of September, the Ninety-Nines add more new names and plaques. The forest is located a mile south of the junction of US 59 and US 73. Call (913) 367-1419 or check out www.ninety-nines.org or the forest's website, www.ifof.org, for more info.

President du Jour

Atchison

Unlike most states, Kansas has two presidential libraries. It also has a presidential loser's library (the Dole Institute in Lawrence, which even has clips of Bob Dole's infamous Viagra commercial) and a gallery of Oval Office wannabes (the Gallery of Also-Rans in Norton; see the Northwest chapter).

The older of our two presidential libraries, the Eisenhower Museum and Library in Abilene, is pretty well known. It's one of 10 presidential libraries administered by the National Archives and Records Administration. It gets thousands of tourists each year.

Our other presidential library, the one that honors our 12th president (no, not Zachary Taylor, he was the 13th and hailed from Virginia) is little more than a 35-square-foot kiosk inside the restored Santa Fe Depot that serves as the Atchison County History Museum. Only a few people see it each year.

I should probably explain. David Rice Atchison served as US president for one short day, which could account for why he's usually left off the official list of former presidents. By a quirk of fate, Atchison assumed office when newly elected president Zachary Taylor, a religious man, refused to take the oath of office on a Sunday.

At midnight on Saturday, March 3, 1849, incumbent James Polk's term ended. Since March 4, when Taylor should have taken the oath, happened to fall on a Sunday, he put it off until Monday, March 5, so no one could accuse him of defiling the Sabbath for something as insignificant as a little oath of office.

Atchison, who was president pro tem of the Senate, was, of course, next in line for the job. During his 24 hours in office, he didn't declare war or appoint any of his cronies to office, but he did turn his "unofficial" presidency into a great story.

The Atchison County History Museum has taken its namesake's lead, turning its "world's smallest presidential library" into a great story as well. The kiosk that serves as the presidential library contains a picture of Atchison, who was born in Frogtown, Kentucky; a Civil War pistol he once owned; the one biography written about him; and a copy of his Senate speeches.

To visit the world's smallest presidential library, go to the Atchison County History Museum, located at 200 S. 10th St. (913-367-6238; www .atchisonhistory.org).

Dreams of Flying High
Atchison

If you've ever thought of flying, Amelia Earhart has crossed your mind. You're in luck if you're visiting Atchison because this is where the famous aviator was born, and her birthplace is now a museum. Step back in time, learn what life was like back at the turn of the 19th century, and get a glimpse of what drove Amelia to take to the skies. Her birthplace is located at 223 N. Terrace St.

There are guided tours, self-guided tours, and virtual tours available. Call (913) 367-4217 or visit www.ameliaearhartmuseum.org for more information.

Staying in the same flight pattern, while you're here, make sure to visit the Amelia Earhart Hangar Museum at 16701 286th Rd. Besides interactive activities, you will see *Muriel*, a Lockheed Electra 10-E, which is exactly like

Down-to-earth living AMELIA EARHART MUSEUM

Amelia's childhood swimsuit
AMELIA EARHART MUSEUM

Dining in Amelia's family home
AMELIA EARHART MUSEUM

the plane Amelia flew on her last voyage. Visit www.ameliaearharthangar museum.org or call (913) 372-0021 to check out these wings.

Glad I Didn't Have to Dust Buckingham Palace
Baldwin City

A tiny 24-by-40-foot chapel in Baldwin City was singularly responsible for England's Great Sawdust Shortage of 1995. But that can happen when you're shipping 25,000 stones across the ocean. Ten thousand pounds of sawdust, Great Britain's entire supply, was stuffed into crates that held the 250 tons of rocks sent by ship, by truck, and by rail to Kansas.

Maybe I should start at the beginning.

In 1864, the Methodist congregation in Sproxton, England, a little town about 100 miles north of London, built a church. For six decades this spunky congregation had been meeting in homes of local parishioners, so having a real building was a big deal. All I can think is that they must have had an awful lot of bake sales. The church prospered (which undoubtedly meant more bake sales) for more than a century. But by 1988 the congregation had shrunk and the tiny chapel was forced to close. About the same time, Baker University in Baldwin City got a new dean. He hated to be pushy, but hey, how could a Methodist college not have a chapel on campus?

Up stepped the husband of Clarice L. Osborne, a banker in nearby Olathe. He was looking for some way to honor his deceased wife, so he threw a cool million in the offering plate to bring the church with no congregation to the university with no church.

The Sproxton church was literally taken apart, and all 25,000 pieces were numbered, packed in crates (with five tons of sawdust), and sent to Baldwin. It was reassembled like Legos and dedicated by Margaret Thatcher (her dad, Alfred Roberts, used to preach at the little church) on October 23, 1996.

To see this miracle of modern masonry, visit the Clarice L. Osborne Memorial Chapel on the campus of Baker University in Baldwin City. The chapel is open Monday through Friday from 8 a.m. to 4:30 p.m. Call (785) 594-8439 for more info or go to www.bakeru.edu/clarice-l-osborne-memorial-chapel.

Tom Sawyer Would Be Proud

Basehor

Tom Sawyer—who raked in a kite, 12 marbles, six firecrackers, a tin soldier, and a cat with one eye for allowing his friends to whitewash Aunt Polly's fence—has nothing on Les and Michelle Meyer. The father-daughter owners of Holy-Field Vineyard & Winery have come up with a fall harvest scheme so clever that loyal customers literally fight over the chance to help them pick grapes.

Reservations (and you simply MUST secure reservations) for their picking Sundays, five late summer and fall Sunday mornings when the entire 15-acre vineyard is picked clean, fill up faster than you can say American and French hybrid varietals. If you wait until the fall to reserve your space, you will definitely be S.O.L.

But then Les and Michelle have been forced to be crafty. Running a winery in a state that didn't even allow liquor by the drink until 1987 is no small feat. In 2001, *Kiplinger's Personal Finance* magazine ran a two-page spread about Holy-Field, raving about its Chambourcin, declaring it the best of 65 nonviniferas they sampled. Needless to say, phones started ringing off the wall. All Michelle could do was grit her teeth and tell the potential customers that Kansas law prohibited her from shipping wine. If they wanted to get a bottle or a case, which many wanted to order, they'd either have to come and get it or send friends.

The Meyers have concocted many a scheme to lure customers to "come and get it." Besides the "sold-out" grape-picking weekends, they offer music at the vineyard every Friday night over the summer, with various food trucks present, weddings, and murder-mystery dinners with such clever titles as "It's a Wonderful Death," "When Irish Spies Are Dying," and "Gone with the Passing of the Wind." They also sell an incredible box of wine-filled chocolates.

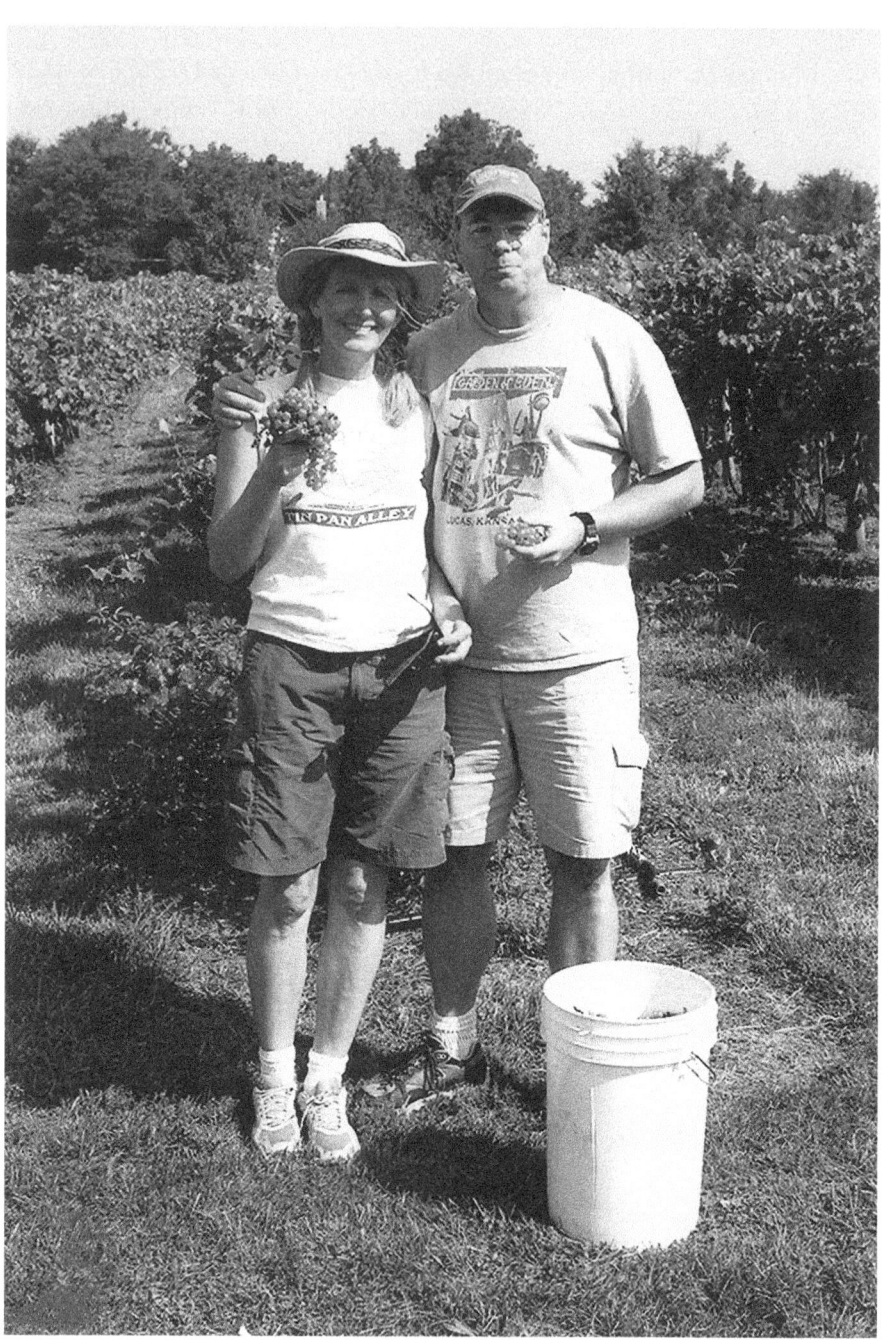

American Gothic without the pitchfork WAYNE RHODUS

The Meyers planted their first vines in 1986, primarily for personal enjoy-ment. As the volume increased and friends insisted, they officially launched Holy-Field Vineyard & Winery in 1994. For 4 years they kept their day jobs. Les was a successful hairdresser. Michelle ran the community blood bank. But then the awards started piling up. In 2005 alone, Holy-Field wines won 31 national and international awards. Now, the awards wall holds well over 1,000 and every year more is added, according to Mandy.

Holy-Field Vineyard & Winery, including its wine production cellar, tasting room, and gift shop, is located at 18807 158th St., just west of Basehor. Call (913) 724-9463 (WINE) or visit them online at www.holyfield winery.com.

Art to Si(lo) For

Belvue

They might look like ordinary everyday silos to the average eye, but to a Kansan, those ubiquitous grain storage bins call to us for more. Make us your canvas, they practically scream. In Emporia, there's a silo that's a spit-ting image of a Coors beer can. Less than a mile away, there's a red-and-white Coca-Cola can.

The Western Resources Oregon Trail Nature Park near Belvue had higher aspirations. The 30-foot silo there has three giant depictions of early Kansas history. There's even a giant map of the Oregon Trail. Onaga art-ist Cindy Martin was commissioned by Western Resources, owners of the 60-acre park, to paint the silo in 1995.

To reach the giant easel, visit Western Resources Oregon Trail Nature Park, a mile east of Belvue, just north of US 24. Phone (785) 456-6100.

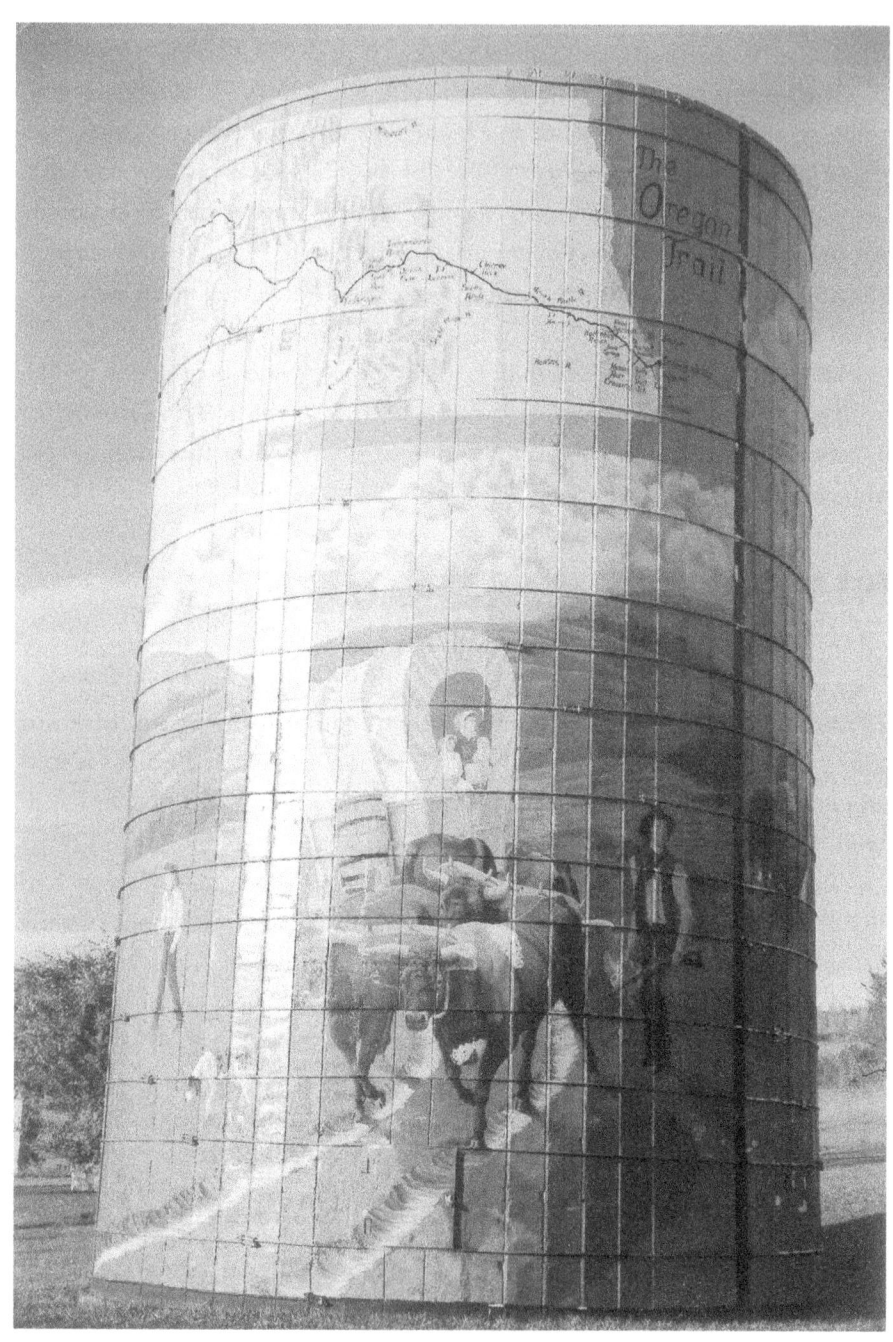

Onaga artist Cindy Martin proves great art doesn't grow on trees.
MARY BETH HOWE-BERNHARDT

Lost Your Marbles? Find Them at "The Moon"

Bonner Springs

Bruce Breslow has heard all the jokes. And he's happy to laugh because while everybody else is losing their marbles, he's busy making replacements. His Moon Marble Company is a one-of-a-kind general store with all kinds of marbles (ever seen marbles with busts of dead presidents inside?), as well as games and toys.

If you call ahead, Breslow will show you his "marble field," two big circles painted on the green carpet, and teach you how to knuckle down.

Ask nicely, and he'll even demonstrate how marbles are made, a unique glassblowing technique that requires a blowtorch, special glasses, and a kiln where the finished products slowly cool off. Breslow's creations, one-of-a-kind art marbles, sell for $50 to $300, but he also sells lots of machine-made marbles (a million or more) that cost a whole lot less.

The most "marble-ous" collection in the Sunflower State
JASON GIBBENS, COURTESY OF MOON MARBLE COMPANY

A woodworker since he was a kid, Breslow started making marbles after he had trouble finding them for the old-fashioned wooden games he was making. Marbles now make up 75 percent of his business.

Most of the marbles for sale are machine-made. In 1997, Breslow was looking for Bumblebees and Boy Scouts, marbles named for their colors. His search led him to a company in West Virginia, where he ordered 8,500 marbles (or so he thought). When the order arrived, it contained 85,000 marbles, and a new career was born.

If you want to tour the marble-ous factory and buy a glow-in-the-dark Moon Marble T-shirt, stop by the store at 600 E. Front St. in Bonner Springs. Call (913) 441-1432 or check out www.moonmarble.com for more information.

Stumps Me: A Retirement Home for Tree Stumps

Council Grove

Council Grove has not one, not two, but three celebrated tree stumps. The town's name, in fact, came from one of the stumps back when it used to be a 70-foot tree. Called Council Oak, the tree with the 16-foot diameter was the official "council site" for the Osage Indians. When government officials decided to seek permission for settlers to pass safely through Osage land, they scheduled a powwow under the tree in August 1825. The big cheese of the Osage, in return for $800, signed a treaty agreeing not to disturb stagecoaches, wagon trains, or others heading down the Santa Fe Trail. Unfortunately, the tree was knocked down by wind in 1958, but its stump is still there, still attracting visitors.

Visitors also can see Post Office Oak, which is also nothing but a stump as of 1990, when the 300-year-old bur oak unfortunately bit the dust. In its heyday, it served as the official post office for travelers on the Santa

Fe Trail. Between 1825 and 1847, travelers going one way left mail in a hole at the bottom of the tree for travelers going the other way. Letters must have been addressed something like, "George Custer, Council Grove Oak."

Which brings us to the third famous Council Grove stump. It's called Custer Elm, and it too is no longer a "real tree." It's named for General George Custer who, before his ill-fated rendezvous at Little Bighorn, owned the land it sits on.

Trivia

Hermit's Cave on Belfry Hill is a tiny rock cave built by Italian religious mystic Giovanni Maria Augustini, who lived there in 1863 before walking 500 miles along the Santa Fe Trail to New Mexico.

Although these stumps are nothing but a shadow of their former selves, they are being treated to a fine retirement under fancy canvases in this historic city on the old Santa Fe Trail. You can pick up a map of historic tree stumps at the Council Grove/Morris County Chamber of Commerce and Tourism, (620) 767-5413, www.councilgrove.com. Council Oak and Post Office Oak are on Main Street, at the 300 and 100 blocks, respectively. Custer Elm is 4 blocks south on Neosho Street, also known as Highway 177.

In-Law Problems

Hiawatha

In the middle of Mount Hope Cemetery in Hiawatha, Kansas, is an extravagant quarter-million-dollar memorial to John Milburn Davis and his wife, Sarah. The memorial, with its 11 life-size Italian marble statues of John and Sarah, attracts nearly 30,000 visitors a year.

Commissioned during the Depression by Davis himself, the expensive cemetery plot was meant to honor Sarah. Or that's what Davis claimed if anybody questioned why all these lavish Carrara marble statues were coming to Kansas from Italy. But naysayers insisted Davis built it to spite his wife's family. Let's just say Sarah's dad wasn't overjoyed when his daughter decided to marry the former San Francisco trolley driver.

Before Sarah died in 1930, the Davises lived a frugal lifestyle. They farmed their 260 acres, saved their money, and refused to buy much of anything, even though they had no children to whom they could leave an inheritance.

After Sarah's death, Davis had a change of heart. He moved the simple Davis headstone from his wife's grave to his brother's plot on the other side of the cemetery. Within a year, the handcrafted marble statues began arriving, each depicting Davis and his wife at various stages in their life together. Davis sent waist, height, hip, and shoe measurements to the Italian sculptors so they'd be realistic in every way. The 11 marble and granite statues include a winged angel version of Sarah in prayer, an empty overstuffed chair, and figures of Davis without his left hand, which he lost to infection.

Needless to say, city fathers were dismayed. They begged Davis to reconsider his lavish spending and to invest instead in the town, which at that time didn't even have a hospital. The eccentric Davis refused, choosing to spend every last penny on the elaborate memorial. He visited the site weekly, and often personally greeted tourists before his death in 1947.

Family feud: John Davis didn't want his money to go to his in-laws when he died, so he "plotted" to spend it on this $250,000 memorial. HIAWATHA CHAMBER OF COMMERCE

Trick or Treat

The oldest Halloween parade in the world, known today as the Halloween Frolic, was started in 1914 in Hiawatha. Mrs. John Krebs, president of the Hiawatha Garden Club, couldn't bear one more year of watching all those costumed trick-or-treaters tramp though the town's flower beds. Rather than fight them, she decided to throw a parade. City fathers pooh-poohed the idea, said it was ridiculous. But it worked, and now, nearly a century later, the parade holds the distinction of being the oldest continuously running Halloween parade in the world. Every year, an effigy of Mrs. John Krebs is pulled through the parade in an antique car with a convertible top.

The parade starts at 7 p.m. every October 31, unless Halloween falls on a Sunday, in which case it's held October 30. For more information, contact the Hiawatha Chamber of Commerce, (785) 742-7136.

Despite his refusal to listen to city fathers, Davis's extravagant memorial has benefited the community. Articles have appeared in *Newsweek, People,* and *Life* magazines, and people troop to Mount Hope Cemetery from around the world.

To pay your respects to Davis and his wife, go east on Iowa Street in Hiawatha from US 73. To learn more about the cemetery and its history, you can call (785) 740-4236.

Starting at the Bottom
Kansas City

John Woods's son Timmy had good reason to send his dad nutritional energy drinks. He was 80, after all, and had undergone five operations. But rather than drink the cases of Boost that Tim, one of six kids, shipped from Omaha, Woods turned them into a team of 24 oxen, 18 feet long. The red plastic bottles, still full (sorry, Timmy), made a splashy art medium.

Of course to John Woods, a former aerospace engineer, pretty much everything was a potential art medium. His first medium, in fact, was the junk he dug up from the bottom of West Lake in LA's MacArthur Park. He owned an antiques store near the landmark lake, and when city officials drained it in 1973 and 1976 for park remodeling projects, Woods hired local panhandlers to poke through its muddy bed. What they brought back was a century's

King of the hill, bottom of the heap

worth of treasure: hundreds of watches, rusty tools, antique toys, corroded trolley tokens, old hotel keys, guns, knives, brass knuckles, and rusty bullets.

"The police confiscated some of the weapons for a while," he said.

Woods patiently cleaned, polished, and cataloged the thousands and thousands of items until one day he started gluing them together, creating whimsical sculptures and three-dimensional maps.

"People call me an artist, but the only thing I know about art is that I'm not interested in it. The only reason I'd ever go to an art opening is if I had a piece in it," he said.

Well, he went to several art openings with pieces and shows, not only in Los Angeles but also in Kansas City, where he moved in 1996. Art patron Bill Wenzel, recognizing Woods's genius, offered him a house next door to his Wenzel Steel Works.

Although he still had banana boxes filled with refuse from MacArthur Park ("We made at least four trips from Los Angeles," Wenzel said), he moved on to other projects such as a 6-by-16-foot rendition of John, chapter 17 from the Bible. He carved more than 10,000 letters with metal tabs to mark the verses.

Much of Woods's works use visual puns such as his *Name Game* (viewers puzzle out dozens of names from an odd assortment of everyday items) or a large piece that used to be in Wenzel's home with dozens of oak letter "E's" in a long pan (Okies from the panhandle) and chairs made of keys (Cherokees).

"His work is magical," said art curator Ginny Brush.

Even though Woods has passed on, his art continues to impress and inspire. John's *Name Game* and other pieces can be viewed at the Grassroots Art Center (www.grassrootsart.net), 213 S. Main St. (785-525-6118).

Gettin' Down and Dirty in the Kansas Heat

Kansas City

If you've ever wanted to start your own vineyard, you might want to volunteer at the Rowe Ridge Vineyard and Winery to see if it's really the sort of thing you want to do.

Back in the 1990s Marc and Pamela Rowe bought 10 acres, west of Kansas City. At the time, it was out in the country. Both held full-time jobs, but they decided to try to grow some vines. Those first vines were planted in 2005. Today, there are 5 acres with approximately 3,000 vines. The Rowes grow nine different varieties of hybrid and American native grapes. "You know, the hardy kind," Pamela said, "the ones that can survive in Kansas."

At first, Pamela worked the winery as an amateur. She had a mentor who taught her the process, someone she could go to who would answer the little and big questions like how long do Concords need to process or what does a diseased vine look like. Pamela's motto is "you learn wine making by doing." When she retired 15 years ago, she moved from amateur to professional. "There's a lot of paperwork when you make that move."

In 2007, the Rowes made their first wines. By 2012, the tasting room was built for those wanting to stop by and sample the 10 wines available. There are dry wines as well as fruit wines. In the summer they serve fruit wine slushies and in the fall they have mulled wine.

Both Marc and Pamela find their peace in the vineyard itself. They both love working outdoors and being among the vines. "It's my summer office," Pamela said, "my tanning salon and gym."

To visit the Rowes, go 1 mile west of I-435 on Leavenworth Road. You can taste their wines and, if you're going to be in the area in late August, perhaps join them in the vineyard and pick some grapes.

Chug-Chug Woo-Woo—Here Comes Food
Kansas City

There's no mistaking a ready order at Fritz's Union Station in Kansas City, Kansas. You'll hear the toot-toot, ring-ring, and chug-a-lug of a miniature railroad car circling the restaurant.

When the train arrives at your table—with burgers, fries, and cherry malts in tow—your order will be dumped off and lowered to the table on a miniature elevator.

Fritz Kropf invented the train back in 1970, not because he had a special affinity for railroads but because he was tired of employees calling in sick. Using a 12-volt heater motor from an old car, Kropf designed an engine that would circle his restaurant, deliver food, and eliminate the need for servers.

Although he now has two patents (on the train itself and on the elevator), it took a while to work the bugs out. The first week, Fritz's newfangled invention accidentally overturned a bowl of chili on a customer's favorite dress.

Fritz didn't conceive his time-saver as an actual train until customers started bringing in railroad memorabilia. The casual drive-in now sports a wide variety of train mementos, from wooden cabooses and train lanterns to railroad station signs. All employees wear red engineer's scarves, customers get paper engineer hats, and the jukebox plays Glenn Miller's "Chattanooga Choo Choo."

Would you like fries with that? MARY BETH HOWE-BERNHARDT

Today, Fritz's is still family owned and operated with two more locations added in the Kansas City area. Carrying on a long family tradition (the restaurant opened in 1954 and celebrated their 70th year of business in 2024), Fritz's still serves the classic burgers with fresh grilled onions and funny names like the Kitchen Sink.

To try the Gen-Dare burger, a popular choice that comes with crunchy hash browns, grilled onion, and melted cheese right on the bun, stop by Fritz's Union Station at 250 N. 18th St. Call (913) 281-2777 or visit www .fritzskc.com.

Popeye Would Be Proud
Lenexa

Every year, on the first Saturday after Labor Day, the Lenexa Historical Society makes the world's largest spinach salad. Using pitchforks and 150 pounds of fresh spinach, 600 fresh mushrooms, 100 cloves of garlic, 12 jars of bacon bits, 75 cups of vinegar, and 50 cups of salad oil, this gigantic salad is mixed in a plastic swimming pool.

Plate-size servings are available at Lenexa's annual Spinach Festival. Once known as the Spinach Capital of the World, Lenexa is where Belgian farmers in the 1930s took their spinach to be shipped to New York and Chicago canneries.

Other zany events at the festival have included Spinach Eve polka dancing, green rock skipping, a dog and owner look-alike competition, and a briefcase throw, which was once profiled by John Madden as one of America's craziest sports. In recent years, Popeye and Olive Oyl have been spotted, stirring the salad, getting it ready for visitors.

The festival is held on the first Saturday after Labor Day at Sar-Ko-Par Trails Park, 87th St. and Lackman Dr. Phone (913) 477-7131 or visit https:// www.lenexa.com/Events-Activities/Festivals-Special-Events/Spinach-Fes tival. You can also google "Spinach Festival Lenexa, Kansas." That'll take you right to the page of events.

The Sunflower Will Come Out, Tomorrow

Lenexa

Tourism in Lenexa suffered a devastating blow in 2008 when Bill Nicks, former director of Lenexa Parks and Recreation, retired and took one of the city's prime tourist attractions along with him. His personal collection of sunflower memorabilia, the world's largest, was proudly displayed in his office at the Lenexa Community Building. Upon his retirement, all 3,556 items—ranging from a 70-pound manhole cover ("I can't divulge where I acquired this piece, but I will say I wouldn't advise jogging in Topeka at night," Nicks said) to a sunflower-shaped flyswatter—were boxed up and taken home to the family basement, a sobering development that realized his wife's biggest fear.

Of course, she should shoulder part of the blame. She's half the reason he started the collection in 1998.

A showcase of Bill Nicks's sunflower collection

Do You Live in a Barn?

Yes, for a while the Adam Legler family did. The barn was built by Legler in 1864 and sat on the Santa Fe Trail, and reports have it that the roof was paid for with cabbage. The family lived on the top floor of the building until their home was complete. in 1972, the barn was deconstructed and then reconstructed in 1983. Today, it is owned and operated by the City of Lenexa and has become the Legler Barn Museum and Depot.

From barn to museum. What an elevation. CITY OF LENEXA

"We noticed we had lots of items with sunflowers around the house—hats, mugs, napkins. One of us said, 'I wonder how many things have sunflowers on them,'" Nicks explained.

The collection blossomed and Nicks became a sunflower celebrity.

"My collection has certainly received more notoriety than it deserves," Nicks said, who appeared on a General Mills billboard, in *Smithsonian* magazine, and on live remotes for the F/X Collectibles channel.

Some of the most unique items in the collection are the sheet music for the 1949 Billboard chart topper "Sunflower," which was sung by Frank Sinatra; an Oscar Wilde perfume card from the 1880s (Wilde considered the sunflower his signature flower); a sunflower ashtray from Paris; and sunflower seeds from Japan.

The good news about the world's largest collection of sunflower memorabilia (Nicks's wife calls it the onliest collection) is it is housed in the Legler Barn Museum and Depot in Lenexa. Nicks still occasionally does presentations. To check the schedule, call (913) 477-7133.

Too Bad Lawrence Welk Didn't Know About This
Manhattan

When Earl Slagle was 10, he got a royal tanning for taking the wheel off his uncle John's new Ford automobile.

It was an innocent mistake. He just wanted to know how the newfangled contraption worked. In 60-some years, Slagle's curiosity didn't wane. Over the years, instead of taking things apart, he put them back together or created them from scratch.

For 35 years, Slagle worked at Kansas State University, first in the horticulture department, then in forestry. Whenever professors needed something—say, a temperature-controlled growth chamber for watermelons, for example—they called on Slagle, who could always figure out a way to build whatever they needed.

After he retired, Slagle turned his attention to his own creative projects. He made everything from 2-by-3-foot Plexiglas bubble machines to catapults for hedge apples. He painted dead apricot trees orange and stenciled still-growing apples with K-State's Wildcat logo. After someone gave him 256 CD-ROMs (probably offering 256 hours of AOL or something), he made what he called "a high-tech tree" with eight arms, 256 hanging CDs, and a glow that would give Francis During's reflector house a run for its money.

"I always have two or three projects going," Slagle said. "I couldn't finish all my projects if I live to be a hundred."

He and his wife, Wanda, lived in a beautiful home in the hills overlooking Manhattan. Earl designed it so there was no sun heating up the house in the summer, but an abundance streaming in during the winter.

Slagle passed away in 2014, but his work lives on at the Grassroots Art Center in Lucas (213 S. Main St.), where several of his art pieces and at least one of his four bubble machines is displayed. Phone (785) 525-6118.

A Bug's Life
Manhattan

Ladies and gentlemen, the thoroughbreds are coming 'round the bend. It looks like . . . oh, my stars . . . it looks like they're neck and neck. Will it be Lane Number One's German Cockroach (*Blattella germanica*) with the two dark stripes, or will it be Lane Number Two's Oriental Cockroach (*Blatta orientalis*) that almost looks black as it streaks by the stands?

At the K-State Insect Zoo in Manhattan, entomologists stage what can only be called the Triple Crown of Cockroach Racing. These derbies, designed to educate and, well, inspire, are held throughout the year at the old Dairy Barn turned Insect Zoo. The K-State Insect Zoo, one of only a few in the world, contains more than 1,000 wriggling, squirming insects, all cared for by a full-time zookeeper.

No need to bring the Raid! Most of the zoo's six-legged denizens are caged in Plexiglas or in cabinet drawers in the demonstration kitchen, where insect cooking demonstrations take place. The Insect Zoo, which consolidates a succession of live insect exhibits scattered around the campus since the school opened in 1863, also has a walk-through tropical rain forest and butterfly garden near a large elm tree. No word on whether or not the derbies serve mint juleps.

To bug out, stop by 1500 Dennison Ave., (785) 532-2847, www.ksu.edu /butterfly.

Rest in Pieces

Maple Hill

When Sarah Ann Oliver died on January 2, 1923, her relatives figured they'd save money on the gravestone by pouring it themselves. Unfortunately, they overlooked one small thing. When they took the stone out of the mold, the letters that looked so perfect in the casting were reversed. So dear old Sarah Ann had to go to the grave with her stone printed backward.

You can find her modest, budget-conscious stone just west of the church that sits in the middle of the Maple Hill Cemetery. Take a mirror to read it. Take exit 341 off I-70, and go left at the intersection. The cemetery is at 2301 S. 34th St.

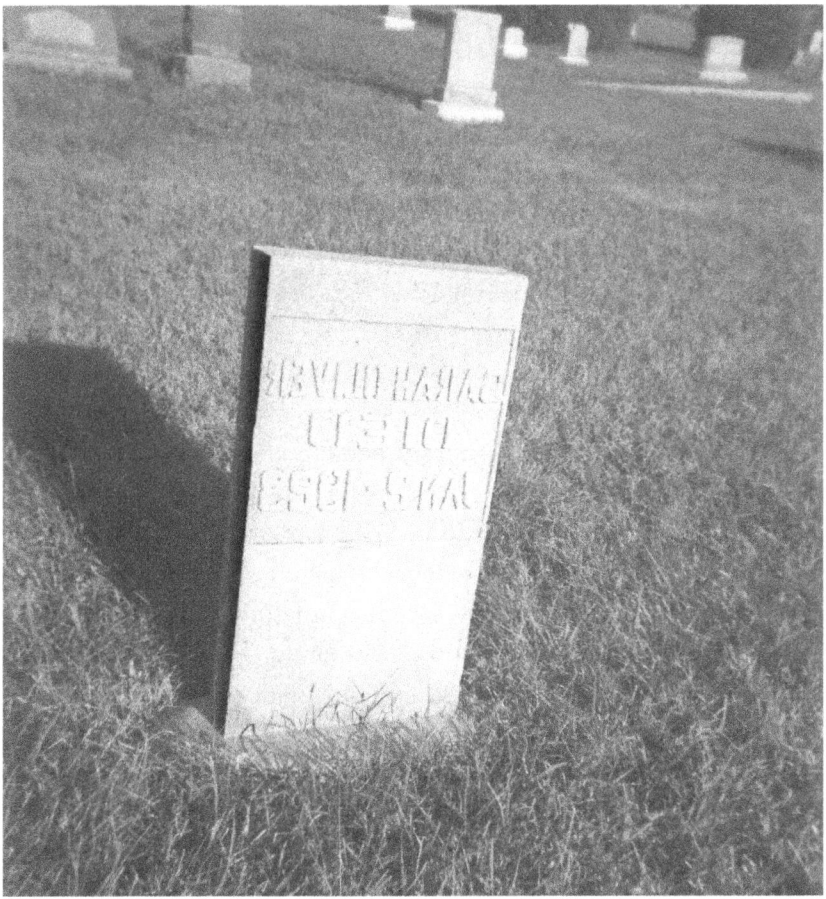

The last time the Oliver family insisted they could "do it themselves" PAM GROUT

Can I Have Your Autograph Before You Starve and Get Eaten by Your Fellow Pioneers?

In May 1846, a westward-bound wagon train got delayed for 5 days while waiting for the swirling floods of the Big Blue River to calm down. This late-May reprieve gave the Donner-Reed party just enough time to carve their names into the sandstone rocks near Alcove Springs. Today, Alcove Springs, as the ill-fated pioneers named this scenic river valley, is not only on the National Register of Historic Places but also has 5 miles of trails through native grasses and wildflowers.

Squirrels in Black

Marysville

Drive in any entrance to this prosperous river town and you'll see big signs proclaiming it "The Black Squirrel City." Indeed, coal-black squirrels have the run of the town, with a city-proclaimed right-of-way on any street, alley, or railroad track. In 1972, city commissioners made black squirrels the official town mascot, granting them immunity from all traffic regulations, freedom to trespass on all county property, and the first pickings of the town's black walnuts.

No one knows for sure where the huge population of black squirrels came from, but the most persistent legend claims a local hooligan unlocked a cage of the dark rodents from a carnival of travelers who camped in City Park for three nights in the 1920s. Evidently, they breed like rabbits, because today most of the town's squirrel population is jet black.

However they got there, there's no question the squirrels are here to stay. Needless to say, the "Black Squirrel Song" is the official town anthem. It goes like this:

Lives in the City Park
Runs all over town
The coal-black squirrel will be our pride and joy
Many more years to come.

Besides the "live" population, there are 51 five-foot-tall black squirrel painted statues scattered throughout town. You can pick up a map at the interpretive site or download one from the town's website that shows where all the squirrels are on parade.

Marysville is located at the intersection of US 36 and US 77.

That's One Heck of a Piece of Corn

Ottawa

From Paul Bunyan to King Kong to "the one that got away," tall tales have always been popular in America. One photographer from Ottawa was particularly good not only at telling tall tales, but at "proving them" with his photographic postcards. William H. "Dad" Martin made his fortune selling what are known today as exaggeration postcards.

That's a Big Baseball

If you are interested in baseball, you should check out the world's largest baseball in Muscotah, Kansas. Located north of Highway 159 on Kansas Avenue, it was constructed from an old steel water tower tank in 2013 to honor Chicago Cubs legend and Baseball Hall of Famer Joe Tinker. The town hoped to put a museum inside the 20-foot-diameter baseball, but that hasn't happened yet. The lack of artifacts will allow you to step inside, spin around, and get a picture inside the massive baseball.

Who says everything's bigger in Texas? FRANKLIN COUNTY HISTORICAL SOCIETY, INC.

After stumbling across some new photography tricks in 1908, Dad started the Martin Postcard Company, which sold more than 7 million postcards with such photos as men riding saddled roosters, pumpkins uprooting farmsteads, and ears of corn that required flatbed trucks for transportation to market.

By superimposing two black-and-white photos and coming up with funny captions such as "Shipping a few of our peaches" or "Harvesting a profitable crop of onions in Kansas," he captured the attention of state secretary of agriculture Foster Dwight Coburn, among others. Coburn, who was already bragging about Kansas's prowess in the fields, sent out hundreds of thousands of news releases claiming such facts as "Kansas sheep have the heaviest fleece" and "Kansas farmers grow more wheat than Belgium and Holland combined."

Soon a rivalry was started with Texas, and tales went something like this: Yeah, Texas grows some big sunflowers, but the sunflowers in Kansas are so big that one night a farmer tied his cow to a sunflower, came out the next day, and thought he'd lost her . . . until he looked up and saw the cow dangling 40 feet up in the air, the distance the sunflower had grown that night.

Martin's whimsical postcards were sent as proof to disbelievers everywhere.

To see some of Dad's giant peaches, stop by the Old Depot Museum at 135 W. Tecumseh St. in Ottawa (785-242-1250) or send electronic versions of the postcards at www.olddepotmuseum.org. The Kansas State Historical Society's Center for Historical Research at 6425 SW Sixth Ave. in Topeka (https://www.kansashistory.gov/p/kansas-museum-of-history/19578)   also curates an impressive collection.

Paris, Kansas?
Rosedale

My friend Ron spent several thousand dollars flying to Paris to see the Arc de Triomphe. He could have saved himself the trip, the money, and the jet lag if he'd only gone to Rosedale, Kansas, instead. Overlooking Turkey Creek, only a short hop, skip, and a jump from the home he shares with his wife, Jana, is a scaled-down but just as pretty version of the famous Paris landmark.

Not that locals pay much attention. Soon after it was built in 1924 to honor World War I soldiers, the WPA came up with a project that required building a 22-foot wall only 82 feet away. Unfortunately, the wall had no stairs, making it next to impossible to get to the Rosedale Memorial Arch. In fact, the groundbreaking drew more people and attention than the monument's dedication 12 months later. Weeds and trees soon overtook the 34-foot arc, which was designed by J. Leroy Marshall, a Rosedale architect. Marshall had made sketches of the "real thing" while serving in the American Foreign Legion.

Lucky for you, the Rosedale Memorial Arch has now been restored to its former glory. You can see it at 35th Street and Booth in the Rosedale section of Kansas City.

They'll Leave ALL the Lights On for You
Shawnee

Put on your saddle shoes, slick back your hair, and get ready for an all-electric blast from the past. The Johnson County Museum of History in Shawnee was the first in the country to preserve and interpret a 1950s suburban home. The entire 1,500-square-foot house, complete with patio

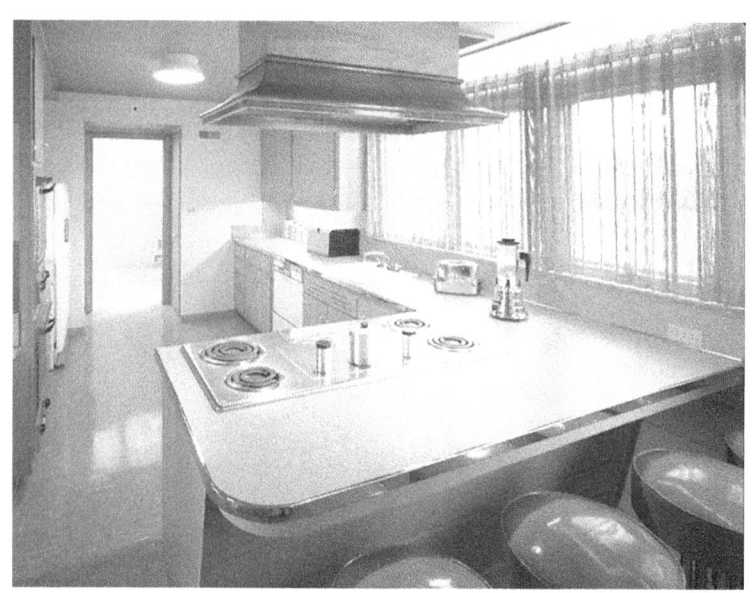

"Modern electric living"
circa 1954
JOHNSON COUNTY MUSEUMS

That dress! Those glasses! JOHNSON COUNTY MUSEUMS

and garage, was moved to the museum from its original site in the Kansas City suburb of Prairie Village. As the centerpiece of the museum's *Seeking the Good Life* exhibit, the house portrays the American dream of owning a home in suburbia. The model home was originally built in 1954, when Ike was president and every kid owned a coonskin cap. Kansas City Power and Light built it to showcase the latest innovations in modern electric living, such as electric curtain openers, waist-high electrical outlets, bed-side remote controls for the coffee maker, and televisions hidden behind slide-away pictures.

To experience the good life, visit the home at the Johnson County Museum of History, 6305 Lackman Rd. If you call ahead, docents dressed in hats and gloves will give your group a tour. Otherwise, you'll have to settle for an ungloved, unchaperoned tour guide. Phone (913) 826-2787 or visit www.jocomuseum.org.

Truckin' A
Topeka

When Topeka health and zoning officials instructed Ron Lessman to pick up the junk on his family's five-generation farm, he took them at their word. He picked up the front ends of six 1940s and 1950s pickups, stuck their rear axles in the ground with 4,200 pounds of concrete, and turned them into megalith billboards, spray-painting his libertarian political philosophy across the doors: rise up, freedum [*sic*] isn't lost.

Truckhenge, as his folk art installation is known, has become a cult tourist attraction, with Lessman giddily leading rambling tours of the trucks, his beer-bottle city (made from thousands of old beer bottles, it whistles and hums on a windy day), his 96,000-square-foot Quonset house, and his newest "henge"—Boathenge—that he erected from old boat hulls.

Built Ford tough TAZ GROUT

"It is a way of saying 'truck you' to the local powers that be," said Bob Cutler, a friend and one of the organizers of Truckhenge's annual free music festival, where bands play in a natural amphitheater on the 56-acre farm. "Truckhenge is Topeka's counterbalance to Fred Phelps and his pickets."

As for Lessman, he's just doing his art.

"I believe in recycling," Lessman said of his penchant for collecting license plates, fossils, rocks, beer bottles, bumpers, and hubcaps and turning them into comical artwork.

Or more useful applications. When the field reviewers from Roadside Attractions asked him if the trucks could be used as a solar calendar, he thought for a moment and said, "Well, the sun does come up here."

If you want to join Lessman and his nose-thumbing, he's at 4124 NE Brier Rd., Topeka, right inside the gate of Victory Sand and Gravel, (785) 234-3486, www.truckhengefarm.com.

Bone to Be Wild

Topeka

Paleontologists piece together bones to create skeletons. Steve Gray, owner of Kickstart Saloon, a Topeka biker bar, pieced together bones he picked up on his motorcycle jaunts around Kansas to make a full-size Harley-Davidson.

The Palencyclist is in a glass-enclosed display at Kickstart. According to the museum-like exhibit, it was made from 10,000 cow and other animal bones and determined, in a meticulous analysis of beer and alcohol spillage, to be the world's oldest motorcycle. Gray claims it was found in 3025 BHD (Before Harley-Davidson).

When asked what compelled him to make the unique motorcycle, Gray answered honestly, "Too much beer."

Kickstart, which also has 150 bras and memorabilia from various motorcycle wrecks on display, is open 11 a.m. to 2 a.m. (the next day) 7 days a week at 2521 N. Kansas Ave., 1 block north of US 24. Phone (785) 232-3422.

Nothing quite like the feel of wind through your hair, bugs in your clavicle . . .

No Shirt, No Pants, No Problem
Topeka

At Lake Edun, a 10-acre lake southwest of Topeka, guests canoe, hike, swim, and play volleyball in nothing but their birthday suits. There's great freedom, members of the private club claim, in not being judged or valued for your designer duds. And besides, there's a lot less to pack for a weekend trip.

Throughout the year, many events are planned. There is the Fancy Easter Hat Group Hike, as well as a reunion where participants are invited to bring their favorite potluck dish. Visitors can participate in the Polar Plunge or help plant flowers and vegetables around the barn in the spring.

So, if you want to get all the way back to nature, in more ways than one, you'll want to check out Lake Edun.

The lake is located at 5501 SW Indian Hills Rd., outside of Topeka. For more information about Lake Edun (*"nude"* spelled backward), you can call (785) 940-0476 or visit www.lakeedun.com.

Only You Can Prevent Forest Fires

Let's hope the Feds don't catch wind of Blind Tiger Brewery's award-winning Smoky the Beer. While we're not sure if it violates the Smokey Bear Act of 1952 that takes Smokey out of the public domain and mandates that all royalties go for education on forest fire prevention, we do know this amber-colored, smoke-flavored beer deserves all the medals it has pulled down since John Dean invented it in Blind Tiger's on-site brew kettle and fermentation tanks. Blind Tiger, named for the Prohibition tradition of hanging stuffed tigers to alert customers to the availability of illegal hooch, brews six hand-crafted, cleverly named ales. Check them out at 417 SW 37th St., Topeka, (785) 267-2739 (BREW), www.blindtiger.com.

They Had to Be Good for Something

Topeka

Environmentalists tell us pull tabs from aluminum cans are dangerous to squirrels, chipmunks, and other curious animals. Herman Divers came up with the perfect solution: He saved the metal rings from beer and pop cans, connected them, and turned them into art.

The retired hospital handyman made everything from a full-size VW bug to a full-size suit of clothes, complete with shoes and umbrella, for both himself and his wife. And maybe there's something about living in the state's capital, because, like Steve Gray, he also made a full-size Harley-Davidson. But instead of bones, Divers's is made out of 179,200 pull tabs.

Divers's unique affinity for pull tabs began in the early 1980s, when he asked the hospital's snack bar attendant if she'd start saving them.

"I told her I was going to make a bedspread. She thought I was crazy," Divers said. "I just figure you can't get into too much trouble when you're working."

When it got harder to find enough pull tabs, Divers branched out into buttons. He made a lamp, a full-size horse, a chair, a button bassinet for his granddaughter, and the cane he used to walk with.

Divers passed away in 2013 (age 90), but to view his amazing pull-tab motorcycle and car (he and his grandson could sit in it), head to the Grassroots Art Center in Lucas, 213 S. Main St., (785) 525-6118, www .grassrootsart.net.

Does this constitute drinking and driving? JON BLUMB.COM

What's a Cajun Like You Doing in a Place Like Kansas?

Troy

When Brandon Adams and his wife, Anita, moved to Kansas from Louisiana 9 years ago, Brandon thought he would continue working as an electrician. Then COVID-19 struck. When work fell apart, he knew he had to do something to support his family, and since he loved to cook, he decided to take his skills on the road—literally—in a food truck. That lasted a couple of years. Finally, he decided to put down roots in a brick-and-mortar building in Troy, Kansas, population 1,000.

Brandon and Anita run the Louisiana-inspired restaurant Cajun Food Coma, and it is a hit. From the crab and shrimp boils to the blackened poor boy sandwiches with sweet coleslaw and Brandon's own signature sauce, repeat customers as well as new customers come to experience swamp-style eats with Cajun flair.

Down in the bayou . . . in Kansas BRANDON ADAMS

While the building is not special, the food is. Anita makes the desserts and according to Brandon, she makes whatever she feels like making that particular day. Everything is custom.

Every Sunday, since the opening of the restaurant, Brandon pulls out the cookbook his grandma and uncles put together for him and makes something out of it. "Being the only grandson and Grandma knowing I like to cook," Brandon said, "she figured I'd like some recipes. I've not made the same thing on Sundays since we've opened."

The restaurant is open 6 days a week. Closed on Wednesday. So, if you're looking for some Southern hospitality and in the mood for some authentic Cajun food, buzz on over to Troy for a culinary experience you won't soon forget. Because business is booming, Brandon and Anita plan on moving their restaurant to Elwood, Kansas, eventually so they can serve more customers. "Things in Kansas move slow, though," Brandon said, "so we'll be here a while longer."

Whispering Giant
Troy

What used to be a 10-story bur oak has morphed into an Indigenous American. Thanks, of course, to a chainsaw and a Hungarian-born sculptor who made it his life mission to carve statues of Native Americans in all 50 states. Peter Wolf Toth calls the monuments he carves out of native trees and stones "The Trail of the Whispering Giants." Toth, who grew up in a family of 11 children, fled Hungary in 1956. He says he has always felt a kinship with the Native Americans who, like his countrymen, were tortured and abused. The statue in Troy, which he started May 1, 1978, took 7 months to carve. The statue's feathers, neck brooch, and headband are composites of those worn by Native Americans from the Kickapoo, Pottawatomi, Iowa, and Sac and Fox tribes that inhabited the area before the white man.

Toth's statue can be seen on the south lawn of Courthouse Square at Main and Walnut.

Smoke signals JAMES S. DICK

What's in a Name?

Valley Falls

Apparently, a lot, if you believe what the folks of Valley Falls have to say. The first settlers landed here in 1854. They found a fall on the Grasshopper River that they planned on having a mill and running a pretty good business on. A town grew up around the mill and Grasshopper Falls would be platted in 1855 and incorporated in 1869. Then disaster struck. In 1870, there was an invasion of grasshoppers. Being an agricultural and farming community, the town didn't think the name "Grasshopper Falls" would be good for business. Nobody wanted to be reminded of an insect that nearly destroyed everyone's livelihood.

So, the town went about getting not only the name of the town changed, but the river too. It took a couple of tries at the town name, but eventually the river was named the Delaware River, after a Native American tribe that used to be in the area, and they settled on Valley Falls for the name of the town.

To celebrate their humble beginnings and keep things real, today the town has a huge celebration every September called Grasshopper Days. Like any small-town festival, there are vendors selling everything from T-shirts to popcorn. Starting in 2025, there will be an artists' alley added to the mix. If you're in the area, they'd love to have you. Hop on over to 409 Broadway St. or simply follow the signs to where all the activity is going on.

Setting the Record Straight

Wamego

If you want the straight scoop on Dorothy, Toto, and the Tin Man (as opposed to the Hollywood version that MGM cemented into our consciousness in 1939), it's high time for a skip through Wamego's Oz Museum.

Oh sure, the museum has the classic movie playing in one of the exhibit areas and displays one of only three remaining flying monkey props (it's made from rubber and has a pipe cleaner tail), but it also has galleries honoring the 13 other Oz books L. Frank Baum wrote, the earlier silent films

We're Off to See the Wizard

Most towns the size of Wamego have let big-box stores bully their way in and steal the show. But thanks to some enterprising business minds, Wamego has managed to keep Lincoln Avenue, its main drag, bustling with locally owned, Kansas-themed businesses. Here's the short list of locally owned products:

Toto's Tacoz serves yellow bricks (burritos smothered in cheese) and courage hot sauce for those with the gall of the Cowardly Lion.

Oz Winery blends such award-winning wines as Run Toto Run, Professor Marvel's Ruby Red, and Witch in a Ditch.

And as for that 9-mile haul from I-70, Wamego simply renamed it "The Road to Oz" in honor of its Oz Museum.

"Most people rely on life's default setting," said Clark Balderson, a longtime Wamego entrepreneur who has built several companies from scratch. "We don't do that in Wamego. We do things our way. We work hard, we think outside the box, and we know that we can make about anything happen."

(one even starred Oliver Hardy of Laurel and Hardy fame as the Tin Man), and board games, toys, and other memorabilia that came out long before MGM got ahold of the Oscar-winning script.

The unique Oz collection, loaned to the museum by Friar Johnpaul Cafiero, a Franciscan priest, has more than 25,000 pieces and is considered one of the world's largest.

To find out the answers to such questions as why the color of Dorothy's slippers was changed from silver (in the book) to red (in the movie), visit the museum at 511 Lincoln, call (866) 458-8686 (TOTO), or visit www.ozmuseum.com.

Shoe-Be-Doo-Be-Doo

Wetmore

A cottonwood tree on John Kissel's Wetmore farm has sole—er, rather hundreds of soles from the sneakers, pumps, clogs, boots, flip-flops, and heels that people have nailed to the old tree. Kissel, who started the "Shoe Tree" in the mid-1980s, leaves a hammer, a can of nails, and a guest book at the base of the tree that has grown adjacent to his family's farm since he was a kid waiting for the mail carrier under its branches. The tree has even inspired a song and an ode to its many glories.

"We get people from all over. They come in limos, buses, and even on horseback," Kissel said, who at 84 could still climb 20 feet into the tree's branches. "We've got a baby shoe, an ice skate, and my old roller skates from 1943."

Recently, the old tree was struck by lightning. While most of it is now gone, there is a large stump that remains with shoes of all kinds still attached. People continue to come to see the relic and add their contribution.

Pome on the Range

I don't know how New York got the nickname "The Big Apple," but whoever coined the term had obviously never been to Wathena, Kansas.

Back in the 1920s, a couple of brothers named Hunt built a two-story wooden apple 3 miles west of Wathena on US 36. This architectural wonder had a ballroom in back, a gas station out front, and groceries and other sundries in between.

When the popular landmark burned down during the Depression, the people of northeastern Kansas were devastated. The Hunt brothers felt obligated to rebuild it, this time a bit larger. When it burned down for the second time on July 12, 1940, the brothers took it as a sign and let "The Big Apple's" memory ease into history's annals.

Shoe Tree Song

Written by Erika Nelson

(Sing along to the tune of "Oh Tannenbaum," aka "Oh Christmas Tree")

Oh Shoe Tree, Oh Shoe Tree
John Kissel's own attraction.
Oh Shoe Tree on 80th and V
How soleful are your branches.
With cowboy boot, sandals, pumps, and clogs
Stiletto heels, and old flip-flops
We nailed 'em to John Kissel's Tree,
The only one in Kansas!

To add your two laces' worth, take Kansas Highway 9 1 mile west of Wetmore; then go north on W for 5 miles to 80th. It's 1 mile west at the junction of 80th and V.

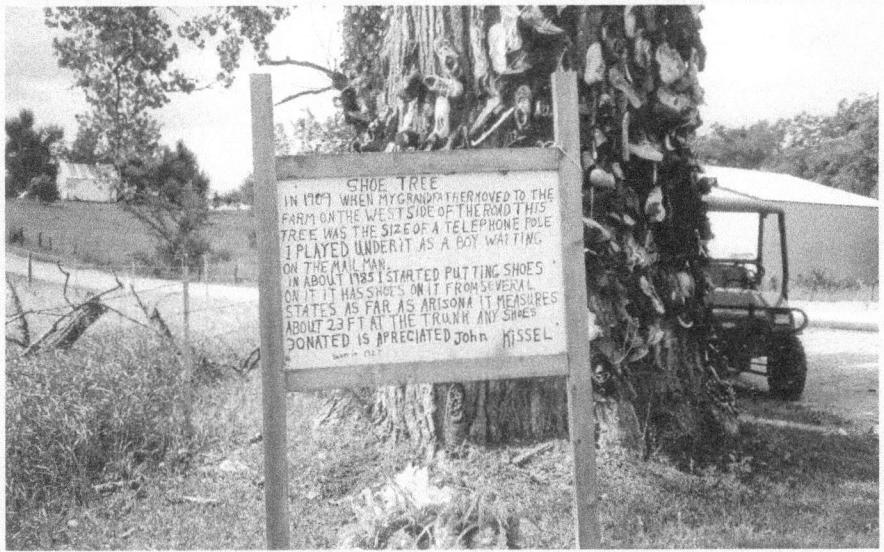

The shoe must go on. JOHN KISSEL

The "Pig" Chill
White Cloud

The piggy bank was invented in White Cloud, a little town of 300 on the Nebraska–Iowa border. In 1913, 10-year-old Wilbur Chapman was devastated when a missionary on leave from a leper colony came to town spouting chilling stories of leprosy's horrible ravages. The missionary, who happened to be an uncle of Wilbur's, claimed chaulmoogra oil could relieve suffering, and that 10 kids could be treated for only $25.

Wilbur took it upon himself to help his uncle's lepers. His scheme, a classic capitalist dictum (buy low, sell high) involved a piglet he named Pete. He bought the small pig for $3, fattened him up on slops, sold him for $25, and donated the entire amount to the American Mission to Lepers.

The news of his selfless act got around, and before you knew it, people around the country began saving their spare coins in pig-shaped containers. Thanks to an article in the *Sunday School Times*, a one-page newsletter distributed to hundreds of thousands of churches, more than $1 million was raised in "pig containers" to fight leprosy. Many of those first piggy banks were known as Pete 2.

The monument to Wilbur Chapman, an obelisk-shaped memorial made of native rock and concrete that was dedicated in 1938, stands just east of the front door of the Community Christian Church on Main Street. (785) 595-3261.

Barn Again
White Cloud and the rest of Doniphan County

The historic barn tour of Doniphan County doesn't have a tour guide or an air-conditioned bus. For that matter, it doesn't even have a bus without air-conditioning. But it does have a brochure that can be picked up at the local county courthouse, 120 E. Chestnut, in Troy. The brochure can also be downloaded at https://dpcountyks.com.

The List Goes On. . . .

Also in Doniphan County:

- Fifty ghost towns
- A lookout along the Missouri River where you can see the four states of Kansas, Iowa, Nebraska, and Missouri. The four-state lookout is 4 blocks from Highway 7, near White Cloud. Follow the signs.
- Wolf River Bob, an ex–Hollywood stuntman, trick bullwhipper, and mapper of the Lewis and Clark Trail, who knows virtually everything there is to know about White Cloud, which he calls "the Switzerland of Kansas"
- A stone where Lewis and Clark, who camped there in 1804, carved their names
- An entire downtown listed on the National Register of Historic Places and used for the filming of the 1973 movie *Paper Moon*

This two-color brochure lists several barns that can be driven by, gawked at, and photographed, including the three-story Godfrey Nuzum barn that is built into a bluff; the Kiehnoff barn that has a unique system of louvers for getting air in yet keeping rain and birds out; and the John Fuhrken barn, an octagonal barn that was touted in the late 1800s by the Department of Agriculture as the "wave of the future."

Indeed, back in the days when the Doniphan barns were built, farmers often put more money into their barns than their homes. But today, barns, though still celebrated as an icon of rural life, are being razed just like family farms (3.8 million farms have bitten the dust in the last century).

Toothpick
Memorials

Kansas Turnpike

North Kasold Drive

South MaDonald Drive

KANSAS RIVER

70

40

Hugh Cameron
Plaque

To Stull
Cemetery

West 6th Street

40

59

● The Sandbar

West 9th Street

● Randy Walker House

South Massachusetts Street

KU Memorial
Stadium

South Iowa Street

Bob Billings Parkway

Natural History
Museum

East 15th Street

Oak Hill
Cemetery ●

Sigma Nu ●

South Kasold Drive

West 19th Street

59

William
Burroughs
House

Haskell Avenue

West Clinton Parkway

West 23rd Street

10

North 1400 Road

10

Louisiana Street

59

North 1300 Road

West 31st Street

North 1260 Road

10

Lawrence

Lawrence

Call it shameless bragging, but people who make Lawrence, Kansas, home believe it is one cool town. Long a stronghold of individuality, this quirky little burg in the middle of the Bible Belt is the only town in America that was started for no other reason than to spout politics. Folks who didn't think slavery was such a hot idea came here in 1854 to put up their dukes and say, "All people have a right to live as they choose."

Even though Lawrence was burned to the ground by proslavery rabble-rousers who disagreed, that sentiment is the predominant theme to this day. It's why some people think downtown looks like a Halloween party, why you see everything from Honk for Hemp signs to Junior League bouffants.

It's why the Lawrence downtown, unlike so many small downtowns, is still vibrant, alive, and attracting such entrepreneurial anomalies as the Waxman candle factory, which has a swing hanging from its rafters, and Local Burger, a hamburger joint that sells burgers made from buffalo, elk, tofu, and, of course, beef—but only beef that's organic and locally grown.

How many towns of fewer than 100,000 can you name that have their own coloring book? Or that put on a community-wide talent show twice a year? Or that host a home tour of the town's old and ugly houses?

There's a different parade practically every month. At Christmas, there's a horse parade. Art cars come out in May. April brings an Earth Day parade. March means an all-green St. Patty's parade. Bike parades happen about any month the local "Take Back the Streets" contingent decides to set up couches on Massachusetts Street, the main thoroughfare.

If it sounds like summer camp, that's a pretty fair description. Lawrence is one big summer camp attracting odd characters from all over the world. Practically any one of its 96,000 inhabitants could qualify for a listing in this book. Maybe that's why Hugh Beaumont, the actor who played Leave It to Beaver's straitlaced Ward Cleaver, left town when he was still in high school.

Of course, the Convention and Visitors Bureau, which loves to roll out the town's honors, tends to bring up the fact that the National Trust for

Historic Preservation includes Lawrence in its dozen distinctive destina-
tions. And when the National Endowment for the Arts ranked cities accord-
ing to number of artists per capita, Lawrence landed in that list's top 12.

But for those who live here, they like it for all its character and its
characters, for the fact that filmmakers like Alyssa Buecker can land HBO
contracts for films starring guinea pigs, for the joie de vivre that prompted
all of K. T. Walsh's neighbors to add umbrellas to their own yards when the
city tried to put a halt to her outdoor art display of umbrellas and bowling
ball sculptures, for the statistic that ranks our county third in the country for
percentage of Ralph Nader voters.

Sure, they're proud of the University of Kansas and all it has to offer,
but they like the fact that in Kansas, they're known as LaLa Land. And they
wouldn't have it any other way.

They Shoot Mermaids, Don't They?

As Willie Shakespeare liked to say, "Beauty is in the eye of the beholder."
That's certainly the case in Lawrence, where people actually look forward to
hurricanes. Of course, the hurricanes in Lawrence only last 15 minutes, involve
rum-laced brightly colored fruit drinks, and abate after drunks dressed in
mermaid costumes jump up on the bar and perform the Macarena.

The Sandbar, a cozy cabana just off the main drag in downtown Lawrence, began offering the fake, but ferocious, indoor storms in 2002. Five
minutes before the Katrina-clone hits, the local hangout slowly fills with
fog and the TV screens flicker to a phony "Channel 69" newscast warning
guests of the impending doom. Wind machines and torrential rainstorms
complete with lightning, thunder, and driving rain continue until a couple of
brave volunteers (believe it or not, customers have been known to come to
blows over who gets to play the Little, or sometimes not so little, Mermaid)
agree to save the day by donning mermaid costumes and dancing on the
long wooden bar.

As far as I know, it's the only indoor hurricane in the world. The Sandbar also has huge tanks of exotic fish, tropical decor, a jukebox with lots of
songs you know by heart, and a gift shop with clever T-shirts and the funky

place's signature costume: bras made from coconuts, what else? In fact, if you can come up with a unique logo to be painted on the coconuts, you win your own bra free of charge.

To experience one of the Sandbar's nightly hurricanes, show up at their intimate, hurricane-swept bar at 17 E. Eighth St. (785-842-0111), or check out their webcam at www.thesandbar.com. The excitement starts at 10 p.m. Central time.

Hanging Out in the Street Never Looked So Good

When you were growing up, I'm sure your mother always told you not to play in the street. But buskers have made an art of it, and in Lawrence they take home the cash. Literally. For those who don't know, the word "busker" means a person who performs music or other entertainment in the street or another private place for monetary donations. You may have seen street mimes or musicians with their instruments and a can or hat for tips on the streets of New York or Dallas, but Richard Renner had an idea that has turned into a life of its own.

"I have traveled to a lot of places and seen a lot of street performers, good and bad," Renner said. "One day it hit me. Why not bring acts here to Lawrence." So that's exactly what he did. The 3-day street performers festival was started 18 years ago this Memorial Day. The festival is held on Friday, Saturday, and Sunday in locations called pitches across downtown Lawrence.

Acts include magicians, musicians, unicycle riding, bed of nails, strong men and women acts, yo-yo tricks, fire breathers, mimes, sword swallowers, poetry and written word performers, plus any other act Renner can find to bring in. Performers come from Canada, England, Germany, and across the US. Food trucks and artists' booths can also be found throughout the festival.

The Lawrence Busker Festival ranks number one among the three other busker festivals across the country. Admission is free. Remember, performers are paid by the tips they make while performing. Anywhere from 30,000 to 40,000 people attend this festival every year. So, what are you waiting for? Next Memorial Day weekend, head on over to Lawrence and watch people play in the street.

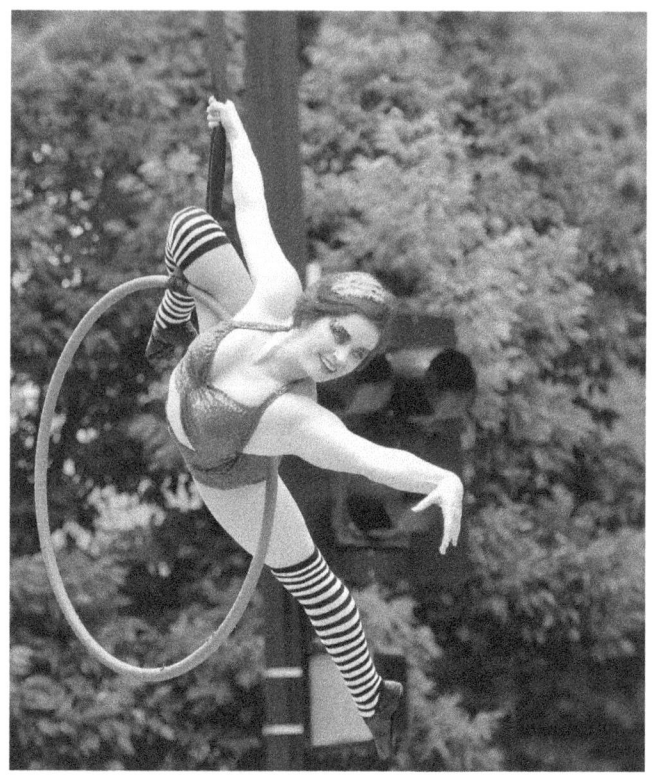

Doing the impossible with a ring
RICHARD RENNER

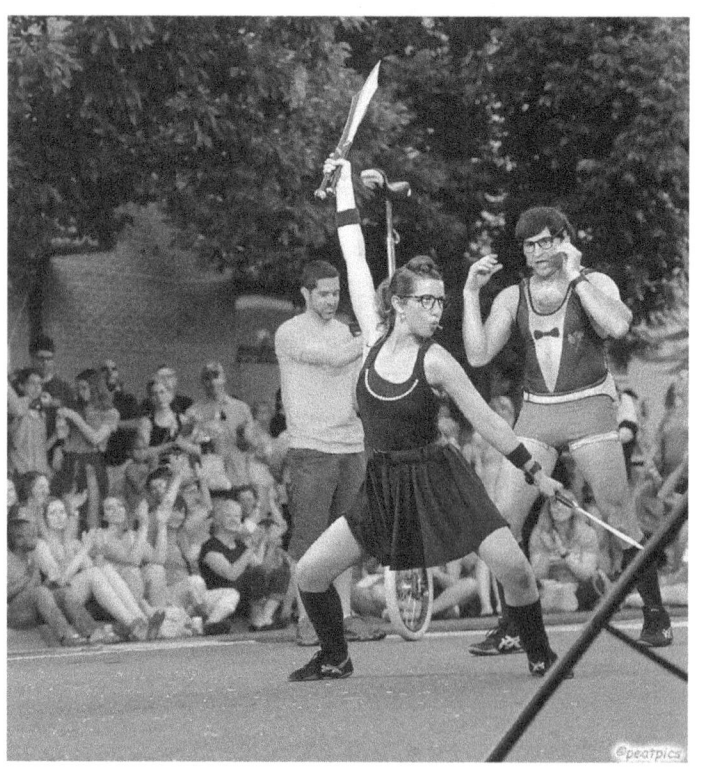

Another thing Mama told you not to do—play with swords.
RICHARD RENNER

To Each His Own

Cawker City may have its Big Ball of Twine, but Lawrence has a Big Ball of Metal. The Big Metal Ball is literally a leftover from the city's industrial days. Sitting just south of the One Riverfront Plaza parking garage, it has become quite an anomaly to Lawrence residents and visitors alike. It sits there alone, like a giant sentinel of times gone by, without a placard or anything posted about what it is or why it is there. People passing by stop and go hmmmm.

However, if you are into paper or papermaking, you might have a clue as to what it is. In 1883, the Lawrence Paper Company was located next to the dam where city hall is today. The drum or large metal sphere was filled with straw pulp; then it was heated with water as it rotated, thus allowing the mixture to combine so the company could make paper and cardboard boxes. Once the paper company relocated and made way for city hall, the Big Metal Ball came to rest in its current location.

As there are other sculptures and works of art throughout Lawrence, the ball has found its own artistic place.

Grave Consequences

No matter where you go to law school (UCLA, Harvard, or anywhere in between), you know about John Wesley Hillmon, a Kansas cattle dealer whose body supposedly lies in a wooden coffin in an unmarked grave in Lawrence.

His body, which was dug up several times and photographed in various stages of decomposition, was the subject of six long, drawn-out court battles, two of which ended up in the US Supreme Court. In fact, one of our legal system's few exceptions to hearsay evidence—an out-of-court statement that's usually inadmissible—owes its very existence to rules put in place after the 1892 US Supreme Court decision in *Mutual Life Insurance Co. v. Hillmon*.

But maybe I should start at the beginning. John Wesley Hillmon, born in 1848, married a Lawrence girl named Sallie E. Quinn. Soon after their 1878 wedding, they set out in a wagon with a compadre named John H. Brown to claim some cattle ranching land in the southwest US. They didn't get any farther than Medicine Lodge when Brown accidentally shot his friend in the head with a rifle he was trying to unload from the wagon. Or so he claimed.

Here lies John . . . or is it Frederick?

Not more than 10 days after he was buried, Hillmon's body was dug up at the bequest of the insurance company that held three life insurance policies in his name. His body was sent to Lawrence, a 290-mile journey by stage and rail, where a coroner, paid by the insurance company, declared that the body, indeed dressed in Hillmon's clothes, was not Hillmon after all.

Insurance fraud at the time was rampant, and the insurance company, in an effort to nip what it claimed was fraudulence in the bud, decided to fight the claims by Hillmon's widow. Only problem? The company conducted its own fraud in trying to prove that the body was one Frederick Adolph Waters. That's where the exception to hearsay evidence came in. The Supreme Court decided to allow a letter that Waters's "girlfriend" produced, claiming that her 24-year-old beau had joined up with Brown and the two Hillmons shortly past Wichita.

To make a long story short, Sallie Hillmon, after 20 years and six trials, finally got the $25,000, a princely sum in those days, the Federal Rules got Rule 803(1)(b) with the oft-studied exception to hearsay evidence, and Lawrence got a veritable legal celebrity right in its own Oak Hill Cemetery.

Oak Hill Cemetery is located 1605 Oak Hill Ave., about 7 blocks east of Haskell on 15th Street.

The Gum Hither Look

In 2003, on the 100th anniversary of the Wright brothers' infamous first flight, the Grassroots Art Center in Lucas staged a *Flights of Fancy* exhibit featuring flying machines made from recycled art. One of the featured attractions was a long-necked bird made from dried grapefruit peels.

The artist who concocted the bird was none other than Lawrence's own Betty Milliken, a yodeling 90-something self-taught artist who, during her lifetime, made hundreds of pieces of art from grapefruit and orange rinds. Her specialty was portraits—cameos that she fashioned out of not only fruit rinds, but out of caulking compound, bread dough, Styrofoam meat trays, and chewing gum. Yes, chewing gum. Her cameos, not more than an inch tall, sometimes sported hats that Milliken knitted, or locks of her own hair. Sometimes she dressed them in photos from magazines. Sometimes she gave them the faces of celebrities—like Joe Namath or Martha Washington. Collectively, her cameos of bubble gum mixed with foot powder and tub caulking were known as "Betty's Children."

How do you make a portrait out of chewing gum?

"Well, first you have to chew the gum," said the colorful Milliken, who passed away August 2005 at the ripe old age of 94. "You gotta get all the sugar out of it. Big Red isn't bad, but Cinnaburst works best."

Born in Detroit, Michigan, to a family of Hungarian immigrants, Milliken grew up really poor (she remembered wearing her dad's barnyard boots that smelled of manure to school) and was a bit of a social outcast. Although she didn't like school, she loved learning. She taught herself art, photography, painting, yodeling, and acupressure, a hobby to which she attributed her longer than usual life. She also played a mean ukulele, banjo, fiddle, guitar, and water xylophone. That's where you set up glasses with varying amounts of water to create different tones.

A sampling of Betty's Children can be viewed at the Grassroots Art Center in Lucas, 213 S. Main St. (785-525-6118; www.grassrootsart.net).

All my children
NANCY HUBBLE

The Jane Goodall of Sock Monkeys

Randy Walker charges a buck to get in the door of his house. And that's a bargain. His home on the east side of Lawrence is a veritable museum of American kitsch.

The avid collector, who works as a chef to support his hobby (he also, not surprisingly, runs a booth at the local antiques mall), has collections of bottle cap men, art deco lamps, purses and hats made from bread bags, 3-D religious art, lamps and ashtrays made from deer hooves, postmortem photos, and velvet Elvises. Of course, he also has nonvelvet Elvis memorabilia, including a lock of Elvis's hair, one of his toenails, a fingernail, and pictures of Elvis's underwear that he took last year in Pigeon Forge, Tennessee.

Walker's most recent pursuit is acquiring the world's largest collection of cow hairballs. So far, he has three, the biggest of which is still dwarfed by the Garden City hairball (see the Southwest chapter). But, unlike the Finney County Historical Museum that only gets theirs out when someone asks, Walker's hairballs are all proudly displayed under glass domes.

Say cheese-y! Randy Walker with his collection of sock monkeys. (Randy's the one in the middle.)

His most famous collection, however, is his zoo of sock monkeys. He owns more than 350 of the monkeys, which were popular homemade items in the 1950s and '60s. He has monkeys with capes, monkeys with hats, even monkeys with eyes made out of seashells.

"They're like people," Walker said. "Even though they're made from the same basic things, every one is a little bit different. Each one has its own personality."

His favorite Christmas card? What else but a picture of himself surrounded by his monkeys, with the greeting, "From my family to yours."

I'm sorry to report that Walker's cockatiel Raoul, the one that could hum the theme song to *The Andy Griffith Show*, kicked the bucket at the ripe old age of 22 (the average cockatiel lives to be 15), but Walker still has him in the freezer.

"I'm trying to get somebody to stuff him, but most taxidermists think he's too small," Walker said.

"I collect American junk. If it's in bad taste or ugly, I probably collect it," Walker said of his interesting addiction. "I collect stuff that shows the human spirit. Creativity just bursts out of people. I love it when people are able to make something out of nothing."

If you can spare a buck and want to see a genuinely original home, now called "Museum of Odd," call Walker at (785) 843-8750. His home/museum is located at 1012 New York St.

Don't Forget to Eat Your Vegetables and Your . . . Art

Most artists use easels and canvas. Stan Herd, an internationally known environmental artist, uses cornfields, tractors, and crops to create his beautiful, albeit large, portraits. He sculpts live, growing crops into designs so huge you can only view them from the air. But get high enough and you'll see 1-acre Amelia Earharts made from perennial grasses and 160-acre Indian chiefs made from squash, melon, corn, and beans.

Although he calls Lawrence home and has designed many artworks here (Lawrence Riverfront Park sports a giant Stan Herd flowerpot fashioned

Crop circle conspiracy? WILL PENDLETON

from rocks), he travels the world creating his one-of-a-kind masterpieces. He once made a giant Absolut vodka bottle the size of 16 football fields that was featured in magazine ads for the Swedish import.

Herd grew up in tiny Protection, Kansas, and won his first art competition (the grand prize was a whopping $1) when he was in first grade. That award was just the first for the artist, who has been written up by *People, National Geographic,* and *Smithsonian* magazines. After attending art school at Wichita State University, he decided he wanted to think bigger. And bigger indeed he has thought.

His first piece of crop art, created in 1980, was a 160-acre portrait of a peace-loving Kiowa Indian chief named Santana.

Herd's murals can be seen in little towns all over Kansas, including Kingman, Dodge City, Wilmore, Topeka, and Protection. You can call (785) 331-6548, or visit www.stanherdarts.com.

Oops . . . Phone Line Stuck in a Tree

Hugh Cameron, known as the Kansas hermit, built a tree house with electricity and a phone. After getting fired from his job in Washington, DC (the powers that be didn't approve of his strident abolitionist views), he walked to Lawrence with the first party of 29 hoping to establish Kansas as a free state. That was in 1857. Although he started a newspaper and served in the territorial congress, he eventually forswore society after a girlfriend jilted him. At 55, he vowed to never cut his hair or beard again.

Cameron lived in a cave for many years, coming out every 4 years to walk all the way to Washington, DC, for the presidential inauguration. By 1907, he decided to move closer to town. He built a retirement tree house at what's now Fifth Street and Indiana. The house had a small dining area, a kitchen, electricity, and even a telephone.

While Cameron's tree house was located at what is now Fifth Street and Indiana, there's a plaque honoring this old war fighter and poet's tree house embedded in the sidewalk at Fifth Street and Louisiana (because it was open and available—we're weird here in Lawrence).

Naked Burroughs

He lived in Paris, London, New York, and Tangier. But William Burroughs, the famous poet and artist who is credited with introducing Jack Kerouac and Allen Ginsberg to the Beat lifestyle, chose Lawrence as home. Indeed, he lived here longer than he lived anywhere—in a modest red frame house where he gardened (one of his typewriters "grew" among the weeds), raised cats, and practiced target shooting. His classic *Naked Lunch*, published in Paris in 1959 and banned in the US until 1962, was one of dozens of books he wrote after he accidentally shot his wife in a drunken William Tell accident.

Living in Mexico to escape US drug authorities, Burroughs bragged to his friends he could shoot a wineglass off his wife's head. Unfortunately, he missed, and his wife died almost immediately. If not for that unfortunate accident, he says, he'd have never started writing (he wrote hundreds of books, from *Ticket That Exploded* to *Wild Boys*) and would not have

Burroughs's bungalow PAM GROUT

become the much-loved champion of freethinkers everywhere. An admitted homosexual and former heroin addict, Burroughs railed against convention all his life. He still influences the counterculture today. Before his death in 1997, hundreds of "worshippers" came to Lawrence to visit, including Ginsberg, Kurt Cobain, and Deborah Harry.

To see the home Burroughs inhabited from 1981 until a heart attack sent him to Lawrence Memorial Hospital, go by 1927 Learnard Ave.

(Red) Dog Day Afternoons

While some people like to exercise with Billy Blanks, Richard Simmons, or Jane Fonda, a huge contingent in Kansas chooses to work out with Don Gardner, a 70-something ex-marine with a bullhorn. His nickname is Red Dog, the class is known as Red Dog's Dog Days, and for more than 30 years he has been leading hundreds of believers through laps and push-ups and other strenuous exercises in the sometimes 100-degree Kansas heat.

Gardner and partner Jim O'Connell (his nickname is Punkin—he was born on Halloween) were trainers for the Lawrence High Chesty Lions football team. They grew tired of all the injuries that plagued players at the start of the season, so they launched this hot, brutal workout to get them in shape.

For some unexplained reason it caught on, and now everyone from police officers to restaurant servers to elementary school kids shows up to be pushed and occasionally sworn at by the infamous Red Dog. In fact, on July 27, 2009, 2,766 people showed up for Red Dog's World's Largest Workout. Today, they average 150–200 people per day over the summer.

The class is free, meets two times a day 4 days a week every summer, and keeps growing every year. They also meet in the fall and winter and every Saturday year-round. There's also a group for those who have moved away. To be brutally punished in person, all you gotta do is show up at KU's Memorial Stadium (11th and Maine). But don't say I didn't warn you. www.reddogsdogdays.org.

Scary Movie 13?

Stull Cemetery is the most haunted cemetery in Kansas and one of the Seven Gates to Hell. Or at least that's the rumor. Stull Cemetery, a tiny, run-down graveyard with nothing but a burned-out church, a couple of trees, and headstones with such names as Wulfkuhle and Hildenbrand, sits innocently across from an old bait shop. But on Halloween night, the tiny cemetery opens up a straight path to the red guy himself.

Stull locals—a quiet, peaceful lot—say the rumors are complete gobbledygook. They've erected a fence and given out $100 fines to anybody who tries to prove otherwise as the property is privately owned. So far, their threats have done nothing to thwart the persistent legends that circulate around the world via the internet. Some say the devil's child is buried there. Others claim a boy who turns into a werewolf haunts the place. Kurt Cobain of the rock group Nirvana made a pilgrimage to the famous cemetery and tested its most notorious legend: that if you throw a bottle against one of the rock walls, it won't break. Or if it does, says the legend, you're next to join the dead. Well, I can't say I was with Cobain the night he threw his bottle, and I wouldn't know whether or not it broke, but I do know he's not around anymore.

If you dare, Stull Cemetery can be found by taking Sixth Street out to 1600 Street and following it west until you feel chills.

Equestrian Elvis Lives On

When the cavalry's burial party arrived two days after General George Custer's ill-fated raid on the Sioux Indians, there was only one living thing left on the Little Bighorn battlefield: none other than a 14-year-old steed named Comanche. Even though seven bullet holes pierced his body, Comanche, who got his name when he was struck in the right hind quarter with an arrowhead and supposedly let out a yell just like a Comanche, was still breathing.

He had already survived the Ku Klux Klan, Kentucky moonshiners, and numerous battle injuries. After he was found wounded on the Little Bighorn battlefield, he was taken to Fort Lincoln and nursed back to health.

The "stuffing" legends are made of KU NATURAL HISTORY MUSEUM

A symbol of American patriotism, for years Comanche made the rounds of parades and festivals all over the country. Like an equestrian Elvis, he was sighted everywhere.

Eventually, Comanche found a permanent home at Fort Riley, Kansas. When he died at the ripe old age of 29, the Fort Riley cavalry had no idea what to do with the famous steed's carcass. Finally, they contacted the taxidermist at the Natural History Museum, who agreed to stuff him for $400. The cavalry never paid the bill, and the mount, except for a brief exhibit at the Chicago Exposition in 1893, has been in Lawrence ever since.

Even in death, poor Comanche has suffered numerous brushes with danger including an attempt by students to steal him and a near drowning, which occurred when a goose being thawed in a sink on the floor above plugged the drain, causing water to pour onto the stuffed steed.

Ever since, Comanche has been proudly displayed for all the world to see on the fourth floor of the Natural History Museum at the University of Kansas in a climate-controlled glass case.

The Natural History Museum sits on the university campus just south of the university union, 1345 Jayhawk Blvd., (785) 864-4450, www.biodiversity .ku.edu.

The (Spooky) Sweetheart of Sigma Nu

Even though fraternities are normally "men only," the Sigma Nu fraternity house of the University of Kansas has a frequent female visitor. Her name is Virginia and, well, she's a ghost. When she was living, Virginia was allegedly the mistress of Kansas governor Walter Roscoe Stubbs, who lived in the house when it was the official state mansion.

In 1911, 17-year-old Virginia was found hanging from a crystal chandelier on the third floor. This was before Barbara Walters, CNN, and other snoopy reporters, so no one knew for sure whether Virginia, who worked for Stubbs as a servant, killed herself or was murdered by Mrs. Stubbs. All we know is that she was cremated and her ashes were stuffed inside the first-floor fireplace. A mysterious plaque in the room that now serves as the fraternity library reads, The world of strife shut out, the world of love shut in.

Virginia has been getting her vengeance ever since. Members of the fraternity, which took over the house in 1922, report regular disruptions, including rattling doorknobs, heavy footsteps, and flashing lights. In April, the anniversary of her death, she's often seen pacing the floors or sitting on steps.

The frat house is at 1501 Sigma Nu Place, (540) 463-1869.

Bowling with Martha

Columbus discovered the New World. Einstein proposed the theory of relativity. Larry Woydziak, a Lawrence firefighter, made it his quest to bowl with Martha in every county in Kansas.

Martha, by the way, is a bag for a mother-of-pearl bowling ball that he bought for $1.95 at a thrift store. It even came with a pair of slightly dirty socks and a 1988 bowling schedule.

As a member of the Kansas Explorers Club, a wild and wacky group that promotes local travel and small-town culture, Woydziak came up with this unusual quest one day at an Explorers conference meeting. He wanted an excuse to see Kansas, so why not do it at the bowling alley?

"Back in the '50s and '60s, the bowling alley was where people in small towns hung out. Thanks to TV and the internet, many of the small-town bowling alleys are closing up," said Woydziak. "Nowhere are people as friendly as they are in the bowling alley."

Indeed, he did make lots of friends—even became quite a celebrity, drawing huge crowds to his 10-line game in each county. He even created a website with a journal called *Larry's Gutter Life*.

For a mere $18.61 (the year Kansas became a state), you too can become part of America's most exciting organization. By becoming a Kansas Explorer, you'll receive six newsletters a year that will inform you about such newsworthy events as Larry's last bowl in Sterling (sorry, you missed that one—it was in June 2001), the Kingman farm machinery Christmas parade, and the round hay bale art competition.

You'll learn the top-secret explorer ritual, get a number (I'm Explorer #2098) and a four-color membership card, and have the chance to attend

Grand Expeditions, explorer conferences where you might come up with crazy schemes like Larry's. Just don't try to eat biscuits and gravy in every county or jog through every county, because those are already taken. You might even win the LuWonderer Award, a 10-inch limestone fence post (the first one was a Barbie doll) that is passed from member to member.

If you "Dare to Do Dirt," a Kansas Explorers motto, check out www.explorekansas.org.

Art Cars Rule

Other than a witty bumper sticker here and there, most of us drive clones, cars that are exact replicas of every other Toyota Camry or Honda Accord.

Not in Lawrence. This town has a whole fleet of what's known as art cars, cars that express their owners' personalities.

In May, all these one-of-a-kind vehicles come out to strut their stuff in the annual Art Tougeau, a wacky art car parade that celebrates folk art, ingenuity, and community spirit.

If it has wheels and any kind of art facade, it qualifies for entry. Sometimes, that means wheelchairs decorated to look like bananas. Or bikes that

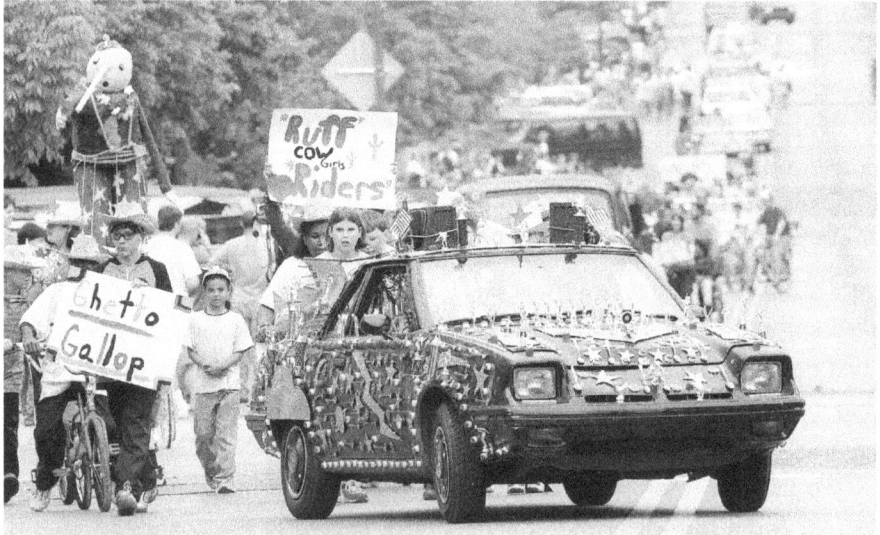

Instead of mpg (miles per gallon), this car boasts spg—stares per gallon.

look like cows. Once, a grade school rigged up a bunch of wheelbarrows and lawn mowers. Another entry added wheels to a couple of refrigerators. But the art cars usually get the biggest laughs, such as the expensive Jaguar decorated from top to bottom in cookies applied with icing. Or the old Chevy that reflects the sun with its new coating of thousands of CDs.

Charles Jones, a county commissioner, started the parade back in 1997 after watching a CBS special called *Wild Wheels*. And yes, he's more than a judge. His art car, although it started as a very normal 1983 Ford Escort, now has hundreds and hundreds of trophies glued to its exterior.

Speaking of trophies, students in an art class at the high school rig up wacky trophies (they use twisted wire and old toy parts) to give out at the end of the parade. As one Art Tougeau fanatic said, "It appeals to the exhibitionist in all of us."

To catch the parade, check the website, www.arttougeau.org, for the date and then show up on Massachusetts Street.

Southeast

Southeast

Anybody who thinks Kansas is backward, conservative, and boring has obviously never opened a history book about southeast Kansas. I dare anybody to malign the state with one of those Archie Bunker–like claims after reading this chapter.

Not only was there a vegetarian commune near Humboldt in the 1860s, 100 years before hippies shocked the middle class with such far-out notions, but progressive ideas like 8-hour workdays and the abolition of child labor were hatched in Girard, a small town Jack London once called "a temple of revolution." Not only that, but the world's first protest march was organized in the southeast's Crawford and Cherokee Counties.

The progressive ideas were touted by the Appeal to Reason, a Socialist newspaper that in 1913 had the largest circulation in the country (750,000). The protest march was staged by 6,000 women, wives of coal miners, who took to the streets in 1921 to protest the miserable pay and abominable working conditions their husbands were forced to endure. Girard, by the way, also had an innovative airplane builder who opened one of the country's first airplane factories in an empty lumberyard. Unfortunately, only one of his 14 designs ever left the ground.

The southeast also has rare white lions, 13 miles of Route 66, and the world's largest piece of hail. For more fascinating facts about southeast Kansas, read on.

Mom-and-Pop Zoo
Caney

When Tom Harvey was 4, he went with his dad, a truck driver, to pick up a load of cattle. They waited and waited until finally the guy who hired them sheepishly sauntered over to the truck to say he was terribly sorry, but his shipment wasn't going to be ready for them after all. He offered to pay him for his time, but Mr. Harvey wouldn't hear of it.

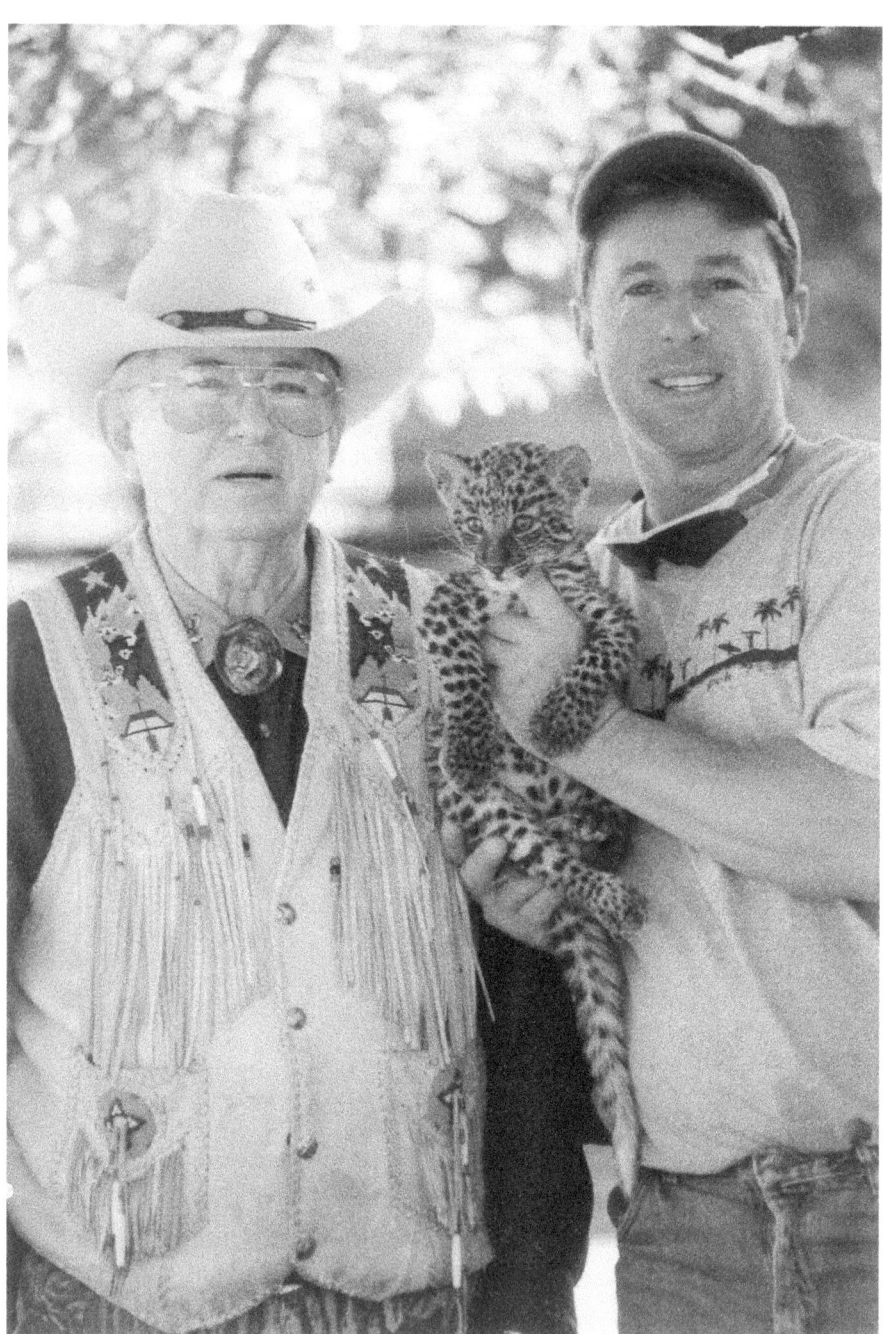

Tame kingdom SAFARI ZOOLOGICAL PARK

"Well, the least I can do is give your son one of these," he said, walking over to a beat-up El Camino.

He opened the door of the old Chevy and showed them a litter of baby deer that had been born a few weeks earlier in the front seat.

Young Tom giddily picked one out, named him Rudolph (hey, he was 4), and took him home, where he made the fawn a bed in his wooden toy box.

"I've had animals ever since," said Tom.

Only now, Tom has exotic animals (70-some) and his own zoo that he runs with his wife, Allie.

"People think since we're out in Kansas that we probably have a couple chickens, a cow, and maybe some frogs," Tom said. Boy, are they in for a surprise when they pull up to the zoo in tiny Caney. Harvey's 10-acre Safari Zoological Park has black African bear cubs, seven rare white tigers, four black leopards, jaguars, and what could be the only white Barbary lion ever born. People come from China, Australia, and countries most of us have never heard of to see the rare menagerie.

Tom's first exotic, a cougar, was just a pet. But then he got a black African bear cub, a lion, and a mate for the cougar.

People came to visit.

"I was taking so many people out to see them that I couldn't get anything done. I decided that I'd either have to get rid of the people or I'd have to let the people help support the hobby," he said.

Some years, the park that he opened to the public in 1994 does better than others.

In 2008, Sassy, one of the white tigers, rejected her three newborn cubs. She decided she'd had enough of being a mom and refused to let them nurse. Isabella, the Harveys' yellow lab who had just had a litter of pups, adopted them, even took over the nursing details. Before long, Harvey, Allie, and the cubs were on the *Today* show, inking book deals, and fielding calls from all over the world.

"We had just had three tough years. I told my wife, hang on. There's a miracle coming," Tom said.

The influx of money has allowed him to renovate the park and add a new leopard habitat.

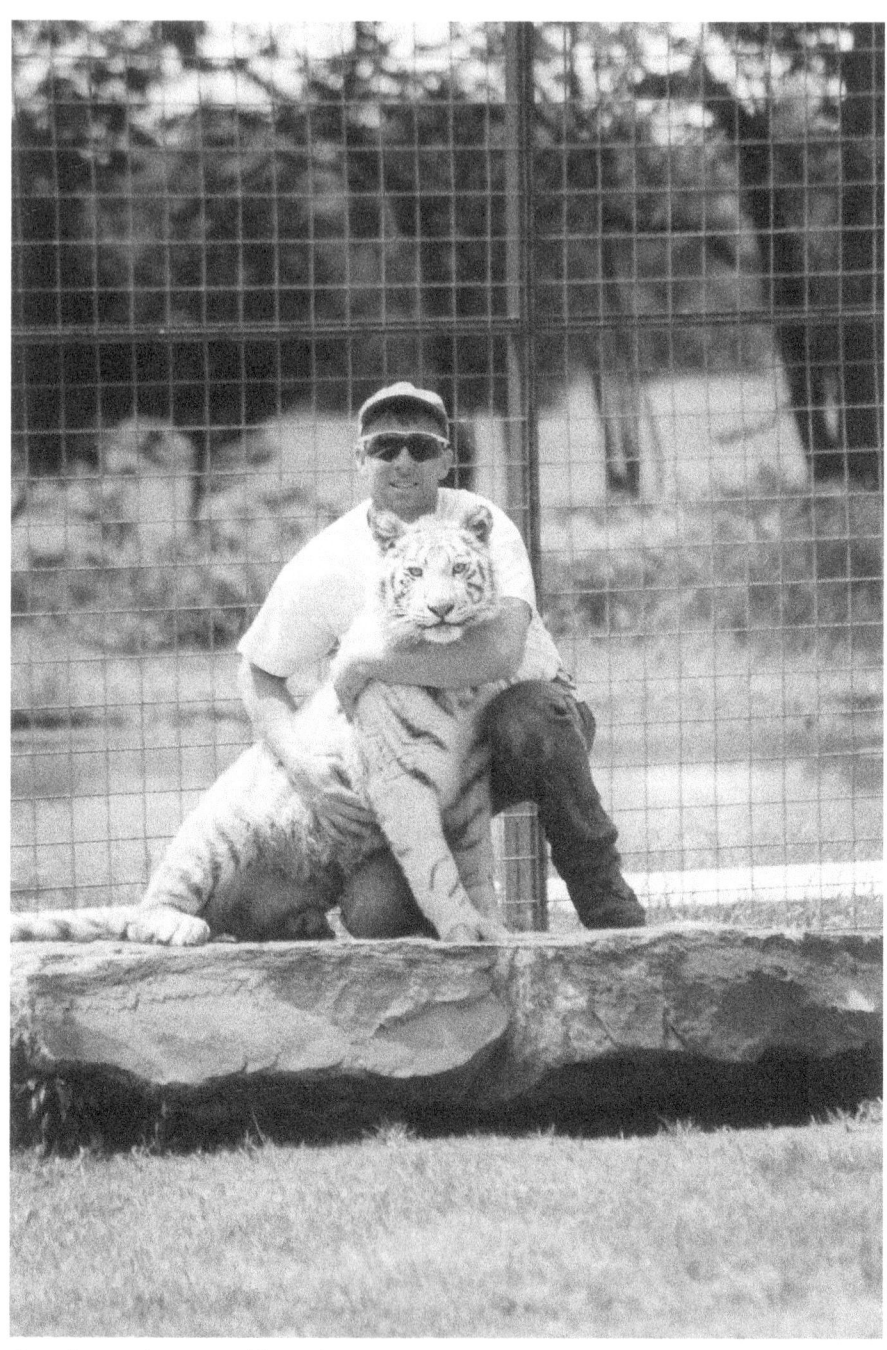

Born free to be nursed by a dog TOM HARVEY

But even with all the improvements, Harvey's zoological park still takes guests on personal guided tours. Anybody who pays the $15 admission is led by Tom, Allie, or one of the volunteers through the park and regaled with funny anecdotes about the animals—when their birthdays are or what they did when they were cubs. Tom has been known to hypnotize the alligators and ride on the backs of lions. If you'd rather feed the animals yourself, you can buy a ziplock bag of, yes, animal crackers. Up close and personal is the best way to describe it. In 2025, the park welcomed wolf pups and fox kits. Visitors can view them, but they're keeping the babes behind glass until they are a little older.

To visit the park, take US 75 to old Highway 166 and go east 1.5 miles. Phone (620) 515-2886 or visit their Facebook page at www.facebook.com/SafariZoologicalPark/#.

Casting the First (and Second and Third) Stone

Cedar Vale

After Lotus Day suffered a heart attack, he decided to retire from his job as a stonemason. He figured his time was better spent "glorifying God." Some might have thought that sending money to starving kids in Africa would have been enough. But not Lotus Day. He wanted to build a cathedral—a tiny stone cathedral that seats exactly 12. When he commissioned the oak pews, he told the woodworker, "I want just enough space to seat the twelve disciples."

So far, the disciples haven't shown up. But when it was available to tourists, thousands of other people from every part of the world showed up. That alone is a miracle, because the church, called Wee Kirk of the Valley, sits in a field off a gravel road that's 6.5 miles from the nearest town. You can still see the church from the gravel road, but don't go climbing any fences; it's private property now. There's a 6-foot marble statue of Christ that was sculpted in Italy, and statues of the Last Supper and Jesus in the Garden of Gethsemane that glow in the morning light.

If you want to learn more about the little church, the ranch it sits on, and the small town of Cedar Vale, stop in and say howdy at the Cedar Vale Historical Society and Museum. It is located at 622 Cedar St.

Lions and Tigers and Scares, Oh My!
Chanute

Chanute's Osa Johnson was the Julia Roberts of the 1920s. When she showed up on the stages of America to sing or talk or show clips from her many safari movies, people came out in droves. Her book, *I Married Adventure,* which was printed on zebra-striped cloth, was a bestseller (*National Geographic* still lists it as one of the best adventure books of all time), and while she was on the vaudeville circuit, she topped fashion magazines' lists of the best dressed.

Of course, no one would have heard of the girl from small-town Kansas if she hadn't married Martin Johnson, a kid from nearby Independence, when she was still 16. Martin, who was 10 years older, met Osa after returning from a 2-year adventure on Jack London's *Snark.* Martin had responded to London's classified ad for a cook, even though he hadn't the foggiest notion how to cook. He got the job and continued to travel even after the *Snark's* 6-year journey was cut short.

That trip whetted his appetite for exploration and, with new bride Osa by his side, he traveled to the remotest corners of the earth. Not only did the adventurous duo pioneer documentary filmmaking, but they also introduced many Americans to new and uncharted worlds. They made nine full-length movies, 17 short features, and at least a half dozen films for the lecture circuit. Their film *The Cannibal Isles of the South Seas* debuted in 1918 and set box office records across the country.

In 1961, a few years after Osa died of heart failure (Martin had died earlier in a commercial plane crash), Chanute opened a museum in honor of the Johnsons. For a while, donations to the museum were collected in an elephant foot with a board nailed to the top.

The Martin and Osa Johnson Safari Museum contains thousands of artifacts collected by the Johnsons on their five forays into Africa and four journeys to the South Pacific.

Their books and all their full-length safari movies, as well as blowguns, elephant-foot banks, and 300 pieces of West African tribal art, are on display at the museum, along with handcrafted African jewelry made on-site.

*Osa's Ark. This zebra-striped Sikorsky S-38 was employed for the Johnsons'
1933–1943 "Flying Safari," their fifth and final expedition to Africa.*
MARTIN AND OSA JOHNSON SAFARI MUSEUM

Fashionably Kansas

American Eagle Outfitters, the brand preferred by teenagers everywhere, came straight to Kansas when developing a new line for 30-somethings. Their Martin + Osa brand, launched in 2006 with 28 stores around the country, features clothes inspired by the early Kansas explorers. Although the brand's cashmere sweaters, shorts, and jackets are slightly updated, a Johnson junkie would notice subtle hints throughout the line: belt buckles with 1910, the year the Johnsons married; labels with S-38, the amphibious airplane they used to traverse Africa; or NC-52, their plane's registration number. The Pittsburgh, Pennsylvania, retailer has yet to open a Martin + Osa store in the Sunflower State (although their largest distribution center employs more than 550 in Ottawa, Kansas).

The museum is located at 111 N. Lincoln Ave. (Highway 39), 2 miles from US 169. Take Cherry Street to Santa Fe and turn right at the next light. It's open 10 a.m. to 5 p.m. Monday through Saturday and 1 to 5 p.m. on Sunday. Phone (620) 431-2730 or go to www.safarimuseum.com.

Ax to Grind

Cherryvale

Back in the early 1870s, Kate Bender and her family built a small barn and house near the Osage Mission Trail, a few miles northeast of Cherryvale. A crude sign on the home advertised groceries.

Kate's parents, both in their 60s, kept to themselves, as did their son, John Jr. Kate, however, was just the opposite. She had an outgoing personality and flashing brown eyes, and she was quite popular with local lads. Advertising herself as a "healer," Professor Katie Bender, as she billed herself, passed out flyers claiming she could cure blindness and deafness. The Benders' little home on the trail had a canvas partition. The family bunked on one side; travelers in need of a meal could sit on crude log benches on the other.

There was just one problem with the partition. Behind it, the Benders would wait with axes and sledgehammers and bludgeon their unsuspecting guests to death. There was a trapdoor underneath the bench if for some reason the sledgehammers didn't finish them off. No one missed the first 10 travelers who disappeared—or at least they didn't suspect Katie Bender, the great healer, of perpetrating any crime. But when William H. York, a well-known doctor from nearby Independence, disappeared, search parties were sent out. When York's brother and a posse tracked him to Bender's store, Katie admitted that he'd stopped by, but she insisted that he had watered his horse, bought a couple of things, and rode on.

Two weeks later, the Benders' home was deserted. When officials went to investigate, they discovered York's body in a shallow grave in the Benders' orchard. Eventually, they discovered the bodies of 10 other victims nearby, including a father and his small daughter, who were all beaten to death with the Benders' tools. The Benders were never seen or heard from again.

To find out more about the murdering family, visit the Cherryvale Historical Museum at 215 E. Fourth St. (620-336-3576) or get a copy of Fern Morrow Wood's book, *The Benders: Keepers of the Devil's Inn*.

Glad They Were Wearing Pads

Coffeyville

Check out the website of any weather service and the name of Coffeyville, Kansas, is sure to come up. That's because Coffeyville, a town just a mile from the Oklahoma border, holds the rare distinction of being the very place on the globe where the most gigundus hailstone fell. You've heard hailstones described as golf ball size or pea size or even softball size. Well, the hailstone that fell on the west end of Coffeyville on September 3, 1970, was the size of a large rugby ball. It had a 17.5-inch circumference and a 7-inch diameter, and it weighed nearly 2 pounds. And the people of Coffeyville can prove it. Wearing football helmets for protection, they rushed out, snagged the giant hailstone, and stuck it in a freezer until meteorologists could get there to measure it.

Eventually, of course, the record-breaking hailstone did melt, but not before the Coffeyville Convention and Visitors Bureau had the foresight to make a plaster cast replica, which now sits in a glass showcase near the front of the Dalton Defenders Museum.

To see the world-record-holding, rugby-ball-size hailstone, visit the museum at 814 Walnut St., just east of the downtown plaza. Call (620) 251-5944.

Crime Doesn't Pay

Coffeyville

It's one of those unfortunate twists of fate. The Billy the Kids and the Son of Sams get all the glory. And their victims, the folks whose lives were cut short, are quickly relegated to the obit pages.

But not in Coffeyville. Here, the proud denizens celebrate the everyday Joes who, on October 5, 1892, stood up to the notorious Dalton Gang when the gang brazenly rode into their own hometown to rob not one, but two banks, in the light of a sunny day. The would-be robbers got delayed by construction, giving every store clerk, farmer, teacher, and innocent bystander time to grab guns and put up a fight. Twelve minutes later, when all the smoke had cleared, eight men lay dead—four of the five Daltons and four defenders whose names are proudly remembered each year in the annual celebration that includes reenactments, pig kissing contests, an outhouse auction, and wheelbarrow races.

And, yes, the townsfolk still take care of their own. When a major industry pulled up stakes in 1998, leaving a 500,000-square-foot building empty and hundreds jobless, the city put together a proposal in two short weeks to lure Amazon to open what was one the company's largest distribution/fulfillment centers at the time.

And as for the men who stood up to the Dalton Gang that October day, they were Lucius Baldwin, a dry goods store clerk; George Cubine, a shoemaker; Charles Connelly, the marshal; and Charles Brown, also a shoemaker.

Emmett Dalton, the youngest of the gang, survived and was sentenced to life in the Kansas Penitentiary. He was pardoned by the governor after 14 years and moved to California, where he wrote books and served as a consultant for the movie industry.

You can see the bullet holes left behind that day in the north brick wall in Death Alley. Visit www.coffeyville.com or call (620) 251-2550 to learn more about Dalton Defenders Days, which is always held the first full weekend of October.

Truth in Advertising

Elk Falls

Writers of travel brochures often exaggerate. When you show up to luxuriate in calm, serene waters, you find chlorine. When you look for the world's largest, you find second best. The Elk Falls travel brochure is nothing if not truthful.

The writers of the brochure call it a living ghost town. For a small fee, they'll scrawl your name on a rock and drop it into a pothole. They'll even make you an honorary citizen. On one condition: that you promise not to move there. They're happy with their population of 101, thank you very much.

To find out more about this teensy tourist town that London's prized newspaper *The Economist* raved about, call Friends of Elk Falls at (620) 329-4440.

Out the Back and Down the Garden Path

Elk Falls

Every year the population of Elk Falls (101, according to my records) grows tenfold on the Friday and Saturday before Thanksgiving. Not because the town sells the world's most scrumptious turkeys (in fact, the closest grocery store is in Grenola, 14 miles away), but because it offers the most unusual "homes tour" available anywhere. I should probably call it the "part of a homes tour," because the only room shown is the backyard outhouse. Not that the town's outhouses are anything to sneeze at.

Every one of them is elaborately decorated and given a name. Postmaster Licia Nichols's entry on the Outhouse Tour (perchance the only working outhouse still used by the US Postal Service?), for example, is called Postal Privy. There's an American flag, a gent built out of Priority boxes, and a story Licia wrote about "neither rain nor snow nor the postman needing to go."

Over the years, the tour has included the Gingerbread Outhouse (the seats on Hansel and Gretel's double-seater were painted red and white, like peppermint candy), a Chamber Pot (this elaborate porcelain throne was thrown by Steve Fry, the local potter), the Flower Pot (once a WPA outhouse, it was redesigned and sat next to the garden at the local B&B), the Nature Calls Outhouse (donated by the phone company, it had a phone receiver rather than a moon cutout on the door and included a little sign urging those who "have to go" to use the competitor's phone books first), and the Pooh Puppy Palace, designed around a fire hydrant. In 2024, favorites included Tomb of King Toot, Crapper Barrel, and Wipe Out. Everybody who comes to town for the festival and buys a button gets a map and a ballot for voting.

In 2008 *American Profile* magazine, well, profiled the Outhouse Tour and "outhouse enthusiasts came out of the woodwork," Fry said. "We got poems and songs and odes to the outhouse from thirty-five states."

Most importantly, the article attracted the attention of Homer Allison, the country's foremost outhouse collector, who donated his entire collection to Elk Falls. So now, the local one-room schoolhouse has been transformed into the Homer Allison Outhouse Museum. Displays include electric corncobs, outhouse signs, and miniature outhouses made of everything from coal to copper.

For more information about the museum or the annual Elk Falls Outhouse Tour, call Friends of Elk Falls at (620) 329-4440.

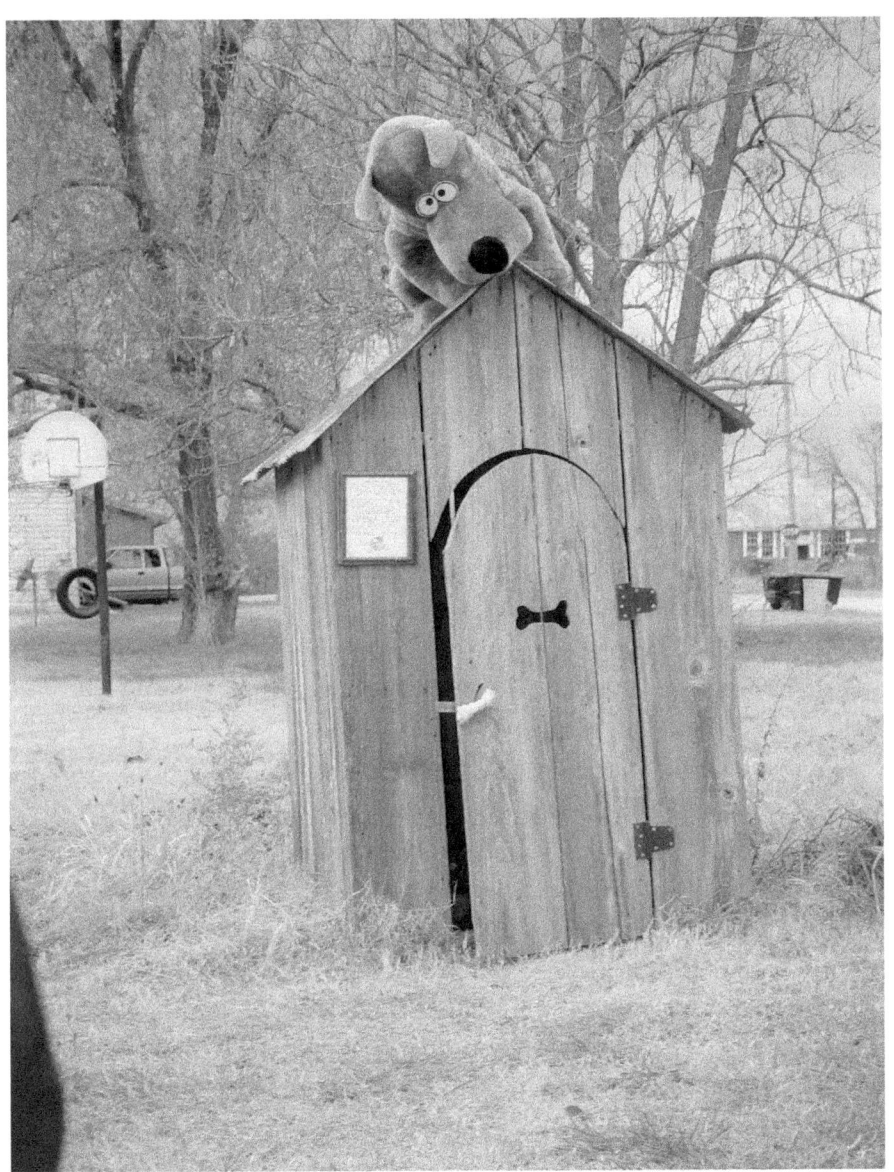

Über fire hydrant STEVE FRY

I Would Have Moved to Kansas Too

Elk Falls

Right outside Elk Falls is a historical marker erected by the State of Connecticut. While most states choose to erect historical markers within their own boundaries, Connecticut erected this one in Kansas to make up for a giant boo-boo it made in 1833.

Even though Connecticut sided with the Yankees in the Civil War, the state came out with a "Black Law" in 1833 to prevent Black students from getting a free education. The law was passed after Prudence Crandall, an educator and human rights advocate, started New England's first academy for Black females. For doing so, she was thrown in jail and endured three long court battles, all the while being harassed and hounded by local mobs. When the vigilantes started in on her students—throwing rocks through windows, setting the place on fire, and refusing to serve her students—she closed the school in order to protect them.

By the time Connecticut repealed the "Black Law" in 1838, Prudence had already moved to Illinois, where she continued the fight for equality and equal education for everyone.

So why is the historical marker in Kansas? In 1874, Prudence moved to Elk Falls with her brother, Hezekiah, to teach Native Americans.

In 1886 the Connecticut legislature, supported by Mark Twain, apologized to Prudence, offered her a $400 monthly stipend, and even agreed to buy her old Connecticut home for her to retire in. She wisely "just said no." She died in Elk Falls on January 27, 1890.

More than 100 years after her Connecticut trials, legal arguments used by her 1833 trial attorney were submitted to the Supreme Court during the historic civil rights case of *Brown v. Topeka Board of Education*. And in 1951 Walt Disney/NBC made a movie about Prudence's life, *She Stood Alone*.

The Connecticut marker is right next to the marker erected by the Kansas Historical Society on US 160 on the west edge of Elk Falls.

Getting By with a Little Help from the Locals
Emporia

In the "olden" days, you could walk down to the local theater, plop down 10 cents, and watch a movie in the afternoon. It may cost you a little more now than in 1930, but you can still go to the same theater locals were visiting almost 100 years ago and take a trip down memory lane.

The Emporia Granada Theatre was built in 1929 and cost $350,000. It had an organ that helped accentuate those early talkies and hosted everything from beauty pageants to vaudeville acts. The Fox Corporation leased it for a number of years; thus, it was known as the Fox Theatre for a while.

While it was a boon to the community in the early part of the century, the theater has had its share of ups and downs. There was a fire in 1959 and for the next two decades suffered from decline and neglect resulting in a leaky roof. In 1982, the theater closed—some thought permanently, especially when it was slated for demolition. Then, in 1984 the Granada Theatre Alliance was formed. Its goal was to restore the old building to its former glory and make it better than it was. In 1985, the building was listed on the National Register of Historic Places and the Alliance got to work on raising money preserving the Spanish Colonial Revival architecture.

The theater reopened in 2008 with new frescoes on the walls, new seats, up-to-code bathrooms, and a new concession area. The ticket office is updated but still in its original location, and the carpet is a reproduction of the original. A 100-year-old patron had a swatch of the original carpet when the renovation was going on, and she offered it as a contribution so the new carpet could be matched.

Today, you might catch a movie (alas no organ, it wasn't replaced after the fire), see a play, or catch a concert or any number of other performances the Emporia Granada Theatre has scheduled. Whether it's for a show, to see the architecture, or just to relive a past space in time, you won't regret the visit. The theater is located at 807 Commercial St., the main drag in Emporia.

Not-So-National Dinosaur Monument
Erie

If you're still trembling from the *Jurassic Park* movies, don't even think about driving south of Erie on Highway 47. From a distance, you'll think you've accidentally stumbled into a time warp. Several massive dinosaurs, some rearing their heads, others tending to their young, are grazing on Robert Dorris's family property.

The retired navy officer built the life-size dinosaurs out of scrap metal. And while they're certainly not real fossils, it would take an expert paleontologist to tell the difference. After studying each dinosaur, Dorris drew diagrams, took pictures of sculptures at museums, and began scouring through piles of scrap metal looking for discarded oil pans, pistons, crankshafts, and other pieces of metal that might make a vertebra or a skull. Among his collection of 15 are *Velociraptors*, a *Pterodactyl*, a *Triceratops*, and a mom and baby *Eryops*.

If you build it, they will come. GRASSROOTS ART CENTER

Dorris's dinosaur fascination began after a visit to the Smithsonian back in the 1980s. "I was looking at the dinosaur skeletons at the Smithsonian," Dorris said, "and I thought, shoot, I could build one of these."

Sure enough, he went home and made a *Brontosaurus* out of bolts, a gift he gave to his wife, Elveta. Next he made a *Teratosaurus* from welded car parts. Mr. Dorris passed away in 2007. While some of his larger creations are still on the property, many have moved to the Erie Dinosaur Park located at Fourth and Walnut.

The family still allows visitors to drive past and take pictures. To visit the modern-day Jurassic Park, drive south of Erie on Highway 47.

Trivia

More than 2,000 wild horses live in Greenwood County's tall grass pastures. The US Bureau of Land Management pays a dollar amount per day per horse. BLM does not provide a suggested rate as there are many factors to pasture these horses. To qualify to babysit what the BLM calls "a natural resource," you gotta have a business plan and a set amount of acreage per wild horse.

Gravity of the Situation

Eureka

If you go to Colby College in Maine, Emory College in Atlanta, and 11 other college campuses across the Eastern Seaboard, you'll find monuments erected by the Gravity Research Foundation, a scientific clearinghouse that awards competitive grants to scientists conducting antigravity research. In return for planting these gravestone-resembling monuments, these 13 small colleges received between $5,000 and $12,000 of stock (which eventually grew to millions of dollars) for gravity research. But in Eureka, the man who started the Gravity Research Foundation erected more than a monument. He built a whole college.

Roger Babson, a self-made millionaire, 1940 US presidential candidate, and the first to predict the 1929 stock market crash, believed Eureka was the safest place in the US to live. He called it the center of "The Magic Circle." He founded Utopia College there 6 years after his unsuccessful presidential bid.

A graduate of MIT and the author of 47 books, Babson became obsessed with gravity at the age of 18 after his younger sister, Edith, drowned in Massachusetts's Annisquam River.

"She was unable to fight gravity," Babson later wrote, "which came up and seized her like a dragon and brought her to the bottom."

Unfortunately, the year after he opened Eureka's Utopia College, a second relative succumbed to the forces of gravity. Like Edith, his grandson drowned in New Hampshire's Lake Winnipesaukee. From that point until his death 20 years later, the eccentric Babson turned all efforts to the study of gravity, a force he believed could be conquered and controlled. Which could explain why Utopia College is now defunct.

But the building is still there, along with lots of beautiful Flint Hill scenery. It is privately owned but is always available for drive-bys if you are looking to follow the history of gravity like Babson.

Nanny Nanny Boo Boo
Fort Scott

Arlington National Cemetery might be more famous, but the National Cemetery in Fort Scott is older. Or at least that's what the sign on the edge of the cemetery says. It was the first of 14 national cemeteries established by President Lincoln. Arlington, that also-ran, was number two. Buried here are 16 Native American Civil War vets, Black soldiers known as buffalo soldiers (their gravestones are shorter), and even some Confederate soldiers, but their graves are at an oblique angle. National Cemetery is located at 900 E. National, (620) 223-2840.

Larger Than Life
Fort Scott

Born in Fort Scott in 1912, Gordon Parks, the youngest of 15 children, became a world-renowned photojournalist, filmmaker, novelist, poet, and composer. In 2004, Fort Scott Community College established the Gordon Parks Center for Culture and Diversity, and in October 2005 Parks himself donated $250,000 worth of photographs to the center. Before then, Parks's works in Fort Scott were displayed at Mercy Hospital.

Gordon Parks, who left Fort Scott when he was 16, bought a used camera in 1938—a camera that launched a preeminent career in photography (20 years with *Life* magazine, to name one of his gigs) and film that included such movies as *Shaft, Leadbelly*, and a movie of his autobiographical novel, *The Learning Tree*, set, of course, in Kansas.

"Parks overcame a childhood filled with racism and poverty and chose to fight back with weapons of his own making—his mind, his creativity, and his art. He devoted his professional life to showing injustice and revealing beauty and in doing so made multiple substantive accomplishments to world culture and diversity," said Jill Walford, director of the center.

The Gordon Parks Center for Culture and Diversity is located at Fort Scott Community College, 2108 S. Horton (620-223-2700, ext. 5850).

Wish upon a Car

Galena

Lana Turner was discovered on a fountain stool at Schwab's drugstore. Natalie Portman was sitting in a pizza joint when an agent signed her to model. Tow Mater, the bucktoothed, redneck star of Disney's 2006 hit *Cars,* was discovered in a Kansas farm field with a tree growing through its middle. Pixar's Joe Ranft spotted the rusted International boom truck that inspired the lovable Mater outside Galena while driving Route 66 for research. Today, the celebrity hunk of rusted metal sits at the north end of Galena's Main Street in front of a 1930s Kan-O-Tex gas station, fully restored. It even runs and, for the right price, will show up at parties.

The old gas station where Tow Mater poses daily with Route 66 travelers (13.2 miles of the Mother Road zooms right through Kansas) has been converted into a diner and gift shop that's stuffed to the rafters with Route 66 souvenirs and such *Cars* memorabilia as Tow Mater himself sculpted from clay. Called Cars on the Route, the diner is run by four Kansas friends who serve hearty road food (a specialty, of course, is Mater sandwiches: tomato, onion, and butter or mayo on white bread) and like to gab over the scrapbook they've put together of the gas station pre-restoration. As for the local celebrity (who has been renamed Tow Tater for obvious trademark reasons), his odometer reads 99,372 miles and his fuel tank resembles a beer keg. The diner is at 119 N. Main St., (620) 202-1615, www.carsontheroute.com.

New York? Where's New York?
Girard

In 1922 the *Chicago Daily News* called Girard (population 2,722) the "Literary Capital of the United States." They knew what they were talking about. Two hugely successful publishing ventures were launched in this tiny burg in southeast Kansas.

The first, *Appeal to Reason,* a radical Socialist newspaper, was launched in 1897. By 1913 it was the largest-selling newspaper in the country, with a circulation of 750,000. Started by J. A. Wayland and masterminded by well-known liberal Fred Warren, who served as editor for 10 years, the *Appeal* printed progressive articles advocating such radical ideas as the 40-hour workweek, the abolition of child labor, and pure food and drug laws.

All of the country's progressive thinkers wrote for the paper, including Jack London, Mary "Mother" Jones, Helen Keller, and Stephen Crane. In 1904, Warren paid little-known reporter Upton Sinclair $500 to write an investigative piece on the meatpacking industry in Chicago. The piece ran as seven weekly installments and was eventually bought by Doubleday, which published it as a book, *The Jungle.* By 1906 the book had become a huge bestseller and had been translated into 27 languages.

Constantly provoking controversy, the paper became a target for politicians and federal investigators. Warren was often thrown in jail, the paper's offices were broken into several times, and smear campaigns by such venerable competitors as the *Los Angeles Times* were waged on Wayland. On November 10, 1912, after newspaper leaks claimed he'd seduced an orphan who then died from the resulting abortion, Wayland died by suicide. His family, who continued to run the paper, eventually won libel suits against several newspapers, including the *L.A. Times.*

The final blow, however, came from J. Edgar Hoover and the Red Scare of 1919. In what's now known as the Palmer Raids, 10,000 Americans were rounded up and accused of supporting Communism. Many were shipped off to Russia. Subscribers got scared and canceled their subscriptions. The paper delivered its last issue on November 4, 1922.

The other publishing empire in Girard was Little Blue Books, a mail-order publishing company that sold small, inexpensive pamphlets of classic literature. Emanuel Haldeman-Julius, co-owner of *Appeal to Reason* after Wayland's death, had the dream of bringing literature to the common working man. He sold 3.5-by-5-inch paperbacks of everything from Greek plays and the complete works of Shakespeare to *Alice's Adventures in Wonderland* and *Jam and Jelly-Making for Beginners.*

Many of his 2,000 titles were reprints (H. G. Wells claimed he made much more money with Haldeman-Julius than with traditional publishers), but he also commissioned original works by such writers as family-planning pioneer Margaret Sanger, who wrote a Little Blue Book called *What Every Girl Should Know,* and Will Durant, who first published *The Story of Philosophy* with Haldeman-Julius.

Set in 8-point type and sold for a nickel, the books with the blue covers were a smash hit. More than 500 million were sold.

Once, while in New York, Haldeman-Julius was approached by two struggling publishers.

"Why," they wanted to know, "are you so successful there in backwater Kansas and we can't make it here in New York?"

Haldeman-Julius advised the men, who at that time were producing crossword puzzles, to publish a hardcover copy of Durant's *The Story of Philosophy.* Mr. Simon and Mr. Schuster took him up on his advice and the rest, shall we say, is history.

Often called "the Henry Ford of publishing," Haldeman-Julius made millions before he drowned in his backyard swimming pool. Little Blue Book fans included Emperor Haile Selassie of Ethiopia and Admiral Richard Byrd, who took a complete set on his expedition to the South Pole.

Although the Little Blue Printing Company burned to the ground in 1978, you can drive by the homes of Haldeman-Julius (east of Girard on Sinnet) and J. A. Wayland (721 N. Summit St.). Back issues of *Appeal to Reason* and most of the 2,000 titles of Little Blue Books can be found in the special collections section of the Leonard H. Axe Library at Pittsburg State University, 1605 S. Joplin St., (620) 235-4882, www.axe.pittstate.edu.

Hubbell's Rubble
Howard

In 1980, Jerry Hubbell signed up for a welding class at Independence Community College. It was a decision that can only be compared to Georgia O'Keeffe meeting Alfred Stieglitz.

"I thought I was taking it so I could work on my farm. You know, fix fences, keep the machines running," he said.

But before he knew it, he was using his welding torch to turn combine augers into mules and silo bottoms into 15-foot *Wizard of Oz* tin men.

His scrap metal creations, dubbed Hubbell's Rubble by the good folks of Howard, take up three city lots and create plenty of traffic. Visitors often stop by the WPA outhouse that he hauled to the site to sign the guestbook.

"It's a two-seater. I call it my office," Jerry said. The guestbook has John Hancocks from pretty much every state in the union.

"I still marvel and wonder how it really happened," said Jerry, who claims he never showed any inclination toward art before the welding class.

Soon after, though, his wife threw a dinner party for several of her gardening friends. As a joke, he welded together a female scarecrow on wheels, covered her with a sheet, tied some balloons to her, and unveiled her for the dinner party guests. He invited the six couples to come up with a name.

Tilly the Tiller, she became. Soon she was joined by a dinosaur, Batman riding a motorcycle, a purple people eater, and a car named Maybelline.

"I just use stuff I find. Very rarely do I pay for anything," said Hubbell, who retired from welding in 2002 upon doctor's orders. Didn't complement his defibrillator, the doc said.

To sign the guestbook in the outhouse office, visit Hubbell's Rubble on Highway 99, just inside the Howard city limits and south of Toot's Drive-In.

Just a Closer Walk with Thee

Humboldt

Humboldt's Biblesta is the largest parade in the world that depicts scenes from the Bible. Then again, it's probably the only parade in the world that depicts scenes from the Bible. Every float, every character, every band member has to be authentically dressed like Moses or Mary Magdalene or somebody else who graces the pages of the Good Book. In 2024, the event celebrated its 66-year anniversary.

The Humboldt High School band usually starts the parade with the gospel classic "Just a Closer Walk with Thee"; then the floats, such as Jonah and a 40-foot whale that squirts water on the crowd, follow behind, circling the town square (if you can circle a town square).

Dr. Arthur Carlson Jr. is credited with hatching the unique parade theme back in 1957. While sitting at a prayer meeting, he suddenly remembered the apostle Paul's words that Christians should take their witness to the streets. The good Christians of Humboldt have been taking it to the streets ever since.

Name a scene from the Bible and it has been featured at one time or another in the parade, which draws thousands from around the world to this little burg of 2,000. There have been floats featuring the Four Horsemen of the Apocalypse, the baptism of Jesus, and the Exodus, a walking float that always includes livestock. Gospel and contemporary Christian music are played on the town square, and a free bean supper begins promptly at 5 p.m.

Events start at 10 a.m. and the parade starts at 1:30 p.m., rain or shine, on the first Saturday in October. Amen.

People See, People Do

Independence

Independence, Kansas, played a pioneering role in America's space program. In 1959, a native of this southeast Kansas town was launched into space in a small capsule atop a Jupiter rocket. The pioneer astronaut, a monkey named Miss Able (there was also a Cain—get it?), survived her short trip of 300 miles at 10,000 mph, paving the way for human space travel.

Although she was not the first animal on a space mission, she was the first that actually lived to tell—er, rather, hoot—about it. Sadly, she died 4 days after her flight, as technicians tried to remove sensors from her heart. The upside is she made the cover of the June 15, 1959, issue of *Life* magazine.

To visit Miss Able's chimphood home, visit Ralph Mitchell Zoo's Monkey Island at Riverside Park in Independence. The 124-acre park also has a unique kiddie playland with concrete dinosaurs and nursery rhyme characters, a carousel that still costs 5 cents, a miniature train ride that will set you back a mere 50 cents, and a miniature golf course that tells the history of Independence in 18 holes.

Riverside Park and Ralph Mitchell Zoo are located at the corner of Penn Avenue and Oak Street. For more information visit https://www.independenceks.gov/286/FORPAZ.

The List Goes On

Also in Independence:

- Shulthis Stadium, the first stadium in the country where baseball was played under lights. The game was April 28, 1930. The Independence Yankees, a farm team for the bigs, built the stadium and then, 19 years later, hired a little-known player named Mickey Mantle, who played his first season there in 1949. The stadium is in Riverside Park.

- The most comprehensive collection of native son William Inge's work. The Pulitzer Prize–winning author wrote *Picnic, Bus Stop*, and the Academy Award–winner *Splendor in the Grass*, to name a few.

- Lots of big historic mansions. In 1901 and 1902, Independence had more millionaires per capita than any city in the country. The millions were made from three things that were discovered in Independence: natural gas, oil, and limestone, which was used to make concrete.

A Sweet Treat by Any Other Name

Madison

If you're from Oklahoma, Missouri, or Kansas, you no doubt have experienced that wonderful, buttery bread aroma drifting from your kitchen. No one would have cared where the sweet, yummy-smelling pastries came from as long as you were able to buy one from a local school band group that was having a fundraiser for an end-of-year trip. But who would have guessed with all the hay baling, farming, and hunting going on across the state, all that confectioner's goodness comes from Madison, Kansas?

Jacob Knobloch and his wife, Krystal, bought the business Kansas Maid, from his parents in 2023. Tom and Jeri Knobloch had owned and operated the business 30 years to the day that Jacob purchased it. You might find Jacob hauling hay June through August, but September through May, you can find him and his 13 employees in the factory in Madison making the different pastries they offer.

Nothing but the best ingredients go into their products. Kansas Maid sources products as local as they can find them, like flour from McPherson,

The cherry on top KANSAS MAID

Kansas, and butter from Nebraska. While they do offer cinnamon rolls and sticky caramel buns, Knobloch sells 33 percent more strawberry cream cheese braids, with cherry coming in second in customer favorites.

Unfortunately, they are too busy to offer tours through the factory, but if you can't find a school, church group, cheer team, or 4-H group in your area selling these delectable goodies and you are passing through Madison, you can find their only retail outlet, Chubby Foods, 2.5 miles from the factory, right there off Main Street. Take your cooler and load up. You'll be glad you did.

But, Captain, I Don't See an Ocean
Neodesha

In the tiny one-stoplight town of Neodesha, 1,500 miles from the nearest ocean, there's a factory with a big sign: THROUGH THESE DOORS WALK THE FINEST BOAT BUILDERS IN THE WORLD. Indeed, Cobalt's 300 to 400 boat builders, mostly farmers, make luxury sport boats, 20-to-29-foot runabouts, with the best reputation in the industry.

When Pack St. Clair, owner of the family-run business that also sells yachts, built his first Cobalt in 1968, he drove it out to California for a boat show. A then-outsider, he was refused admittance, but since he'd poured his last dime into building the boat, he figured he might as well stick around. He parked it in a gas station across from the boat show where everybody could see it. Sure enough, a San Ramon, California, dealer took one look at his boat's sleek lines and ingenious flowing power hump and signed on to be the first dealer. Today, the company has 100 dealers across the globe, makes 2,600 boats and $125 million per year, and happily gives tours to anyone who shows up at the factory in Neodesha.

"We know from experience that once a customer sees what we do here, realizes the work ethic involved, we've got 'em for life," said Alex Barry, regional manager of the western US.

Call ahead and they'll take you on a tour at 1715 N. Eighth St., (800) 468-5764, www.cobaltboats.com.

Abbie Hoffman, You Weren't the First

Pittsburg

The world's first protest march occurred in southeast Kansas. It was December 1921 when nearly 6,000 women, wearing ragged coats and carrying their babies, marched to protest management's decision to replace their coal mining husbands with scabs, most of them fraternity boys from local colleges. In those days, there were 517 mines in southeast Kansas; the miners, who often worked lying on their sides, were lucky to make $1.25 a day. Conditions were wretched, pay was arbitrarily withheld, and more than 200 miners in Crawford and Cherokee Counties were injured or killed in 1921 alone.

The protesters, wives of the miners who were already striking, got mad. They blocked the entrances to the mines with American flags, beat on the bosses with brooms, and sang songs of solidarity in French, Slovene, German, and Italian. The panicked governor of Kansas set up a command post

Communes in Kansas

In Bourbon County, you'll find Vegetarian Creek, named for a former Kansas commune, Octagon City. The Vegetarian Settlement Company bought 16 square miles of farmland in the Kansas Territory in 1862. The ambitious company, which originated in New York, planned an octagonal community with 102 wedge-shaped farms of 16 acres each. Many vegetable-loving settlers bought shares in the company, which promised an eventual hydropathic estate, an agricultural college, a scientific institute, and a museum of curiosities to go along with the farmland. Although the company had good intentions, most of what it promised never materialized. Miriam Davis Colt, one of the shareholders who traveled from New York to Kansas, published a diary of her life at the commune titled *I Went to Kansas: A Thrilling Account of an Ill-Fated Expedition to Fairy Land.* There is also a historical marker, *"Sad Saga of Vegetarian Creek,"* at 1140 Arizona Rd. that commemorates the failed utopian dream.

at Pittsburg's Stilwell Hotel, and the state militia, including a machine gun company, was activated.

The nation had never seen anything like it. "Near-anarchy," said the *New York Times,* which dubbed the women "The Amazon Army." The press raced to southeast Kansas from around the world.

By the end of December, 49 of the women had been arrested and jailed, shots had been fired, and the local union had sent its miners back to work. The Kansas coal industry began its long slide into oblivion, and the Amazon Army was largely forgotten.

Thanks to Lawrence artist Wayne Wildcat, who is part Yuchi Indian, a 10-by-12-foot mural of the march was recently unveiled. You can see it at the Pittsburg Public Library, Fourth and Walnut Streets, (620) 231-8110, www.pplonline.org.

Whole Lotta Cluckin' Going On
Pittsburg

Not 100 yards from each other in a virtual ghost town are not one but two wildly successful fried chicken restaurants that together seat more than 800 people. What's more, they've been wildly successful for more than six decades.

Chicken Annie (aka Ann Frances Rehak Pichler) and Chicken Mary (Mary Zerngast) both started frying chicken in their homes when their coal mining hubbies lost their jobs. Annie's husband, Charles, lost his leg in March 1933 while sitting on a railroad coal car. Because the coal mining companies could no longer use an amputee, Annie, with three small children at home, was forced to think quick. She opened her three-room home to her husband's former coworkers, who gladly paid her 15 cents for a mug of home brew and a ham or veal sandwich. Before long, the Pichlers had to add more rooms and more items to the menu. By 1934, Annie was serving three pieces of fried chicken, German potato salad, German coleslaw with garlic, green peppers, a tomato slice, and bread for a whopping 75 cents.

In 1941, Chicken Mary, who lived across the street, had a similar string of bad luck when her husband, Joe, came down with a strange illness that caused him to lose his job. She too opened her kitchen table and began attracting coal miners, who would knock on the door anytime, night or day, to hustle a meal. Within 4 years, she and Joe moved a pool hall they picked up cheap from a nearby mining camp to the lot next door. Although they originally called their pool hall turned restaurant Joe's Place, it soon became known far and wide as Chicken Mary's because Mary, who was 5 foot 1 and just about as wide, was a real character who pinned her apron on with two safety pins.

Today the mining camps are closed and the restaurants are run by the Chicken ladies' kids and grandkids. Located 5 miles north of Fourth Street and Broadway on US 69 and 3 miles east on US 160, both are open 4 to 8:30 p.m. Tuesday through Friday, 4 to 9 p.m. Saturday, and 11 a.m. to 8 p.m. Sunday. Chicken Annie's, (620) 231-9460, www.chickenanniesoriginal .com; Chicken Mary's, (620) 231-9510, www.chickenmarys1942.com.

Between a Rock and a Hard Place

Sedan

Nobody knows for sure who built England's megalithic ruin known as Stonehenge. Some claim it was the Druids. Others say Merlin himself conjured up the ancient rock formation.

Thanks to the conveniences of modern civilization, we will never need to question the genesis of Prairiehenge, the half-acre earthwork that overlooks a valley just west of Sedan. Barring some unforeseen disaster, we will always know that this tribute to the tallgrass prairie and the Osage Indians was built by artist Stan Herd, who spent a year forming the 13-ton limestone rocks into two overlapping circles.

Commissioned by A&E personality Bill Kurtis, who owns the 10,000-acre ranch where it rests, Prairiehenge was strategically designed in what Kurtis calls "the secret meadow" of his Red Buffalo Ranch. He bought the ranch, near his boyhood home, soon after 9/11, to get back in touch with the land. "When towers fall, you reach out for some permanent anchor," he said. "Here you can feel the pulse of earth beneath your feet."

Bet You Didn't Know They Were from Kansas

- Dennis "The Menace" Mitchell. In Hank Ketcham's 1990 autobiography, he explained that 5-year-old Dennis, his patient parents Henry and Alice Mitchell, dog Ruff, and cat Hot Dog actually live in Wichita. Henry works at a local aeronautical engineering company and George Wilson, the grouchy neighbor, is retired from the post office. The naughty but lovable Kansan has appeared in at least two movies, a television series, and a daily comic strip that is still run in 1,000 news-papers in 48 countries.

- Superman. Like Dennis, Superman grew up "secretly" in Kansas. In a 1986 *Man of Steel* comic book, the superhero made the comment, "At heart, I'm just a boy from a small town in Kansas." Before that announcement, readers just knew he was from "Smallville," some-where in the heart of America. Producers of Christopher Reeve's 1978 film filled the screen with wide-open fields of waving wheat, grain elevators, and even a Kansas Star passenger train to be outrun by the teenage orphan from planet Krypton. In ABC's *Lois and Clark,* the crime-fighting investigative reporter often flew home to Kansas to visit his Smallville parents.

- The Birdman of Alcatraz. Although he's known for his stint at the Alcatraz penitentiary in San Francisco, Robert Stroud, the "Birdman of Alca-traz," spent more than 30 years in the federal penitentiary in Leav-enworth, Kansas. Transferred there in 1912, he received extension diplomas from Kansas State University in mechanical drawing, engi-neering, mathematics, music, and theology. In 1920 he began study-ing birds and was soon publishing articles and books about birds and their diseases.

- Olive Oyl. Marilyn Schreffler, who did the voice for Popeye the Sailor's cartoon girlfriend, was born in Wichita, graduated from Topeka West, and attended Topeka's Washburn University. Besides being Olive Oyl,

Schreffler appeared in numerous TV commercials, including some for Alka-Seltzer and Dole pineapple.

- Mary Ann. You're a true trivia expert if you know Mary Ann's character in *Gilligan's Island* used to work at a department store in Winfield, Kansas.

- Smokey Bear. Artist Rudolph Wendelin first drew Smokey (this was before he was a real bear) in Atwood, Kansas.

- The first husband of the Duchess of Windsor. Earl Winfield Spencer Jr., who was married to Wallis Simpson before she married the dethroned king of Britain, was born in Kinsley, Kansas.

- The creator of Geech. Jerry Bittle, creator of the popular syndicated comic strip, got his first job as a professional artist at his hometown newspaper, the *Wichita Eagle-Beacon.* In the early 1980s, he created *Geech*, a comic strip based on his memories of Kansas. Artie, a regular character in the strip, sometimes wears a sweatshirt from Bittle's alma mater, Wichita State University.

- Dennis Hopper. It was cowboy movies at the Saturday matinees in Dodge City that first inspired Dennis Hopper to take up acting. He was born in Dodge City and grew up on his grandparents' farm nearby while his father was away in the military.

- The creator of Porky Pig. Melvin "Tubby" Millar was often found by his family in Portis, Kansas, doodling cartoons on the side of his homework. His talent took him to Hollywood and a job with Warner Bros., where he created many Looney Tunes characters, most notably Porky Pig.

- Buster Keaton. His Kansas birth was a bit of an accident. As acrobats, his parents were appearing in a traveling tent show with magician Harry Houdini. While spending the night in Piqua, a windstorm blew down their tent; their son Joseph (he didn't earn the name Buster until he was a toddler) was born a few hours later in the church where they took shelter. The star of more than 100 silent movies returned to his birthplace only once, when he drove through town in his chauffeur-driven limousine.

(Continued from previous page)

- Emmett Kelly. The famous circus clown was born in Sedan and lived there until his father quit his job with the railroad and bought a farm in Missouri.

- Vivian Vance. Born Vivian Jones in Cherryvale, this actress who had to agree to wear frumpy clothes and be 10 to 20 pounds overweight in her most notorious role as Lucille Ball's sidekick, moved to Independence when she was 2. Her parents opened a grocery store there.

- The Scarecrow in The Wizard of Oz. The actor Fred Stone, who played the Scarecrow on Broadway, lived in a string of Kansas towns with his father, a traveling barber. His first performance was as a tightrope walker in Topeka when he was 11.

- The actor who played Charlie Chan. Sidney Toler, who made 22 appearances as the clever Chan, was raised in Kansas. His parents owned a grocery store in Anthony in south-central Kansas.

- Erin Brockovich. The real Erin Brockovich was born and raised in Lawrence, Kansas. Her parents still live there.

- Hugh Beaumont. Dad to Wally and "The Beav," Beaumont's Ward Cleaver was also born in Lawrence. When he was in high school his family moved to California, where he was discovered in a Hollywood talent search. After retiring from acting, he moved back to the Midwest (Minnesota) to raise Christmas trees.

At last count, Kurtis was grazing 1,000 head of cattle and 60 buffalo on his ranch.

Although groups can make arrangements to visit Prairiehenge, the blackjack oak grove where Prairiehenge rests is not officially open to the public. To find out more, contact Kurtis's Red Buffalo Gift Shop, 107 E. Main, (620) 725-4022, http://theredbuffalo.com.

Ma, Pa, Laura, and Mary Were Here
Wayside

Of Laura Ingalls Wilder's nine books, *Little House on the Prairie* remains the most popular, having spawned a popular TV series and sold some 5 million copies since it was published in 1935. The "little house" Wilder wrote about (if it were still standing) would be in Wayside (if it were still a town). Lucky for true *Little House*–philes, the little house, which was really more like a 14-by-16-foot log cabin, has been authentically re-created in the very spot where it once stood. There's also a well that Pa and Mr. Scott dug; Sunny Side school, an 1871 schoolhouse where Laura would have gone had she been old enough; and a post office where she might have sent a letter had she known how to write back then.

When the log cabin was erected by Pa Ingalls in 1870, it was the 89th residence in Rutland Township. Laura lived there from 1870 until 1871, when her family learned that they'd mistakenly built the durn thing on property belonging to the Osage Indian Reservation. They moved back to Wisconsin, never knowing that 6 months later the land was opened to homesteaders and, therefore, they could have stayed.

To see the cabin that looks an awful lot like the one Michael Landon and Melissa Gilbert hung out in, visit the Little House that sits 13 miles southwest of Independence off Highway 75. Call (620) 289-4238 or visit www.lhopmuseum.com for more information.

The Big Dipper
West Mineral

In its heyday, Big Brutus, a 16-story coal shovel, could lift out enough coal to fill three railroad cars with every scoop. But that was to be expected of a monster machine that weighed 135 tons, took a year to assemble, and required three men just to operate it. Twenty-four hours a day it ran, working hard for the Pittsburg and Midway Coal Mining Company, which paid $6.5 million to have it built and hired 150 railroad cars to bring it to southeast Kansas from Ohio.

But by 1974, coal prices dropped to $5 a ton. It cost $12 a ton just to use Big Brutus (the crazy thing used enough electricity to power a city with a population of 15,000), so the big cheese at the Pittsburg and Midway made a savvy business decision: Better shut the old shovel down. They tried to pawn it off on interested buyers, asking $5 million, but nobody even made an offer. It was too big to move (even disassembling it would cost a small fortune), so the company eventually donated it to a nonprofit in West Mineral, offering to paint it black and orange, company colors, for free.

Today it's a popular tourist attraction, drawing 30,000-plus visitors a year. Brooke Shields was one of those 30,000, and you can see her autograph ("To the miners. Love and kisses, Brooke Shields") in the visitor center. The visitor center also has old mining drills, historical pictures, and Little Giant, the world's smallest working replica of an electric mining shovel. Little Giant was built by a hobbyist back in the 1930s. It took him 11 years to finish, not too hard to believe when you realize it has 30,000 rivets and 2,000 bolts. The visitor center also offers yo-yos, Frisbees, playing cards, and even Christmas ornaments with pictures of Big Brutus.

Dig this. In its heyday Big Brutus could fill three railroad cars in a single scoop.

Cows in Space

In 1897, the Yates Center newspaper reported that Alexander Hamilton had come out of his house one afternoon to discover a cigar-shaped UFO hovering over his farm. According to the article, spacemen from the ship had roped one of Hamilton's calves and were trying to hoist it on board.

The article had verification from Yates Center's leading citizens, who vouched for the veracity of Hamilton's claims. For nearly 100 years, it was considered one of the best-documented UFO cases on the books. But there was just one problem: It was all a big hoax.

It seems Hamilton, along with his vouchers, belonged to the local liar's club. Once a week, they got together and attempted to outdo each other with tall tales. Hamilton's calfnapping story was so good that the paper published it as a joke. Little did they know that thousands of people around the world would be dumb enough to believe it. It wasn't until 1977 that Jerry Clark of *FATE* magazine published the real truth.

Guests willing to fork over $10 can make the breathtaking climb to the top. One couple even exchanged wedding vows up there.

You can't really miss a 160-foot orange-and-black coal shovel, but its exact location is 6 miles west of the K-7 and K-102 junction, then 0.5 mile south. Call (620) 827-6177; www.bigbrutus.org.

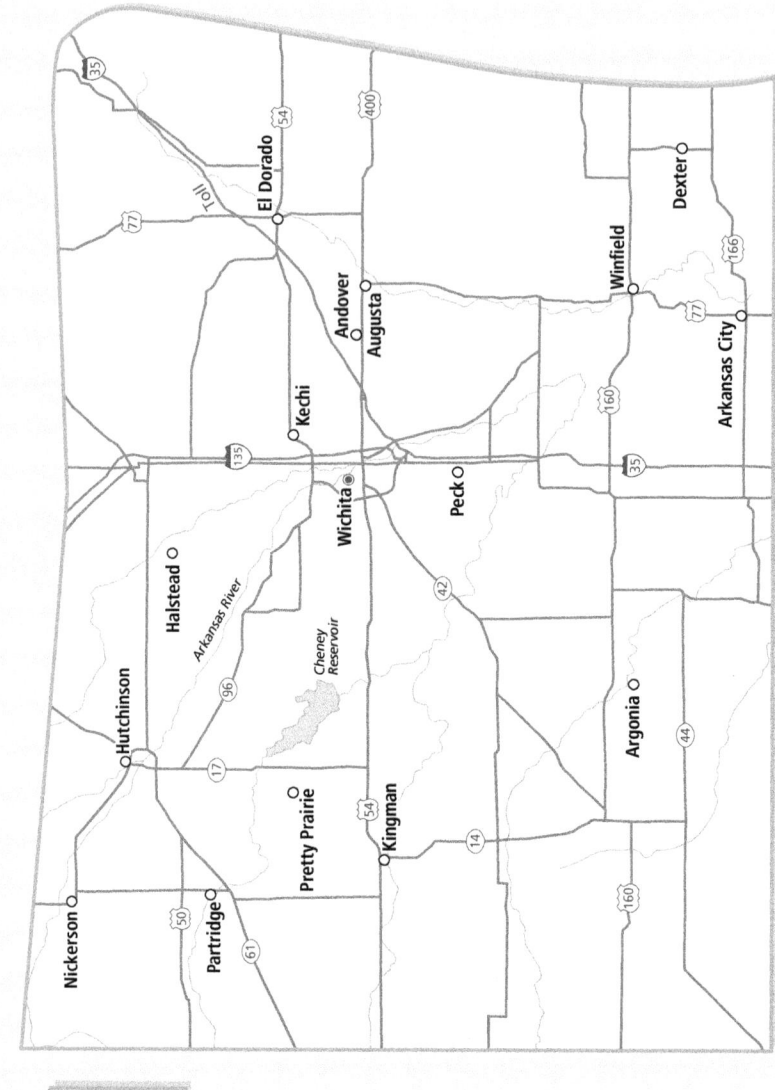

South Central

As hard as I try, I just can't rein in the superlatives when talking about south-central Kansas. There are just too many world's largests and world's firsts in this part of the state to remain humble.

For starters, the world's largest collection of space suits and the world's largest piece of salt can be found in one south-central town.

And if that wasn't enough, the world's first female mayor was elected in Argonia and the world's first Pizza Hut was established in Wichita.

So if you notice a tendency to brag, forgive me.

Of course, I prefer to call it editorial honesty. When I say south-central Kansas is one of the best places in the world to buy elderberry wine, I'm not exaggerating. When I drop names like Albert Einstein (whose brain lived on in Kansas long after his death), Frederic Remington (who got his artistic inspiration on a sheep farm in south-central Kansas), and Peter the Great (his very own autograph resides in Wichita), I'm not pulling a fast one. Basically, I'm telling it like it is. South-central Kansas is one heck of a place.

Rocket Men

Argonia

Turns out, NASA isn't the only organization launching rockets. K.L.O.U.D. Busters, a group of Kansas rocket enthusiasts, launch high-powered rockets that regularly break the sound barrier. In fact, their 40-acre "rocket pasture" outside Argonia has been approved to launch rockets up to 50,000 feet. Of course, you have to get an FAA-approved waiver if you're going higher than 25,000 feet. Five times, the Kansas pasture has been chosen to host the prestigious national Tripoli Rocketry Association's L.D.R.S., which any rocket scientist worth his boosters can tell you stands for "Large and Dangerous Rocket Ships."

At least once a month, the 100-plus members get together to fly their home-built rockets, many taller than them, with engines creating 16,000 pounds of thrust and reaching Mach 1 speeds. Not all rockets are as tall as Paul Bunyan. Experimental rockets are sometimes fashioned out of Legos or old footballs. With a state-of-the-art launchpad that can lift up to 64 rockets simultaneously, the club regularly hosts rocket drag races. There's a public address system, a tent for spectators, and FM broadcasts of the launch control officer's countdowns and play-by-plays.

K.L.O.U.D., in case you're wondering, stands for "*Kansas Lower Orbital Unmanned Delegation*". AirFest, an annual 4-day event held every Labor Day, promises ground-shaking, flame-shooting fun.

The rocket pasture is located on Highway 44, 7 miles south of Argonia, 1 mile east of Argonia Road. Contact them at K.L.O.U.D. Busters, Inc. c/o Science Education Center, 1321 E. Douglas, Wichita, KS 67211-3812, (316) 682-1921, www.kloudbusters.org.

Guess That Nomination Backfired

Argonia

The first woman mayor was elected in Kansas in 1887, 33 years before women nationally received the right to vote. Town drunks thought it would be funny to put the name of Susanna Salter, head of Argonia's Temperance Committee, on the ballot for mayor. Unbeknownst to her, Salter was elected by two-thirds of Argonia's voters. It turned out to be a joke that backfired on her nominating committee: The first thing Salter did was ban the sale of alcohol and close the town's bars.

Other Kansas women have gone on to be "firsts," including Amelia Earhart, Rena Milner (the first woman city manager), Mabel Chase (the first woman county sheriff), Julia Archibald Holmes (the first woman to climb Pike's Peak), Lucy Hobbs Taylor (the first woman dentist), Georgia Neese Clark Gray (the first woman US treasurer), and Minnie Morgan (the first to head an all-female city government).

To see the brick home that Susanna Salter lived in when she reigned as the country's first female mayor, visit 220 W. Garfield St. in Argonia. Even though she never ran for office again and eventually moved to Oklahoma (where she died in 1961 at the age of 101), her Argonia home is on the

National Register of Historic Places and operates as a museum. To arrange a tour, call (620) 435-6564 or visit www.salterhousemuseum.org.

Nothing Stays Lost Forever
Arkansas City

If you are interested in history, lost civilizations, and proving they existed, you ought to check out Etzanoa. They are doing an archeological dig there and finding all kinds of fascinating things, like everyday Indigenous living supplies and Spanish chain mail, the kind worn by 16th-century Spanish soldiers.

In 2015, Wichita State archeologist Don Blakeslee started a quest to find where Etzanoa, also known as "The Great Settlement," a Wichita Tribe settlement, was located. After following clues and studying 16th-century maps, he and his team headed south to where Spanish conquistador Juan de Oñate's expedition led him in 1601. Oñate wrote about the people he found in today's area of Arkansas City comprising around 20,000 inhabitants. He also wrote about a battle with the Etzanoa people. That battle took place in a 3.5-square-mile area along modern-day Country Club Road. After a 5-hour battle with the Indigenous people here, Oñate withdrew his expedition forces and headed back south. His limited number of men seemed outnumbered by the vast amount of forces he met.

Today, discoveries continue. With each foot of dirt removed, more comes to light about who lived in the area and how they lived. Bone tools, chain mail, pottery large and small, animal bones like bison and box turtle remains, canon shot, stone tools, obsidian, and a small piece of turquoise have all been found on the site.

As the dig sites now are on private property, folks like you and me can't visit the sites, but they hope to have adult student classes in the future. They are also going to be opening an Etzanoa Visitor Center in June 2026. This center will have pictures of the dig and more information about Etzanoa's history, where it was and how it was discovered again. If you would like more information, you can contact Georgia at (620) 666-0069.

Items found in the dirt
ETZANOA CONSERVANCY

Learning about history the natural way ETZANOA CONSERVANCY

63 Careers and Counting

Arkansas City

If you go to Canon City, Colorado, you'll find a tourist attraction called Buckskin Joe's. It's probably a fine establishment, probably has lots of Wild West tomfoolery. But I have a problem with it because the real Buckskin Joe, the one who could play 16 musical instruments, turn somersaults over the backs of horses, and hit small objects with a bow and arrow, was actually from Arkansas City, Kansas.

I can't make the argument that he never left Ark City. He made numerous expeditions into the silver fields of Colorado, the wilds of Honduras, and the depths of Nova Scotia, but his home base for all of these adventures was none other than Arkansas City, Kansas.

Edward Jonathan Hoyt (aka Buckskin Joe) was one of the first to homestead the area now known as Arkansas City. He built a home there, owned a grocery store there. Customers often had to wait on themselves, because Buckskin Joe and his partner were usually turning flips in the gymnasium they built in the back.

> ## Trivia
>
> Famed actress Elizabeth Taylor celebrated her first Christmas in Arkansas City, where both her maternal grandfather and grandmother (for whom she was named) lived. She also attended Ark City's Roosevelt Elementary when she was 9.

He served as US Marshal for the newly opened Oklahoma Territory, led expeditions into Indian country, and ran a beekeeping operation, all from Ark City.

For fun, he strung a wire from the town's two tallest buildings and walked the tightrope. One summer, when crowds of kids gathered, he pushed a wheelbarrow across the tightrope, stopping in the center to start a fire. After his third daughter, Belle, was born, he offered to take her across the wire with him. His wife wisely refused.

From Ark City, he formed the Cow Horn Band, the Ragged Ass Militia (so named because many of its members fought in tattered overalls and underwear), and his very own Buckskin Joe's Wild West Shows that had bronc riders, bucking horses, wild steers, and a bona fide "Pete-haw-e-rat" Indian village.

To find out more about Buckskin Joe, visit the Cherokee Strip Museum, located 1.6 miles south of the intersection of US 166 and US 77. Phone (620) 442-6750.

Keeping It Twisted in a Good Way
Augusta

If you've ever ridden a motorcycle, you know the feel of wind through your hair and the freedom of riding down the road with no confinements. The guys at Twisted Oz Motorcycle Museum has taken that freedom and well, put a twist on it.

"We are motorcycle people [speaking of his volunteers] who like bikes," Kelly Modlin, owner of the museum, said, "and want to educate people and preserve the history of the motorcycle."

Modlin started the museum in 2016. He has two buildings and over 6,000 square feet with bikes from before the 1920s. There are from 144 to 160 bikes, ranging from Harleys and Indians to Norton, Curtis, and Pope. The museum has bikes no one else has, like one of the first Indian Six bikes in the world. And there are only two. "I like to get toys never seen before," Modlin said. "I'm that guy."

People come from all over to see the bikes. After all, Twisted Oz is rated one of the top antique motorcycle museums in the world. It's nothing for people to drop in from England, Australia, or New Zealand to check the place out.

But if you're thinking all that's at Twisted Oz is motorcycles, you'd be mistaken. The museum also houses memorabilia from "Joyland," an amusement park that used to be in Wichita. It was a big part of the culture around these parts. Get good grades and you'd get a pass to Joyland.

Twisted Oz is located 12 miles east of Wichita in Augusta, 601 W. Seventh. The museum is open Friday and Saturday from 10 a.m. to 4 p.m. or by special request. Modlin doesn't box himself in, nor his guests.

"You know we've always been told think outside the box," Modlin said. "I was never allowed in the box."

Flying High Another Way

Dexter

In 1903, a local natural gas company, Gas, Oil, and Developing, discovered a large well reserve of natural gas beneath William Greenwell's farm near Dexter. Discovering this natural gas resource meant an economic boom to the area. The whole town turned out to watch the natural gas light up. But there was a problem. When they tried to light the gas, it would not burn. A Kansas University professor took samples back to the college after hearing about the perplexing problem. After all, the survey showed there was a lot of natural gas in the area. Two chemistry professors, Hamilton Cady and David McFarland, stepped up to the challenge of finding out what was going on. After 2 years of studying the issues, in 1905, the two discovered that the gas had helium in it.

Helium wasn't a bad discovery. After all, helium played a huge role in World War II with the use of blimps. So, a large plant was built in Dexter where they separated the helium from the natural gas. Helium is still used today in everything from balloons to magnetic resonance imaging (MRI). Unfortunately, the well and plant in Dexter is no longer operational, but you can still visit where it all started.

In downtown Dexter at Helium Memorial Park, you can see the original helium pipe. There are benches there for you to sit and contemplate the history of that most unusual find. Be sure to also visit the historical marker at the intersection on Kansas Highway 15 and Highway 166. The marker gives history of the helium well and helium plant that was constructed there.

First Thing You Know, Ol' Jed's a Millionaire . . .
El Dorado

In 1918, the oil fields of El Dorado produced 10 percent of the world's oil. Many lucky ranchers who leased their land to Cities Service became over-night millionaires. Oil wells were being dug at the rate of 3.5 per day.

Oil Hill, a company town with 2,500 people, was the largest town in the world without so much as a shred of municipal government. It didn't need one. The company built swimming pools, golf courses, schools, gyms, stores, and post offices for their many employees who unloaded trainloads of pipes, erected wood and steel derricks, and managed machine shops that kept the oil wells going. The El Dorado oil field covered 34 square miles and contained 1,800 producing oil wells.

By 1957, Oil Hill, like other lease towns in Butler County, was gone. All that remains today are sidewalks, abandoned flower beds, a company garage, and a Quonset hut.

But never fear, the history of black gold, Texas tea is available at El Dorado's Kansas Oil Museum, just 2 blocks from downtown. You can't miss the 100-foot steel oil derrick (it still works) and the 10 acres of historic oil field equipment. It's open Thursday through Saturday at 383 E. Central Ave. Call (316) 321-9333 or visit www.kansasoilmuseum.org.

She Says That's Her Gall Bladder, but I Can See Right Through Her

Halstead

She's almost 50 but doesn't look a day over 28. Valeda III, the life-size transparent talking woman of the Kansas Learning Center for Health in Halstead, has taught thousands of Kansas kids how their veins and arteries work. She has shown them her own nerves, her own heart, and her own lymphatic system, all of which light up when she mentions them in her 15-minute presentation on "how the body works."

Valeda has nothing to hide. KANSAS LEARNING CENTER FOR HEALTH

Trivia

Kansas is known as the Sunflower State. It should be since it ranks third in the US in sunflower production. That is third to North and South Dakota, respectively. The state grows both oil and non-oil varieties with the northwestern part of the state having most acres planted.

According to the National Agriculture Statistic Service (NASS) 2024 State Agriculture Overview, Kansas has a booming sunflower crop. Over 10,000 acres were planted with 9,800 harvested acres. That's 1,005 pounds per acre bringing in over $1.5 million in revenue. Most sunflowers are planted in the northwest part of the state, but you can find them in the west, central, and south as well. And who hasn't driven down I-70 and not seen the sun worshippers lined up like a troop of soldiers following their leader, the sun?

Products made from sunflowers are wide and varied. Everybody I know has taken a handful of those seeds and popped them in their mouth for a snack at one time or another. The seeds themselves can be used for oils, butters, and flours; used in cereals, granolas, salads, and pastas; and used for topping breads and muffins. Some of the smaller seeds are used as birdseed. They are so versatile, what's not to love?

Mounted on a rotating pedestal, Valeda is the featured attraction of this center for health, which was started years ago by the Hertzler Foundation, named for Arthur Hertzler, a Kansas doc who traveled the state in a horse and buggy.

Valeda, of course, didn't travel in the buggy. She wasn't even made until 1965, when a German student model in Cologne allowed a transparent rubber compound to be slopped on her body and left until it dried.

Valeda, who is 5 foot 7 and would weigh 145 pounds if she weren't made out of plastic, has several sisters around the country, but according to the folks at the Learning Center, she's the only one who still talks. One of her siblings in Chicago was almost named Cassie, the Lassie with the Glassy Chassis.

Trivia

In 1929 the Haven High football team beat local rival Sylvia High 256–0.

Lucky for Valeda III, who was named after her Chicago sister, they opted for Valeda instead.

To get a personal audience with the transparent woman, visit the Kansas Learning Center for Health at 505 Main St. in Halstead, open 10 a.m. to 4 p.m. Monday through Friday. Admission is $8 for adults and children. Under age 3 is free. Phone (316) 835-2662 or visit www.learningcenter.org.

Has Nike Heard About This?

Hutchinson

If you can run around Hutchinson's Grain Elevator J in less than 3 minutes and 43 seconds, you'll have just beaten the world record for a mile. The grain elevator holds 18 million bushels of wheat (enough to fill 5,400 railroad cars). One lap around the huge concrete structure makes an even mile, and a time of 3:43 or less beats the record set by Hicham El Guerrouj in 1999. Maybe you should try out for the Olympics.

You can find Hutchinson at the intersection of Highways 96 and 61, and you can't miss the grain elevator. Take your running shoes.

Now That's Some Impressive Yard Art

Hutchinson

The Kansas Cosmosphere and Space Center, an affiliate of the Smithsonian, has some yard art you probably won't find at just any Home Depot. I mean, how many yards have you seen with a 70-foot Redstone rocket by the front door? Or a Titan II rocket by the flower garden? The Cosmosphere also has

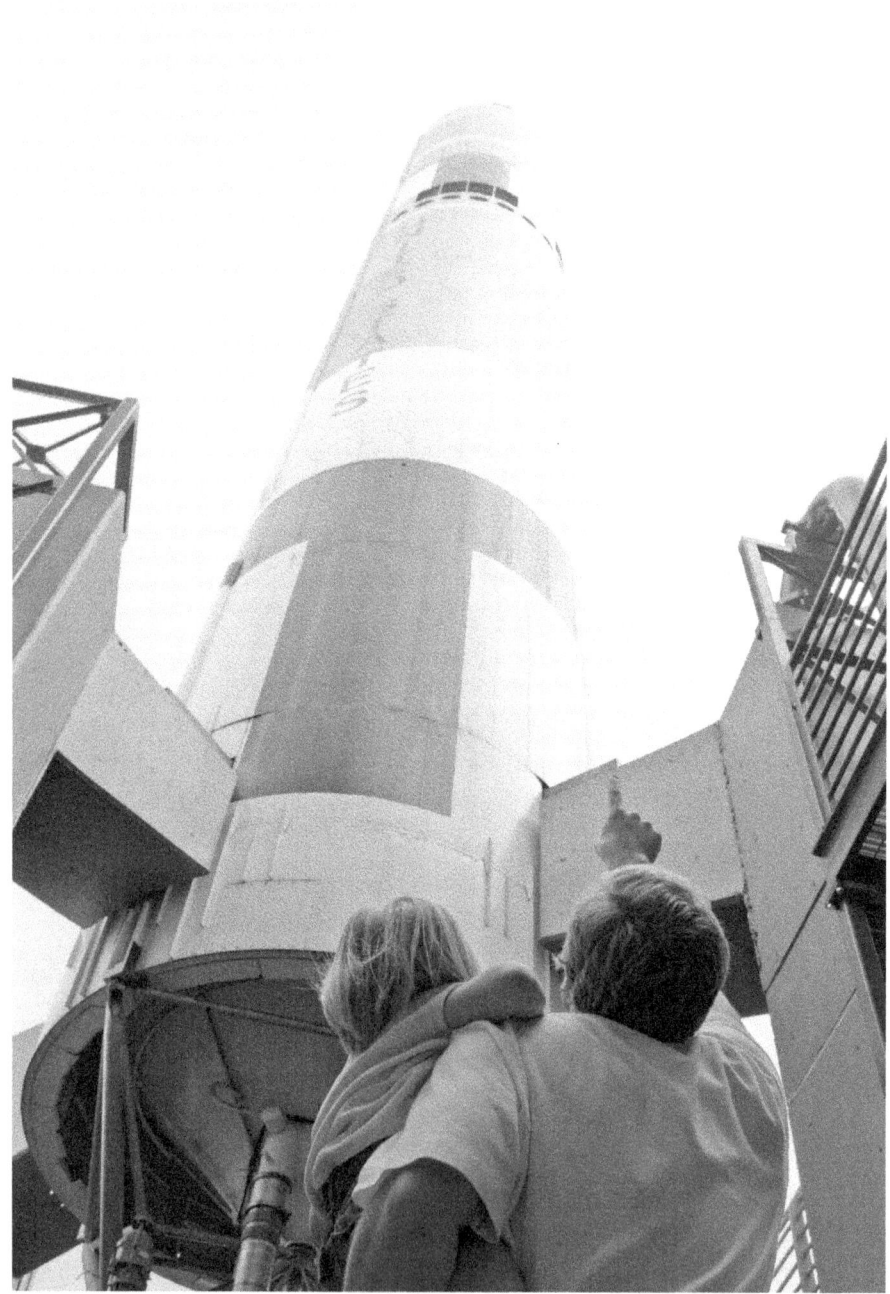

Yard art bigger than the yard COSMOSPHERE

an SR-71 Blackbird, a spyplane that flew at speeds above Mach 3.2; that maybe doesn't qualify as yard art, but you can sure see it from the street.

Started in a poultry barn in 1962, this world-famous space museum has lots of amazing exhibits, including the world's largest collection of space suits, an astronaut training jet, the actual Apollo 13 command module, and a full-scale space shuttle replica. Second only to DC's National Air and Space Museum in number of space artifacts, the Cosmosphere also offers space camp for kids of all ages, leases space artifacts to museums all over the world, and even consults with Hollywood when they're filming space movies.

The Cosmosphere is located at 1100 N. Plum in Hutchison (800-397-0330; www.cosmo.org).

Lost Shaker of Salt

Hutchinson

California and Alaska had a gold rush. Colorado had a silver boom. In Kansas we had a salt boom. It happened in 1887, soon after Ben Blanchard accidentally discovered salt. He was hoping for oil.

Once the word got out that Kansas had the world's largest piece of salt (it's 100 miles long by 40 miles wide), salt miners flooded to Hutchinson. At one time, there were more than 26 salt companies in Hutch, producing up to 44.1 million tons of salt each year. Blocks of salt were cut whole from the 10-to-12-foot veins. Worry all you want about running out of oil, but Hutchinson's 10-to-12-foot veins of pure salt will keep the country in salt for 250,000 years.

Hutch's salt boom came just in the nick of time to save the little town that was started in 1871 by a Baptist minister who marked out the streets with buffalo skulls and threatened to reclaim the deed of any property owner who dared drink hard liquor or even carry it onto his property. Not a popular statute in the wild Kansas frontier.

The Strataca Underground Salt Museum makes Hutchinson the only town in the US with a museum that's 650 feet below the ground. The museum, still a working salt mine, tells the history of Hutchinson's salt mines and how they played an important role in everything from the Interstate

Commerce Commission (the Elkins Act of 1903 was the result of an ICC hearing in Hutch that pitted the "Trusts," nine companies owned by the owner of Morton Salt, against the independent salt producers) to nuclear testing during the Cold War. Thankfully, the tests conducted by the Atomic Energy Commission didn't use real radioactive waste.

Today, there are more than 14,000 uses for salt. The museum, with 100,000 square feet of gallery space, is the only museum in a working salt mine—a mine that stretches for 67 miles, part of which is used (because of its 68-degree temp and 40 percent relative humidity) to store the original reels of classic Hollywood movies. The Strataca Underground Salt Museum is located at 3504 E. Avenue G (620-662-1425; www.under groundmuseum.org).

Confucius Say: Don't Throw Rocks in Glass Houses
Kechi

If you search on the internet for Rollin Karg, the industrial engineer turned glassblower, you might think he lives in Miami or Portland or in one of the other 300 cities that have galleries with his work. But you'd be wrong.

Karg, one of the premier glassblowing artists in the world, lives and works in Kechi, Kansas (population 940), in an outdoor studio behind his home.

A former engineer for Cessna, Karg turned his glassblowing skills (he also dabbled for a while in photography and ceramics) into a full-time business in 1983. He and his wife, Patti, who also blows, saw some Steuben glassmakers in Corning, New York.

Rollin said, "Honey, I'd like to try that."

Patti said, "Yeah, sure."

But the next thing she knew, he was signed up for a glassblowing class at Emporia State University.

"He made one paperweight and he hasn't stopped since," said Patti, who runs the business along with Rollin and several glassblowing apprentices.

Visitors can see glass being blown Monday, Tuesday, Thursday, and Friday from 10 a.m. to 3 p.m. Or you can tour the gallery (Karg's works plus those of 50 other artists are displayed) from 9 a.m. to 5 p.m. Monday through Saturday. To get there, take exit 14 off I-35 and head 2 miles east. Karg Art Glass is at 111 N. Oliver, at 61st and Oliver (316-744-2442; www .rollinkarg.com).

Rollin Karg's "glass act" ROLLIN KARG

I Do . . . but Only If
Kingman

When Glenn Stark proposed to his wife, she said "sure"—upon one condition: She wanted not a traditional wedding band, but a wedding ring carved from wood. After all, wood carving was such a part of Stark's life that a ring made of anything else would never fly. Besides, to marry Stark would mean living in a basement home with a wooden Will Rogers, Abe Lincoln, a cigar store Indian, and Hagar the Horrible.

Stark, a prolific wood-carver and cement artist, started carving wood as early as second grade. He told his mom that shaping things with his hands was as much a part of him as wanting to breathe. He saw ideas in everything.

"I can see designs in veneer on doors. In clouds, in water and animals. I have too many ideas. Almost as many as there are stars," he said.

Although Stark passed away in 2014, he worked in many fields before moving to his unusual home on the outskirts of Kingman. He worked as a Baptist minister, a navy seaman (he was in Pearl Harbor on December 7, 1941), a carpenter, a stonemason, a bricklayer, and a sign painter.

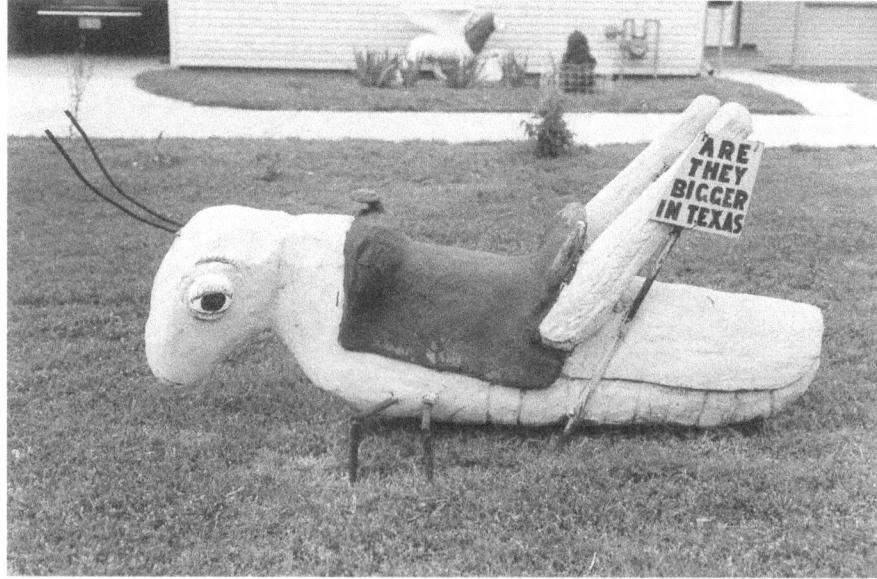

The first sign of a grasshopper plague? STEVE SCHULTZ

Even though his artwork can be found in nearly all 50 states, Stark never really considered himself an artist. But I encourage you to take one look at his pieces and then decide.

He sculpted a giant grasshopper, a winged griffin, a Native American couple, a bear on its hind feet, a buffalo, a steer, two prairie dogs, a 4-foot catfish hanging from a tree limb, and two totem poles. They used to be displayed in his front yard until his passing, then moved to a park in downtown Kingman. Recently the sculptures were placed in storage until the town can find someone to restore them.

Until that happens if you want to see Stark's work head to the Grassroots Art Center in Lucas (213 S. Main St.; 785-525-6118).

But Honey, There's a Kangaroo in My Bed . . .

Nickerson

When Sondra Hedrick says to her husband, "This place is a zoo," she isn't kidding. Her husband, Joe, a former rodeo clown and bullfighter, decided that rather than stock his ranch with the typical cows and chickens, he'd go for kangaroos, zebras, giraffes, yaks, chimpanzees, and pygmy goats.

For years, Hedrick didn't open his unusual ranch to the public, even though it caused more than a few cases of whiplash for travelers zooming down Highway 96. Rather, Hedrick rented out his animals for petting zoos and Christmas parades (his fallow deer make excellent reindeer). He gave camel and pony rides and promoted races of his ostriches, camels, and pigs.

Finally, in 1992, Hedrick gave in. He agreed to open his Exotic Animal Farm on weekends, even added concession facilities and a bed-and-breakfast with a frontier facade of a bank, saloon, grocery store, and livery stable.

And unlike Embassy Suites, where you look out from your room into a courtyard of plants and fountains, at Hedrick's you look out into a courtyard filled with kangaroos and wallabies. It's undoubtedly the most unique bed-and-breakfast anywhere in the world. Each of the eight rooms is decorated in safari motif, with mosquito netting, zebra sheets, painted ostrich eggs,

Just two of the permanent residents of Hedrick's Exotic Animal Farm.
HEDRICK'S EXOTIC ANIMAL FARM

and llama-wool foot warmers. And after a big, hearty breakfast, you'll get a tour of Hedrick's 700 animals, or at least those that aren't on the road in a pygmy goat race or a Girl Scout petting zoo somewhere.

If you want to be kissed by a camel or licked by a llama, hurry to Hedrick's Exotic Animal Farm, 8 miles northwest of Hutchinson on Highway 96. The mailing address is 7910 N. Roy L. Smith Rd., Nickerson, KS 67561. Phone (888) 489-8039 or visit www.hedricks.com.

Feeling Fine on Elderberry Wine

Peck

Forget flu shots! Drink elderberry wine instead. According to an article in *Good Housekeeping*, elderberry wine is every bit as effective at boosting your immune system. Plus, it's a heckuva lot easier (not to mention much more fun) to administer. Hic.

The largest producer of this medicinal wine is located in none other than Peck, Kansas, an hour or so from Carry Nation's hometown of Medicine Lodge. Wyldewood Cellars Winery was started in 1994 by John Brewer, a PhD scientist, and his sister, Merry Brewer, an industrial buyer, neither of whom has had a cold or a virus since they started drinking their own wines. Their mother, a nurse, planted the 1,000-acre family ranch with elderberries in the late 1980s. At the time, she had no idea why, just that she knew they were good for treating everything from upper respiratory infections and diarrhea to sunburns.

John, who made wine as a hobby, decided to try using his mom's elderberries instead of grapes. Eight years and 200 formulas later, he took the results to his friend Mike Martini, a famous Napa Valley winemaker, who couldn't tell the difference between elderberries and grapes.

Hippocrates, who used to prescribe elderberries back in the 5th century BC, would be pleased. In fact the Romans used to say that anyone who grew elderberries would die of old age rather than illness.

If that's the case, the Brewers, who have already landed 500 awards for their wines (including a sales-boosting "best buy" in *Wine Enthusiast*

Trivia

Our Gang celebrity Carl "Alfalfa" Switzer, the freckle-faced kid with the lick of hair that stood up straight, used to be a local in Pretty Prairie, Kansas. When he got too old to be in the short films, he married a local girl whose dad owned the town's feed store, bought a farm a few miles out of town, and settled there. After his divorce from the local gal, he moved back to California. His life didn't improve much. He was arrested for cutting down trees in Sequoia National Park in 1958, then a month later was shot in the stomach over a $50 debt. Most everyone who used to know him in Pretty Prairie is dead, but that doesn't stop the locals from bragging they had a celebrity living in their town.

magazine and being served at the 2002 Winter Olympics), will need to buy a bigger ranch just to house all their awards.

Wyldewood Cellars Winery also makes elderberry jams and jellies, elderberry concentrate, and wines from blackberries and native Kansas sand plums. It's open 9 a.m. to 6 p.m. Monday through Saturday and noon to 5 p.m. on Sunday. Take exit 33 off the Kansas Turnpike. Call (316) 686-9463 or visit www.wyldewoodcellars.com for more information.

Pyramid Power
Wichita

You might suspect that a pyramid in the middle of Wichita could seem a bit jarring, but at the Center for the Improvement of Human Functioning, it fits right in. The rest of the center's eight buildings are geodesic domes, designed by the late, great humanist Buckminster Fuller to be energy efficient and require no internal support. There's not a right angle anywhere on the center's 4 acres. Even the road leading up to Dome 1, where you'll find the Taste of Health restaurant, the Gift of Health gift store, and a

The Great Pyramid of Wichita GREATER WICHITA CONVENTION AND VISITORS BUREAU

Trivia

Arnold Schwarzenegger, former he-man and governor of California, sent his 1987 Wagoneer to Wichita so Jonathan Goodwin,
self-described gearhead, could convert it from running on normal
gasoline to biodiesel, doubling its fuel efficiency. Goodwin con-
verts about six cars a month. A recent project was turning Neil
Young's 1959 Lincoln Continental into a plug-in hybrid that gets
up to 100 mpg.

sign that declares, SOME OF THE MOST WONDERFUL PEOPLE PASS THROUGH THESE
DOORS, is highly curved and is flanked by signs that say DESTRESS TO 25 MPH.

The mission of the center (aka the Riordan Clinic) is to stimulate an epi-
demic of health. Their 45 full-time doctors, therapists, and researchers treat
up to 500 patients a year in holistic and natural medicine. The center was
started in 1975 by Olive W. Garvey, an innovative thinker who at 65 became
CEO of her husband's business, Garvey Inc.

Tours of the unique facility at 3100 N. Hillside Ave. are given Monday through Friday at 1:30 p.m. A nutritious, fiber-laden lunch can be had
between 11:30 a.m. and 1:30 p.m. at Taste of Health. Phone (316) 682-3100
or visit www.riordanclinic.org.

That Slant in Your "F" Indicates an Aloof and Impartial Demeanor

Wichita

If you're a handwriting analyst, you could do worse than plunking down the
$10.95 admission fee for the Museum of World Treasures. There, you can
analyze the signatures of the first 43 US presidents (they're still waiting for
Obama's), Joe DiMaggio, Peter the Great, Charles Dickens, Sir Isaac Newton, rocker Charlie Daniels, and many famous historical figures.

This three-story brick museum with all the famous signatures started as the personal collection of Dr. Jon Kardatzke, a Wichita physician who finally consented to share his 40-year collection with the public after friends kept insisting. His unique presidential signatures collection started with an autograph of Thomas Jefferson that he picked up at an auction in Beverly Hills while completing his Roman Caesar gold and silver coin collection. After he had all the presidents, he expanded into European royalty, authors, composers, scientists, and military leaders.

At the museum that Kardatzke first opened in a former Holiday Inn (he has since moved to a building five times as large), handwriting analysts

You look like death warmed over GREATER WICHITA CONVENTION AND VISITORS BUREAU

can supplement their research with other Kardatzke antiquities, some more than hundreds of millions of years old. Among other things, Kardatzke's collection includes one of only four complete *Tyrannosaur albertosaurus* skeletons in the world, a Mayan burial urn, the shrunken head of a 19th-century Ecuadorian man that was once worn around the neck for good luck, an Egyptian mummy from the royal tombs in Thebes, and the silver bowl from which Hitler ate his last meal before dying by suicide.

Kardatzke got interested in collecting coins when he was 16. You know those T-shirts, MY PARENTS WENT TO JERUSALEM AND ALL I GOT WAS THIS CRUMMY T-SHIRT. Well, Kardatzke's parents were smart enough to bring back something more compelling when they visited the Holy Land in 1956—six gold Roman coins, including one of Herod the Great that, Kardatzke said, "infected me with a love for ancient history for life."

A few years later, Kardatzke's parents took the kids along on a trip to Greece, and Jon, who was scraping around near the Acropolis, found a cup handle buried in the soil. A Greek official grabbed him by the shoulder and informed him that digging was prohibited, but let him keep the cup handle anyway. He has been hooked ever since.

The 36,000-square-foot Museum of World Treasures is located in the Farm and Art Market in Old Town at 835 E. First St. (316-263-1311; www.worldtreasures.org).

Harold and Kumar Should Have Gone to NuWay

Wichita

It's no big secret that Wichita is the "Air Capital of the World." Since 1919, more than 250 million planes have been built here, including the first commercial plane (the Laird Swallow), the first business jet (Bill Lear forsook Switzerland for Wichita when launching his Learjet), and more than 40 percent of the airplanes in the sky today.

Another stellar distinction that Wichita claims is not quite as well known. Wichita also happens to be the "Fast-Food Chain Capital of the World." Or, rather, more fast-food chains were launched here than in any other city in

Trivia

Before he became a legend of the Old West, Wyatt Earp served as a police constable in Wichita. His main responsibility was rounding up stray dogs. Earp had a bad habit of pocketing the fines he collected rather than turning them in to the city, so when he left for Dodge City in 1872, the accounting office withheld his last paycheck.

America. Pizza Hut, of course, was started in Wichita in 1958. But long before that (1921, to be exact), the very first fast-food hamburger chain was launched in Wichita. Yes, White Castle began in Wichita when Walter Anderson, a cook, and Billy Ingram, a real estate agent, formed the White Castle System of Eating Houses. This, I hasten to point out, was 33 years before Ray Kroc even met the McDonald brothers.

Although White Castle didn't gain quite the financial status as its yellow-arched imitator, it was the first to establish uniformity (can you say chain?) at its many locations. White Castle eventually bailed and set up headquarters in Ohio, though no one argues that it was the first fast-food chain restaurant.

Since then, Wichita has spawned a plethora of fast-food chains, including Spangles, Bionic Burger, and my personal favorite, NuWay Cafe. I prefer NuWay because it contents itself to remain small and local. At last count, there were two NuWays in Wichita, both serving the restaurant's trademark crumbly ground beef sandwiches and homemade root beer. You often have to wait for a seat at the vintage U-shaped counter with the vinyl and metal stools.

If you want to see the restaurant that a writer for *National Geographic* raved about, visit the original NuWay at 1416 W. Douglas Ave. (316-267-1131; www.nuwayburgers.com).

Kansas Wins the Pennant for . . . New York?

On July 28, 1911, Charles Victory Faust, a 30-year-old hayseed from Wichita, showed up on a practice field for the New York Giants. They were in St. Louis preparing to play the Cardinals. Faust, wearing a black suit and a tall black hat, approached John McGraw, the manager for the Giants, and informed him that a psychic had told him that if he pitched for the Giants, they'd win the pennant. McGraw, who believed in omens and charms, decided to give the man a chance. After a couple of pitches, it was obvious that Faust not only knew nothing about pitching (he used an odd double windmill), but that he'd never played the game of baseball. Nevertheless, as the team was boarding the train for a stand against Chicago the next day, Faust was there, complete with uniform. He dressed, ate, practiced, and traveled with the team from that day on. Although he was only allowed to play one inning against the last-place Dodgers, McGraw gave Faust credit for, sure enough, winning the pennant that year.

Faust stayed on the team, and the Giants won the pennant for the next 3 years. In 1915, Faust died in a psychiatric hospital, and the Giants, who suffered their first losing season in 15 years, finished in last place.

Einstein's Brain Slept Here

When Albert Einstein died in 1955, his body was cremated. Twenty years later, while reading through some of Einstein's papers, an editor from the *New Jersey Monthly* noticed that Einstein had requested that his brain be preserved. No one at the small Princeton hospital where he'd died knew anything about it. In 1978, the editor sent a reporter to find out what had happened to the famous scientist's brain. The reporter eventually tracked down a Princeton pathologist, Dr. Thomas S. Harvey, who had indeed removed the brain. When the reporter found Dr. Harvey, he was working in Wichita at a medical testing lab. After much pressing, Dr. Harvey reached into a cupboard, pulled out a cardboard box labeled *Costa Cider,* and withdrew two mason jars filled with formaldehyde and bits and pieces of Einstein's brain. Scientific studies were performed on the brain, although Dr. Harvey, who now lives in Florida, still has most of it. In 1997, he put the brain in a Tupperware container, stuck it in the trunk of a rented car, and drove to Berkeley, California, to show the brain to Einstein's granddaughter.

Pizza Mixed in Baby's Bathtub Becomes World's Largest Restaurant Chain

Wichita

One night in the late 1950s, while Frank and Dan Carney were working in their widowed mom's Wichita grocery store, a fight broke out at the bar next door. The landlord of that building, fed up with noisy tenants, suggested to the elder Carney that her sons, students at Wichita State University, open a small, quiet restaurant there instead.

Borrowing $600 from their mother, the Carney boys, ages 19 and 24, decided to serve a popular new food called pizza. While mom sewed red-and-white-checkered curtains, the young men rounded up a baby's bathtub in which to mix the dough. They also hustled an old oven that eventually melted the handles off the door. They named their restaurant Pizza Hut, mainly because that's all they could fit on the sign used by the building's former occupant, the B&B Lounge.

From the day it opened in the summer of 1958, the pizzeria was a success. Within a few months, the college boys were raking in $1,000 a week, and by 1977 they had sold it to PepsiCo for a cool $300 million.

The first Pizza Hut was located at Kellogg and Bluff Streets, but it has been moved to the campus of Wichita State University and sits as a museum at 2090 Innovation Blvd., (316) 978-4488. Admission is free.

Dem Bones

Winfield

By day, he's a diesel mechanic. By night and just about any other time he can find a spare moment, Barry Patton is one of the world's premier double-fisted bones players. Yes, I said bones—as in skeletons, as in dense, hard, calcified tissue. And yes, Patton has played this unusual musical instrument with everyone from country singer Vince Gill to the Louisville Philharmonic Orchestra. He even sells a bones video teaching wannabes how to master the rare percussion instrument that originated in Egypt in 1600 BC. Bone rattlers, as they're called, traditionally used cattle ribs, but in medieval Europe, oxen ribs were all the rage. Barry has preferred to make most of his 15 sets of bones out of hedgewood, although he still plays the set given to him by the old-timer who taught him how to play nearly 40 years ago.

When Barry was 14, bones player Cecil Hiatt (known far and wide as Oklahoma Bones after he picked up the skill from an Old West medicine show) accidentally slammed Barry's finger in a car door. He felt so bad that he gave Barry a set of bones to make up for it. Barry, thanks to the broken finger that required a splint, had lots of time to practice.

Cecil saw promise in his young student, so he took Barry under his wing. As Barry said, "Bones have taken me to more places and introduced me to more friends than I ever dreamed possible."

Kansas Was His First Inspiration

Frederic Remington, the famous western artist of some 3,000 sketches, paintings, and sculptures, got so bored on his 160-acre sheep farm outside Whitewater that he began sketching cowboy scenes, some on the door of a neighbor's barn.

Originally from back East, Remington moved to Kansas in 1883 on a "get rich quick" mission. A friend from Yale insisted there was money to be made in sheep farming, an occupation that didn't appeal to Remington for much longer than 9 months. After running a bar and a grocery store in Kansas City, he finally convinced his childhood sweetheart to marry him. By 1885, they were back in New York, and Remington was selling his cowboy sketches to *Harper's Weekly* and other magazines.

Catch Barry's act at the Walnut Valley Festival in Winfield the third weekend in September, or check out his Facebook page at www.facebook .com/barry.patton.370/.

Modern-Day Land Rush
Winfield

Land rushes, a popular method for distributing property in the late 1800s, are still popular in Winfield, at least every September when thousands of campers line up to find the best camping spot for the annual Walnut Valley Festival. They come up to three weeks early to get their numbers and await the 8 a.m. starting gun that marks Land Rush, which starts an entire week before the official music begins.

The festival, a nearly 4-decade tradition that attracts the country's best acoustic musicians, features six stages of nonstop music, a big arts and crafts exhibit, and 4 days of national flat-picking championships. But the festivalgoers, many of whom haven't missed a single one, are the real

The Walnut Valley Festival—where Florida's pink flamingos go to retire!

troupers. They decorate their campsites with intense planning that would give Martha Stewart pause. There are castles, tropical paradises, "log cabins," and re-creations of granny's back porch.

Walnut Valley Festival is held the third weekend of September at the Cowley County fairgrounds. Call (620) 221-3250 for more info, or check out the festival's website at www.wvfest.com.

Morrowville

Scandia Belleville

Courtland Cuba Washington ⬡36

Republican River

Concordia

⬡9 ⬡15

Solomon River ⬡24

Delphos

⬡81 Longford *Milford Lake* Fort Riley

Minneapolis

Lincoln Beverly Junction City

⬡40 Abilene ⬡77

⬢70 Salina

Ellsworth *Smoky Hill River* ⬡15

⬡14 Lindsborg ⬢135

Marion Lake

⬡56 McPherson Canton

⬡56

Inman Goessel Florence

North Central

North Central

Dwight D. Eisenhower, five-star general and 34th president of the US, used to say that the proudest thing he could claim was being from Abilene.

After reading about his stomping ground in north-central Kansas, I think you'll see why. North-central Kansas boasts such natural wonders as house-size rocks, buffalo herds that run wild, real cowboys, and a proud military history that goes back to the US Cavalry.

And if that wasn't enough, Ike's hometown of Abilene holds the stellar distinction of owning the world's largest spur, a spur so big that two Chevy Silverados, each with a load of 16 screaming cheerleaders, can drive underneath it at the same time. But what's even more amazing is that the ginormous spur, fashioned from an antiquated swamp cooler, wasn't even there to add to Ike's pride. The award-winning spur didn't get erected until three decades after the famous Kansan's death.

And while I'd hate to start any rumors, there's also a scintillating under-wear show in Junction City, just 30 miles northeast of Abilene.

Homeopathy for Beginners
Abilene

If you had a bunion, a backache, or a sick horse back in 1899, there's a good chance you'd turn to A. B. Seelye. After all, he's the guy who came up with Wasa-Tusa, Fro-zona, Ner-Vena, and hundreds of other home remedies that back in those days answered that perennial question: How do you spell relief?

From Abilene, Kansas, where he ran the A. B. Seelye Medical Company, the crafty entrepreneur dispersed 400 wagons carrying 100 patent medi-cines to a 14-state area. Back then, it was the biggest medicine company in the country, the equivalent of Eli Lilly today.

"The label on Wasa-Tusa said it cured anything," said Terry Tietjens, who bought the Seelye mansion and lived there with Seelye's two unmar-ried daughters after they got too old to run the place. "You used it for your cold, your horse, your wife—it didn't matter."

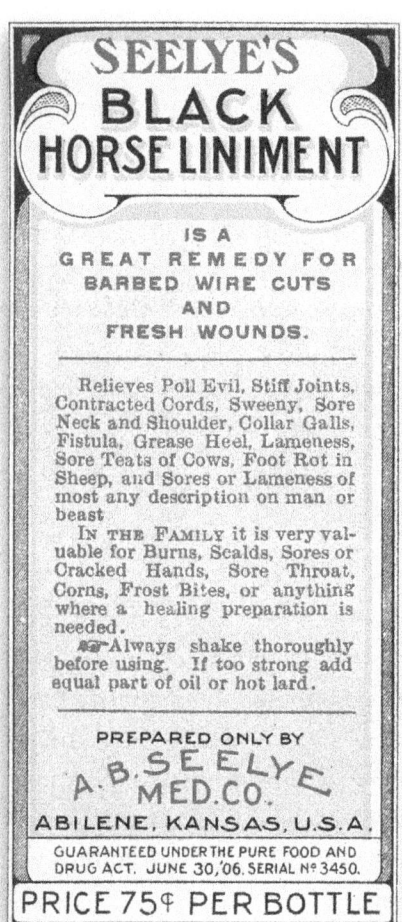
The cure for what ails you TERRY TIETJENS, SEELYE MANSION

The old vats and recipes for all of Seelye's cure-alls (from salves, potions, and lotions to talcum powder, perfume, and extracts) are on display at the Patent Medicine Museum. Most folks come to ooh and aah at the mansion, a 25-room beauty with a bowling alley in the basement and what some say is the world's largest nutcracker collection (they're put out every Christmas), but I'm partial to the crazy medicines, most of which contained 87 percent alcohol.

To see the medicines that were "good for man or beast," visit the Patent Medicine Museum, located behind the mansion at 1105 N. Buckeye St. in Abilene. Phone (785) 263-1084 or visit www.seelyemansion.org.

Fits and Spurs

Abilene

Heaven knows, a writer of *Curiosities* books is keenly aware of all the giant creatures along America's byways, from Bemijidi, Minnesota's 10-foot Babe, the Blue Ox, to Blanchester, Ohio's 68-foot Hermit Crab (the Freedom Worship Baptist Church that owns it claims 60 people can sit within its shell), but I've yet to see one big enough to need the 28-foot spur, the world's largest, owned by Abilene's Wild Bill Hickok Rodeo Arena. They didn't have any trouble landing the stellar designation from the Guinness folks, being as there's not a lot of competition. Abilene, Texas, of course, has the world's largest Spur and Bit Show, and Waco, Texas, recently sold in an auction what they called the world's largest collection of spurs (including a double diamond pair worn by John Wayne), but nobody seems to be in the running for the title of world's largest singular spur. Weighing in at more than 2,000 pounds, the Abilene spur is an impressive piece of hardware, big enough for a semitruck and a trailer to pass under with nary a scratch.

Originally constructed in New Mexico out of a derelict swamp cooler, the monstrous spur came to Kansas with Larry Houston, who built it after watching a friend's little boy drive a toy truck under a normal-size spur. He sold it to the Central Kansas Free Fair folks, who immediately recognized its potential. It welcomed fairgoers until 2017 when it was moved and now sits in front of Rittel's Western Wear, LLC. You can see the spur at 1810 N. Buckeye St.

Still getting along RITTEL'S WESTERN WEAR

We Are Family

Belleville

Not saying that the Pawnee Indians were antisocial, but where one of their village is located might lead certain folks to believe that they were. It's almost in the middle of nowhere. Twenty minutes west of Belleville sits the Pawnee Indian Museum. The museum area covers about 7 acres of the 10 owned by the state. Kansas has owned the property since 1901.

A band of Pawnee called the Kitkehahki settled in this area around 1770 and stayed until about 1802. When archeologists began excavating the area, they were able to uncover approximately half of the village. It consisted of dome-shaped earth lodges the Pawnee used to live in. In total they found 22 lodges and 40 storage pits. The museum itself is built over the remains of one of the large lodge depressions. The building was built in 1966 and opened in 1967 as the museum. Its floor is open, and all artifacts were left where they were uncovered. Besides what is in the floor of the museum, there is a bull bison robe, items made from bison bones, and other items waiting for visitors to discover. Events are held throughout the year like Mountain Man Rendezvous and Pawnee and other Native American lectures.

So, if you find yourself on US 36 outside of Belleville, turn north on Kansas 266 for 8 miles and you will end up at the Pawnee Indian Museum. It's totally free and perhaps you will see that we, as the family of man, are not so different after all.

Trick or Treat

Beverly

After writing several books about roadside oddities, I have come to the conclusion that making animals out of farm implements is not that out of the ordinary. In fact, I'd venture to bet there's not a state among us that doesn't have at least one or two zoos full of rusted-out lathes and motorcycle gas tanks. Not that every last one of them isn't impressive.

But when I found out about Jim Dickerman's Open Range Zoo, off Kansas Highway 18, I knew I was onto something unique. For one thing, Dickerman's zoo has the world's largest dragon. Jim's Dream Dragon IV, made from an antique McCormick threshing machine, is 60 feet long and 20 feet tall. Its tail even moves up and down in the wind. Not only that, but all of Dickerman's scrap metal animals glow in the dark. Most creators of discarded-metal menageries are content to leave them rusted and weathered.

Dream Dragon IV is at mile marker 106 off Highway 18, about 0.5 mile east of Beverly. But if you want to see all of Jim's outdoor creations (the Kansas Canary, Bug Lady, and Break Out, to name a few), pick up a map at the Grassroots Art Center in Lucas (785-525-6118).

Trivia

When new townsites in Kansas were surveyed and plotted, promoters commonly offered a free lot to the first house in the new "city." A. F. Horner built a house in Brookville and then sledged it across the plains to Florence, and on to Newton and then Hutchinson.

I'll give you two guesses. Which one is Jim Dickerman? STEVE SCHULTZ

Before Daytona

On his 19th birthday, four-time NASCAR champ Jeff Gordon took his first national Midget Title in Belleville on the town's famous Belleville High Banks. Built in 1910, this 0.5-mile dirt track, billed as the world's fastest, has hosted horses and motorcycles, as well as such famous race car champs as Parnelli Jones, A. J. Foyt, Tony Stewart, and, of course, Gordon, who "ran wide open, jumped the cushion, and never stopped lifting" for his Midget Title in 1990.

Happy Birthday, Mr. Gordon. JAMES S. DICK

Where the Buffalo Roam

Canton

If you go to the Bronx Zoo, you'll probably hear a story or two about William Hornaday. He was the zoo's first director, an avid conservationist, and the guy who started the American Bison Society at the zoo's Lion House in 1905.

He started the ABS because buffalo that once roamed American prairies were threatened with extinction. Thanks to frontiersmen like Wyatt Earp and Bat Masterson, who shot them for $3 a hide, the 1905 buffalo census reported a mere 1,000 buffalo left. Hard to believe there were once 70 million of them. Some herds in the good old days were as big as the state of Rhode Island.

Hornaday was savvy enough to recognize that if somebody didn't step in, the once prolific buffalo would soon be gone forever. In fact, the herd he started at the zoo in October 1899 eventually restocked bison herds in Oklahoma, Montana, South Dakota, and Nebraska.

I tell you this story to illustrate a point. Kansas also had a conservationist who recognized the need to preserve buffalo. In fact, the Kansan rounded up his herd of bison in 1859, when Hornaday was only 4 years old. But how many people have heard of John Gault Maxwell?

If you go to the Maxwell Wildlife Refuge, a 2,800-acre preserve north of Canton, you'll probably hear about Maxwell and see 200 descendants of his herd, which was willed by the family to Kansas Wildlife and Parks.

The refuge also has elk, a 20-foot lookout tower, a 1.5-mile hiking trail, and a 46-acre fishing lake. Show up on a weekend (be sure to call ahead) and you can even ride on what Friends of Maxwell call a "modern-day covered wagon." It's actually a tram that seats 20, but boy, are you in for a treat: bison, wildflowers, and prairie just as it was 200 years ago.

If you give them enough notice, the Friends of Maxwell will even serve you a campfire barbecued buffalo dinner, complete with beans, potato salad, and cobbler.

The Maxwell Wildlife Refuge is 6 miles north of Canton on 27th Avenue. Call (620) 628-4455 or check out www.maxwellwildliferefuge.com.

Napoleon's Own Curtain

Concordia

You can go to the Hall of Battles in the Palace of Versailles to see Horace Vernet's famous painting of Napoleon at Austerlitz. Or you can head to Concordia, Kansas, where the painting is displayed on a three-story, 32-foot-wide curtain.

Napoleon "made it" to Kansas thanks to a turn of events that started in the late 1800s. It seems one Colonel Napoleon Bonaparte Brown (no relation to the French general) moved to Concordia to open a bank. By 1900, the town had prospered thanks to its four major railroads, and the rich banker decided it needed a grand opera house. On September 17, 1907, the magnificent 650-seat theater with eight box seats and two balconies opened for a performance of *The Vanderbilt Cup*.

Much to Brown's surprise, his son Earl presented him with the gigantic curtain bearing a picture of his namesake. Unfortunately, both men died within a few years and their widows, who didn't get along, sold the stunning theater. It survived by showing movies until seven decades later, when someone got the harebrained idea to restore it.

By this time, the giant curtain had suffered rain damage ("Napoleon looked like he was having a bad mascara day," said former curator Susie Haver), so $9,000 was raised to make a reproduction.

The Brown Grand Theatre is open Tuesday through Friday. It's located at the west end of downtown, 310 W. Sixth St. For a schedule of events or theater tours, call (785) 243-2553 or visit www.browngrand.org.

Take That, Andy Warhol

Cuba

For a town of barely 200, Cuba has gotten more than its 15 minutes of fame. In the past decade, this little Czech community where you can see one end of Main Street from the other has been featured twice on CBS and once in an 18-page spread in *National Geographic*. Maybe it's because its annual March fundraiser (a rockathon with 7 days of nonstop hours of dueling rocking chairs) is, well, a curiosity. Eighty miles from the nearest mall, Cuba's denizens have also been known to stage frog races and blind-folded lawn mower sprints and ride horses into bars.

Maybe it's because you can't get authentic Czech bologna and jater-nice just anywhere. Or maybe it's because its historic Ceska Narodni Sin (Bohemian National Hall) has a backdrop of Prague's Old Town Square, a roller rink, and a senior citizens' center, and, at one time or another, has hosted high school football games and Lawrence Welk. Visit the store at 301 Baird St., or call (785) 729-3632 to find out how you can volunteer for a half-hour time slot in the world-famous Cuba Rock-a-Thon. Oh, and if you're wondering why a community of Czech-speaking immigrants would name their town Cuba, no one really knows, but the most popular theory is that a visitor entranced the settlers with tales of Cubans fighting the Spanish for their freedom, a cause they knew well after escaping a region under Austria's thumb.

Working the counter at the Cuba Cash Store JAMES S. DICK

First Presidential Fashion Adviser

Delphos

Lincoln's famous Cooper Union Address, the speech that propelled his bid for presidency, was first given and practiced in Kansas. Between November 30 and December 7, 1859, Lincoln toured Kansas, giving the same basic Cooper Union speech in Troy, Doniphan, Atchison, and Elwood.

Grace Bedell, an 11-year-old girl from New York who later moved to Kansas, really liked the Republican candidate, but she thought his image needed some polishing. She wrote him a letter a month before the election, suggesting strongly that, with his skinny frame, he ought to try a beard.

"All the ladies like whiskers," she wrote, "and they would tease their husbands to vote for you." She also mentioned that although several of her brothers were going to vote for him no matter what he looked like, she thought she could persuade a couple of her other brothers to vote for him if he grew a beard.

Ever gracious, Abe wrote her a letter thanking her for the fashion advice, and sure enough, by the time he was inaugurated, he was sporting a full beard, the first American president ever to do so.

Bedell treasured her letter from Lincoln and stored it in a vault in the bank her husband ran in Delphos. Despite offers as high as $5,000, she refused to part with it. Finally, after her death, a television producer bought the famous note for $20,000. Today, a copy of both her original letter and the one Lincoln wrote back are part of a memorial at the northwest corner of City Park on the town square.

Yippee Ti Yi Yea

Ellsworth

A huge cloud of dirt bellowed up from the hooves pounding their way into town. Whistles, grunts, moos, and the occasional "yah" could be heard as the cowboys moved their herds along the Chisholm Trail and the Ellsworth Cattle Trail to the feed yards and processing centers in Ellsworth. The town would be packed by late May and June of each year. Cattle buyers would be on hand to buy stock for their ranches or to send to stockyards back East by way of the Kansas Pacific Railroad. By 1873, Ellsworth led the way in the cattle industry, bringing 220,000 head of cattle and a lot of money to the area. It also brought a lot of gambling, brothels, and saloons to the area as well. By 1875, all those profits shifted to Dodge City, leaving the Ellsworth cattle boom a memory.

The National Drovers Hall of Fame is all about keeping not only Ellsworth drover history alive but pay homage to the nation's lucrative cattle history. Their mission statement "recognizes the unique history of the cattle drive era by honoring the drovers, cattle, horses, men, women, railroads and cattle towns" that shaped the beef industry. Preserving the history of the cowboy way of life is what they are known for and they take their mission very seriously.

They are in the process of building a museum that will showcase the history of drovers, the cattle drive, the part railroads played and how it all came together into the American beef industry. Until then, you can visit the Ellsworth Signature Insurance Building at 115 N. Douglas Ave. to check on their progress.

Fine Dining, Harvey-Style
Florence

If you saw Judy Garland in the movie *The Harvey Girls*, you already know about the famous waitresses who wore black dresses and white aprons and could serve a four-course dinner in 30 minutes flat. But you might not know that the first hotel opened by Fred Harvey was located in Florence, Kansas.

Called the Clifton House, the majestic hotel opened in 1878 with fine china, silver, and furniture imported from Europe. The chef, Bill Phillips, even left a job with Chicago's tony Palmer House to come to Florence, where he paid local kids to supply him with prairie chickens and quail.

The Clifton House, which survived only 22 years, was reopened in 1971 as a museum. Now, officially known as the Harvey House, it is located at 221 Marion St. You can celebrate the history by attending the Harvey House Picnic. Every summer, the last Saturday before the Fourth of July, the Florence Historical Society holds the picnic to raise funds for the operation and maintenance of the museum. You'll find a choice of fried fish, mountain oysters, and an abundance of side dishes made from some of the best local cooks. Tours through the museum and dinners for groups can be arranged by reservation by calling (620) 878-4296 or (620) 382-4191.

Trivia

Our 16th president, Abraham Lincoln, who visited Kansas in 1859 while brushing up his Cooper Union speech, remarked that if he ever decided to move west, he'd hightail it straight to Kansas.

Hail to the Chief

Fort Riley

When Chief, the last cavalry horse on government rolls, died in 1968, the army gave him a proper burial with full military honors. The color guard showed up, the commanding general gave a speech, and a cavalry band at his graveside played such military hits as "Hit the Leather," "Block Horse Troop," and "Sabre and Spurs."

They even buried him standing straight up, with full military tack, including blanket rolls, canteen, and rifle. The vault is underground, so you can't exactly see Chief, but a statue, *Old Trooper Bill,* modeled after Frederic Remington's pencil sketch *The Cavalryman,* marks the grave.

The proud bay gelding's burial site is catty-corner to the Custer House, the native limestone military home (or one just like it) that General George Custer and his wife, Libby, lived in while stationed here in 1866. Right across the parade field is the US Cavalry Museum, which recounts a proud history of America's military horse soldiers that served from the Revolutionary War until 1950.

To see the ghost rider, take exit 301 off I-70 and follow it to the Main Post. You'll see the clock tower for the US Cavalry Museum and 270 historic stone buildings. Phone (785) 239-2737; www.home.army.mil/riley/.

As If One Cracked Bell Wasn't Enough

Goessel

On April 1, 1996, Taco Bell ran an ad in several American newspapers. The ad reported that the Taco Bell Corporation, in an effort to reduce the national debt, had purchased the Liberty Bell and was renaming it the Taco Liberty Bell.

The public, not noticing the April Fool's Day date, was outraged, just as they should be. Even though it's cracked, the Liberty Bell is a proud symbol of American freedom. It's such a great symbol the Smithsonian Institution commissioned the Mennonite Heritage Museum in Goessel to make a full-scale replica of the Liberty Bell out of Turkey Red wheat.

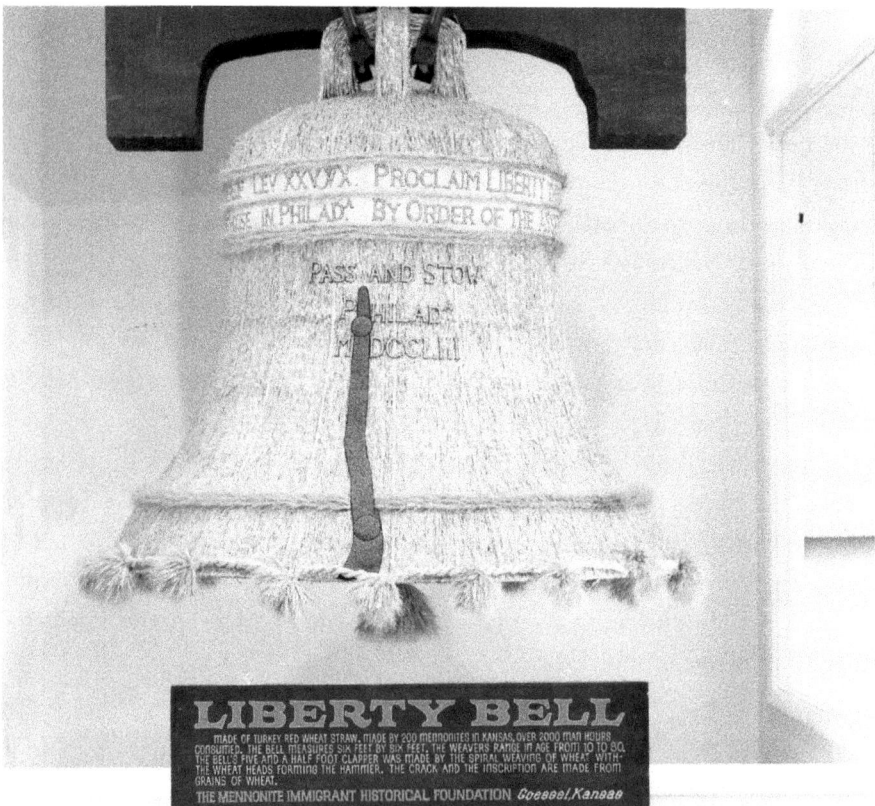

For whom the wheat bell tolls SCHMIDT STUDIO AND MENNONITE HERITAGE MUSEUM

Designed by Marie and Martha Voth, twin sisters who also happen to be straw artists, the wheat bell is the spitting image of the one that, despite Taco Bell's claims, still hangs in Philadelphia.

Members of the Mennonite community near Goessel spent 2,000 hours weaving the straw bell. Although it sat in the Smithsonian for several years, it's now back in Kansas at the museum's Turkey Red Wheat Palace. The Wheat Palace also tells the history of the 400 Ukrainians who immigrated to the area in 1874 from Alexanderwohl in Russia (now Ukraine), each carrying a bushel of wheat.

The Mennonite Heritage Museum is located at Highway 15, 11 miles north of Newton on I-35. Call (620) 367-8200 or visit www.goesselmuseum .com for more info.

Grassroots Tourism

Inman

The only reason people think Kansas is flat and dull is because nobody has bothered to tell them otherwise.

But here's the deal: The only real difference between Kansas and, say, Arizona is an $8 million advertising budget. We have natural wonders, award-winning golf courses, we even have our own Grand Canyon. It's called Arikaree Breaks, and the only reason you've never heard of it is because our boys in Topeka can't see the value in getting the word out.

If Arikaree Breaks, Rock City, or Monument Rocks were in any other state, there would be fancy brochures, tour guides, and million-dollar websites. Half of our natural wonders are on dirt roads, in the middle of some cattle rancher's pasture. To get close enough to take a photo, you often have to crawl over barbed wire or retaining walls. I guess the flip side is you don't have smelly, diesel-belching tour buses blocking your view.

About 20 years ago, Mil and Marci Penner decided to correct this glaring deficiency. They figured if legislators couldn't see fit to pony up line items for an advertising budget, they'd just do it themselves. They'd settle for word of mouth, start a grassroots effort.

They'd publish tour guides—whole books, mind you—with listings of things to do in Kansas. The first step was convincing Kansans themselves they had something to offer.

"The going notion was that if you wanted culture or something to do, you'd have to go to Denver or Kansas City," said Marci, who has become a missionary to the uninformed of Kansas.

When their *Kansas Weekend Guide*, the first of several books, came out in 1990, they staged what they thought would be a small book-signing party at their Inman farm. They invited museum curators, cafe owners, B&B operators—the people they wrote about in the book. Even though it was a rainy, miserable day in November, more than 1,000 folks showed up.

"We knew then that something must be done," said Marci, who, with her dad, started the Kansas Sampler Foundation in 1993 for the sole purpose of preserving and sustaining rural culture.

To say their grassroots effort is working is an understatement.

Each year, the Kansas Sampler Foundation (along with dozens of Kansas communities) sponsors the Kansas Sampler Festival, an annual event that is best described as a living travel brochure. Representatives of rural communities all over Kansas show up to strut their stuff, to give Kansans a "taste" of all the great things to see and do in Kansas. There are covered wagon rides, threshing demonstrations, snake pits, and singing nuns, 50 strong. There are historical reenactors, folks like Amelia Earhart and Calamity Jane. There's Kansas cuisine—ostrich, verenike, bumbleberry pie, and alfalfa sprout enchiladas, to name a few.

Besides the festival, the Kansas Sampler Foundation sponsors the Kansas Explorers Club (see the Northeast chapter), the *We Kan!* newsletter, the 8 Wonders Program, and the *Get Kansas* blog.

The Penner farm that was homesteaded by Marci's great-great-grandfather in 1874 is now home to a full-time Kansas Sampler Center. The hog shed, chicken house, barn, silo, and windmill have been replaced with a pond and deck, 60 varieties of Kansas trees and shrubs, flower gardens, and a reconstructed prairie. The grain elevator has been converted into a wood shop and Kansas display center, where Marci and Mil work like

Kansas farmers during a drought to remind us of everything we have to be proud of.

To get the straight scoop from Mil and Marci, write them at the Kansas Sampler Center, 972 Arapaho Rd., Inman, KS 67546, call (620) 585-2374, or visit www.kansassampler.org.

Pardon Me, but Your Slip Is Showing
Junction City

The Geary County Historical Museum just might host the most unusual fashion show on earth. Called the Undercover Story, the fashion show features models wearing vintage women's underwear from the late 1800s up to World War I.

There are bloomers and petticoats, chemises and corsets. The models don't make Christy Turlington–size wages, and Victoria's Secret certainly hasn't been trying to lure them away. All of the Junction City models are volunteers, members of the local historical society, some of them 80 years old. Since Gaylynn Childs, the museum's director, came up with the idea in 1988, they've performed their not-so-risqué fashion show all over the state.

In the 40-minute show, each of the garments gets a little commentary as the husband of one of the models plays piano tunes from each item's era.

Unfortunately, the famous underwear (like a lot of my unfamous underwear) is getting fragile and doesn't travel well, so the museum has had to restrict the fashion shows to the museum itself at Sixth and Adams Streets in Junction City. Call (785) 238-1666 if you'd like a sneak preview, or visit www.gearyhistory.org.

One Man's Castle
Junction City

Retired algebra teacher Don Kracht had no idea he was building a medieval empire when he started digging a pond in the back of his Junction City lot. He just reckoned he'd transform the back 2 acres of his 4-acre plot into a pond, since nothing seemed to grow there anyway. Heck, after

The Middle Ages in the middle of the county DON KRACHT

The proverbial castle in the air has been grounded. DON KRACHT three decades of teaching school, he figured he could use the scenery. But before he knew it, the pond had an island in the middle—and the island started looking deserted.

"I had the moat. I had the wooden drawbridge. I guess it wasn't too big of a leap to start thinking about a castle," Kracht said.

So in 1992, after staring at his island for 4 years, he began building a medieval castle, stone by agonizing stone. It might have ended up a small castle, except a crumbling rock house from the 19th century went on the market. Kracht picked it up for a song and began dismantling it and hauling it to the island.

"I was working on the castle and this woman comes by and asks, 'When did it start falling down?' I had to tell her it was going the other way," Kracht said with a laugh.

Kracht's castle is four stories tall and has towers, turrets, and a draw-bridge. He included a beer tap (in case he got thirsty), a hot tub (should those stone-hauling muscles get sore), and a cannon (should warring kingdoms come calling).

Today, Castle Island is privately owned so you can't get a tour inside. You can, however, get a view from the outside by driving by. It is located off I-70 at exit 295.

Flag Still Flying High and Proud

Lincoln

Every Fourth of July, Lincoln holds a huge parade. Every year, one of the prides of Lincoln is in that parade, the Kansas state flag. You may think, well yeah, the flag should be flown, but this flag is special. The very first Kansas flag was designed and made right here in Lincoln.

Hazel Avery was a humble woman. Working as a seamstress and running her own business, Ladies Ready to Wear, Avery never sought fame. But when the call went out that Kansas needed a flag, she accepted the challenge. As a member of the Daughters of the American Revolution, she

Avery's flag on display LINCOLN COUNTY HISTORICAL SOCIETY

was already steeped in history and knew how to find out about the history of her state. As a seamstress, she was skilled in sewing and applique and used those skills to design and make her flag.

When it was finished, she entered it in a contest. Unfortunately, her flag did not win. Of course, that's not the end of the story. For a while, the Kansas flag wasn't a flag at all, but a banner. Then on the Fourth of July in 1925, during the annual parade in Lincoln, Avery's flag was flown. People were so impressed by its design, they contacted their legislators and in 1927, Kansas adopted Avery's flag as the state's official ensign. It featured the Kansas state seal with a sunflower perched above it, all appliqued on a blue background. In 1961, the word "Kansas" was added underneath the seal. Today, Avery's flag flies at the Capitol and continues to grace every Fourth of July parade in Lincoln. In July 2025, on the 100-year anniversary of the flag flying in that first parade, Kansas governor Laura Kelly proclaimed July 4, 2025, as Hazel Avery Recognition Day.

If you want to see the flag yourself, show up at Lincoln's next Fourth of July parade or contact Dana Waters (785) 524-9997 for more information.

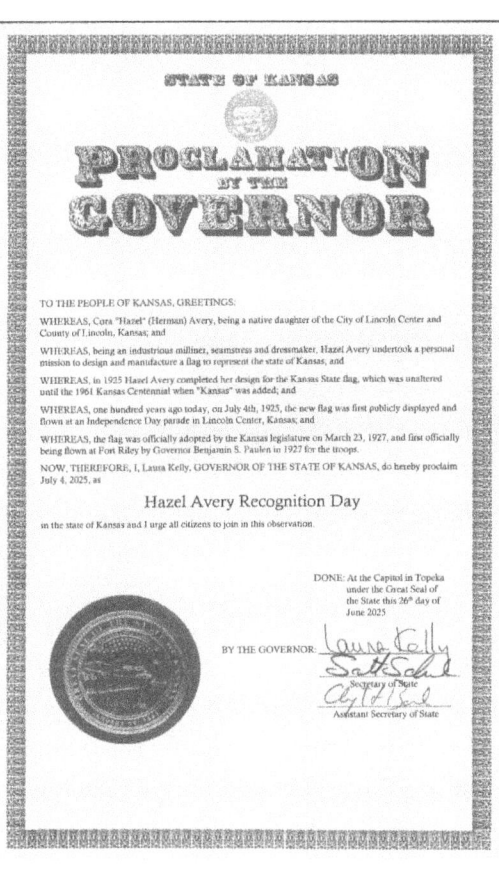

STATE OF KANSAS

PROCLAMATION
BY THE
GOVERNOR

TO THE PEOPLE OF KANSAS, GREETINGS:

WHEREAS, Cora "Hazel" (Herman) Avery, being a native daughter of the City of Lincoln Center and County of Lincoln, Kansas; and

WHEREAS, being an industrious milliner, seamstress and dressmaker, Hazel Avery undertook a personal mission to design and manufacture a flag to represent the state of Kansas; and

WHEREAS, in 1925 Hazel Avery completed her design for the Kansas State flag, which was unaltered until the 1961 Kansas Centennial when "Kansas" was added; and

WHEREAS, one hundred years ago today, on July 4th, 1925, the new flag was first publicly displayed and flown at an Independence Day parade in Lincoln Center, Kansas; and

WHEREAS, the flag was officially adopted by the Kansas legislature on March 23, 1927, and first officially being flown at Fort Riley by Governor Benjamin S. Paulen in 1927 for the troops.

NOW, THEREFORE, I, Laura Kelly, GOVERNOR OF THE STATE OF KANSAS, do hereby proclaim July 4, 2025, as

Hazel Avery Recognition Day

in the state of Kansas and I urge all citizens to join in this observation.

DONE: At the Capitol in Topeka under the Great Seal of the State this 26th day of June 2025

BY THE GOVERNOR: *Laura Kelly*

Scott Schwab
Secretary of State

Clay Barker
Assistant Secretary of State

All Packed Up and No Place to Go
Lincoln

In the Lincoln Cemetery on the east end of town, there's a gravestone shaped like a suitcase. It marks the grave of a 19th-century traveling salesman. His epitaph reads, Here is where he stoped [*sic*] last.

Carved out of post rock limestone, the unusual headstone is living proof that the artist's rock-carving skills were superior to his spelling abilities.

The traveling salesman's name was J. S. Jacobs. In 1891, when he was only 42, he kicked the bucket while staying at Lincoln's old Windsor Hotel. Nobody could locate his relatives, so businessmen around town passed a hat and came up with the funds to honor the hardworking but family-less salesman.

It's a cute story. But it's not exactly true. Turns out old J. S. Jacobs was a traveling salesman, but he did not die without family. It's also doubtful he stayed at the Windsor. Why would he? His parents, Henry and Mary Jacobs, lived right in town. When they died in 1901, they were buried (albeit without suitcase gravestones) just north of J. S. in the same plot.

To pay your respects to either J. S. or the limestone suitcase, visit the Lincoln Cemetery at the east end of town on Highway 18.

They Call the Show *Messiah*
Lindsborg

It's pretty easy to get posters of Miley Cyrus or Robert Pattinson. But have you tried to get a poster of George Frideric Handel lately? Not a simple task.

Unless you happen to be in Lindsborg, Kansas, where they sell a poster of his most enduring composition, *The Messiah*, which they've been performing for more than 120 years.

This little town of 3,000 hasn't missed an Easter season since 1882, when Alma Swensson, wife of Carl Swensson, the new pastor at the Bethany Lutheran Church, rounded up 75 local farmers, housewives, and shopkeepers to perform the famous musical that Handel wrote in 1741.

Reverend Carl saw *The Messiah* performed in Illinois and decided it would be a fitting musical for his newly formed Bethany Oratorio Society. So what if they didn't have a piano and had to use a tuning fork?

The chorus has grown a bit (there are now more than 300 volunteer singers and a 50-piece orchestra) and improved a bit since that first choir of farmers and shopkeepers. In fact, the Bethany Oratorio Society has become so renowned that the performance has been nationally televised more than a few times, and the group has been invited to perform at Carnegie Hall.

There are other events like the Messiah Art Exhibit, Soloists Recitals, and various plays throughout the month of April that you may want to check out as well.

To order tickets for the show, which takes place every Palm Sunday and Easter in Bethany College's 1,900-seat Presser Hall, or inquire about other events, call (785) 227-3380 or visit www.bethanylb.edu.

Castles in the Air

Lindsborg

Kansas is known for its flying houses. We have L. Frank Baum to thank for that. But the architectural wonder that many people have yet to become acquainted with is the Kansas castle. We have dozens of them. In Glen Elder, for example, there's a stone castle car wash. Sedan boasts the world's tiniest castle, although it has been locked in an abandoned building ever since Alyce Youngblood fell and broke her hip, forcing her to close the Lost Mine Confectionary. And in Wichita, there's a 28-room castle complete with a 300-year-old staircase imported from London. It doubles as a bed-and-breakfast.

But the most surprising castle is the three-tiered stone fortress that sits in the middle of nowhere. Well, it's not nowhere. It's in a 26-acre park of wildflowers and native grasses 4 miles northwest of Lindsborg.

It's called Coronado Heights, and some folks might lead you to believe that Francisco Vásquez de Coronado, the famous Spanish explorer, built it when he came to Kansas looking for the seven cities of gold. Don't believe them.

Coronado did camp on the Smokey Hill Buttes where the castle is located, and he did write a glowing letter to the king of Spain describing Kansas as the best and most lush land he'd ever seen (not too surprising when you realize his search in 1541 only took him through Arizona, New Mexico, Texas, and Oklahoma). But alas, the castle was actually built in 1936 as a WPA project, along with outhouses and dams.

But no matter. There's a monument to Coronado at the castle, as well as a map of his North American trip, 85 winding steps, and picnic tables long enough to seat a reunion of Liz Taylor's husbands.

To visit the castle, take Highway 3 north out of Lindsborg to Winchester Road. Go west on Winchester about 4 miles until you see the park entrance. For more information, check out the Smoky Valley Historical Association at www.smokyvalley-history.org or call the Lindsborg Kansas Convention and Visitors Bureau, (785) 227-8687; www.visitlindsborg.com.

Follow the Dala Brick Road

Lindsborg

The Swedish Dala, an orange horse whose saddle and reins are painted with flowers, is a long-standing Lindsborg tradition. The Swedish town brought the horses from Dalarna, a Swedish province where they were first carved by lumberjacks for their kids.

Lindsborg has been hanging them on porches and lampposts since the 1950s. I dare you to find three Lindsborg homes or businesses without at least

Orange you glad I didn't say orange Dala again?

one Dala printed with either a last name or the traditional Swedish greeting, *Valkommen.* Even Lindsborg police officers have Dalas on their badges.

In 2000, the Dalas got wind of the Chicago "Cows on Parade" and threw off their orange shackles. Ken Sjogren and Ken Swisher, owners of Hemslojd, a Swedish import business, carved a 4-foot Dala, stuck her in the back of a truck, and drove all around the country looking for fiberglass companies that could reproduce her.

Soon, Queen Kararina Ditto, as she's known, spawned Dalallama Tele-comma, a Dala with a third eye and telephone handsets, and Uppsa Dala Airways, a Dala with wings, tail assembly, and electrically powered running lights. There's also Hello Dala, Salvador Dala, Dalalujah (which, of course, celebrates Lindsborg's tradition of singing *The Messiah*), Dalamatian, a fire-house Dala that's white with black spots, and Herd It Through the Grape-vine, a Dala with grapes and news items.

There are many wild Dalas, each of which was unveiled with a story, a song, and a cast of crazy characters—from the Flintstones to Mrs. Olsen and Juan Valdez. When Uppsa Dala Airways was unveiled, for example, airline peanuts and paper airplanes were passed out.

Lindsborg, planet of the Dalas, is on US 81 south of Salina.

Oh, Give Me a Home Where the 61-Ton Buffalo Roam

Longford

I've got some tragic news for the folks of Jamestown, North Dakota. You know that concrete buffalo you've been calling the world's largest? Well, it's not. There's a bigger one in Kansas.

It's not that we want to take away your glory. In fact, we wouldn't dream of advertising our buffalo. There are no signs. No brochures. It's not even located on a main thoroughfare. Unless you follow the directions closely (and even then you'll probably stop a farmer to make sure), you'll never in a million years find it.

It's located on a 2,000-acre buffalo ranch at least 16 miles from the nearest interstate. It was built in 1978 by the ranch's owner, Ray O. Smith, and his brother, and if it makes you feel any better, Smith called his a

"Smithalo," not a buffalo, and it got hit by lightning about the same time the governor and 3,000 Kansans showed up to dedicate it.

Smith, who died in 1999, was a real character. His favorite comment was, "I'll tell you how smart the white man is. He killed off all the animals that could support themselves out here and replaced them with cows that need to be fed three times a day." He raised not only buffalo but lions, elk, and bear, too. For a while, he brought in extra income by putting one of his 18 lions in people's laps and taking photos. Before Smith made the buffalo, he created a rock Christmas tree attached to a motor so it could spin in circles and a 37-foot concrete map of North America. He even hauled a rock from each of the 50 states and 10 Canadian provinces to put in his geographic rock garden.

Our big buffalo is located on the highest rise on Smith's Circle 3 Ranch, which is now being run by Smith's son. From the 1,450-foot rise, you can see 40 miles. When you visit, be sure to give the North Dakota buffalo a wave.

Nine Lives and Counting

McPherson

For years, linguists have attempted to trace the lineage of the "cats have nine lives" proverb. Egypt, the most likely candidate, bombed. Perhaps they should have come to McPherson where one cat—one very big cat—had at least nine lives.

His first life was as Leo, the MGM movie mascot that roars during opening credits. McPherson's Leo wasn't the first lion the venerable movie company used. That was Slats, who is buried somewhere in New Jersey. The McPherson lion was the second Leo of six that have been chosen so far. His real name was Jackie, and while on a publicity tour for MGM under his assumed name of Leo, he survived a plane crash in the Arizona desert and a boat sinking on the Mississippi.

> **Trivia**
>
> What lion doesn't have an entourage? Leo's entourage includes a complete skeleton of a saber-tooth tiger, a giant ground sloth, a dire wolf, a collection of early Bibles, and the first man-made diamond, created by a chemistry professor at McPherson College.

The Lion King BRETT WHITENACK AT MCPHERSON MUSEUM

He finally ended up in Kansas—or rather, his hide did—in the 1930s after bank president Francis Vaniman added the Leo rug to his animal skin collection. After Vaniman died, his house became the local museum and his prize animal skins became the skeleton for the museum's African collection.

For a while, Leo was spread out on a black leather exam table, but museum guests kept plucking out bits of fur, so now he's under glass in his own special downstairs case.

The McPherson Museum is located at 1111 E. Kansas Ave. Call (620) 241-8464 or visit www.mcphersonmuseum.com.

Car Bright, Car Light, First Car I See Tonight
McPherson

Jay Leno used to like to joke that unlike most guys in Hollywood who have one car and 36 girlfriends, he has only one girlfriend (actually a wife, Mavis) and 36 cars.

And some of the cars in his three football-field-size warehouses near Burbank, California, have been worked on by antique auto restorers from McPherson, Kansas. Since 1997, the former late-night host has provided a yearly full-ride scholarship, including tuition and room and board, to McPherson College's antique auto restoration program—the only program in the country that offers a college degree in the field of antique automobile restoration. But Leno, who also serves on the program's advisory board, isn't the only celebrity involved with the program. In past years, students have worked on cars owned by Nicolas Cage, Prince Ali Kahn, and Indy car driver John Hollandsworth.

The one-of-a-kind program has been around since 1976, when a McPherson oil tycoon couldn't find anyone to restore his extensive antique car collection. The program has been written about in *Popular Mechanics* and has been featured on the History Channel and, of course, *The Tonight Show* with Jay Leno. One student each year wins an internship to work at the Mercedes-Benz Classic Car Center in Fellbach, Germany.

The program is conducted at Templeton Hall at McPherson College. Call (800) 365-7402 or (620) 242-0486 for more information or visit www.mcpherson.edu/autorestoration/.

Chim-Chiminey
McPherson

If you grew up in the Midwest, it's quite likely that somewhere in your scrapbook is a parent-snapped photo of you and your siblings in front of a 36-foot-tall Happy Chef. At one time, there were more than 56 Happy Chef statues in seven Midwestern states. Kids dining at the once popular family restaurants could even push a button at the base of the three-story statue and hear a recorded message from the Happy Chef himself.

Unfortunately, most of the Happy Chef statues have been disassembled and sent to that big scrap heap in the sky. Except for the one in McPherson, where a former Happy Chef found himself in a whole new profession. Thanks to Vaughn Juhnke, owner of Chimney Specialists, the McPherson Happy Chef is now a chimney sweep wearing a top hat and a black tuxedo. And the spoon, well, it was replaced with a chimney sweep brush. The giant spoon, said Juhnke, won a coveted spot in the McPherson History Museum.

And while the Happy Chefs couldn't win any world's largest awards (after all, they were competing with 55 clones), Juhnke's chimney sweep is widely regarded as the world's largest. In 2002 when a local hooligan climbed up on the sweep and added a, well, let's just call it a "giant anatomy lesson," *Penthouse* magazine got wind of the prank and offered Juhnke $1,000 (he paid a mere $20 for the fiberglass chef) for a photo and story. Juhnke's foreman caught the added body part right away and took the papier-mâché digit down, but not before pictures of it circulated on the internet. Juhnke wisely turned the magazine down, but his giant sweep sans anatomy lesson has made the comics in New York and a magazine in Germany.

Juhnke said that in some ways the Herculean chimney sweep changed his life. I know it has for many people traveling south or north on I-35. It's a landmark for travelers. You can see the sweep for yourself just north of exit 54 on I-35.

The Stone Age

Minneapolis

In these days of million-dollar PR budgets, it's refreshing to find a genuine geological wonder without a concession stand. In fact, when you drive to Rock City, a national landmark with 200 huge rocks (some the size of a house) in the space of two football fields, you usually get lost. The signs are tiny, the roads are dirt, and you start to wonder what fool notion ever propelled you into wanting to see these sandstone concretions in the first place.

Until you arrive. Then you're just dumbstruck. How did these huge rocks get here? And furthermore, what in the heck are you supposed to do with them? You can't exactly skip them. You can't build houses out of them.

About all you can do is name them after what they most resemble and then crawl on top. If you can make it.

But first, you have to deposit your $3 contribution in the rusted money box and sign your name in the guest book, a 39-cent notebook like the kind you used in second grade.

Once you've done that (and you'll probably be the only one there), you're free to wander around Turtle Rock, Kissing Lips, the Twin Sisters, and the other 197 monster rocks. When people say there's no place else on earth like it, you'd better believe it. Because no one paid them to say it.

Rock City is 3.6 miles southwest of Minneapolis. Watch for the Rock City signs, and bring binoculars and your camera.

We built this city on rock, not roll.

"It Was Not Overly Pretty, but It Was Stout"
Morrowville

Lots of city parks have antique locomotives for kids to crawl on, but in Morrowville, the city park has a big red-and-silver bulldozer. I'm sorry to report you can't crawl on it (it's surrounded by a chain-link fence), but considering the fact that the world's first bulldozer was built right there in Morrowville in 1923, it's a small price to pay.

Farmer James Cummings was innocently watching his corn grow one day when he noticed the Sinclair Oil Company was having trouble laying pipes. Getting the pipes in the ground was no problem—newfangled technology took care of that. But to put the dirt back in the trenches, Sinclair workers relied on mules and dirt slips. Cummings wrote to the folks at the company and told them he had a better idea.

They cheered him on, and said, "Show us what ya got." Cummings wasted no time hooking up with J. Earl McLeod, a local draftsman. Scoring parts from local junkyards, they developed the world's first bulldozer. So what if it was made from the frame of a Model T, some old windmill springs, and other odds and ends? It worked, or as McLeod said, "It was not overly pretty, but it was stout." It was enough for the Sinclair Oil Company to award the rest of the pipe contract—from Deshler, Nebraska, to Freemont, Missouri—to Cummings and McLeod.

> ### Trivia
>
> Between 1890 and 1929, flour mills sold their wares in fabric flour sacks with art deco, silk screens, and other beautiful labels such as Kiowa's State Line Milling Company, which used a Kiowa Indian in its logo.
>
> Salina, at one time, milled more flour than anywhere in the country.

A replica of the first bulldozer is located at Cummings Park on Main Street.

No Special Sauce, Lettuce, Cheese— and Certainly No Sesame Seed Bun
Salina

Whatever you do, don't ask for cheese. The cook at Cozy Inn, a 12-foot hole-in-the-wall that sells nothing but hamburgers, is apt to bonk you on the head with his greasy spatula. Not only would a slice of cheddar wreak havoc on his 85-year-old gas-fired cast-iron griddle, but it would be a sacrilege to the institution of the Cozy, a 2.5-inch burger that comes with catsup or mustard on a plain bun. Period.

The secret of these three-bite burgers is the onion. Each two-ounce ball is slathered with an onion mixture that's run through the meat grinder. You can't sit at one of the joint's six stools for even a minute without smelling like a Cozy for the rest of the day. And if you happen to order a few extra, do not—I repeat, do not—leave them in your car. Even Glade Super Fresh has its limitations.

For a while, nearby downtown businesses forbade employees to eat there. After all, they didn't want their businesses smelling like Cozy Inn. But now there's what the cooks call "the wimp window," so you can pick up a bagful to go without facing the curse of the permeated wardrobe.

Loyal customers run in and out, yelling, "Give me five" or "I need a dozen." A former governor of Kansas who grew up in Salina, once ordered 500 Cozies for a staff meeting. Legends surround the place. A pregnant woman in troubled labor allegedly ate a bagful and her baby popped out. A man dying of heart failure requested one last meal of Cozies with all his siblings.

To grab a bagful, visit Cozy Inn at 108 N. Seventh St., (785) 825-2699, www.cozyburger.com. Just don't ask for cheese.

Hedge Funds
Scandia

If you want to make a class of second graders giggle, read them the assortment of names for a hedge apple. The puckered, neon green fruit of the

It seems these hedge apples grow all throughout Kansas. People have reported buying land and that land being taken over by the hedge apple trees. Getting rid of those trees is nearly impossible, so industrious Kansans decided, if you can't kill 'em, share 'em. You can find these paragons of parasite eliminators by googling "hedge apple" or asking one of your Kansas neighbors if they have any. I'll bet they do and I bet they'll be more than happy to share.

Osage orange tree (*Maclura pomifera*) has been called monkey brains, monkey balls, mock oranges, may apples, rootwood, naranjo chino, horse apples, brainfruit, greenbrain, and hedgeballs. Since you can't really eat them (they're not poisonous, but they're about as tasty as tree bark), making second graders laugh is about the only use for this prolific Kansas fruit that can be found in a lot of Kansans' backyards.

Even Martha Stewart gave the ugly fruit a nod, running an article titled "Enjoying Hedge Apples" in a Thanksgiving issue of her foo-foo *Martha Stewart Living* magazine.

Although the EPA doesn't like people to say, many folks swear by the hedge apple's pesticidal properties. Put one or two in the window well or behind the couch and you can kiss spiders, fleas, and other pests goodbye. As a matter of fact, one lady who moved into an apartment overrun by roaches started using the fruit and said it took care of not only the roaches, but crickets and ants too. There's even been a claim they keep mice away.

Kansans have always known what to do with hedgewood—it makes a termite-resistant fence post, it puts on one heck of a spectacular light show when burned in a fireplace, and it even makes good guitars, mandolins, and bows.

Originally planted for fencing (farmers claimed hedge was "horse high, bull strong, and hog tight"), hedgerows became obsolete with the invention of barbed wire in the 1880s.

You Heard It Here First

Kansans tend to keep their inventions to themselves. They come up with things for their own amusement, not because they're hoping to mass-market them and eventually sell them to a big company like General Motors for $10 million. They make things because they need them and because they know they can.

Take Jule Lorenzen, for example. He used to live by himself in a school-house outside of Galva, Kansas, that he rented for $15 a month. He liked to hang glide, and because Galva had a population of 664, most of whom were over age 60, it wasn't exactly easy finding a tow—especially on a Tuesday afternoon when the wind was just right for making contact with thermals. So Lorenzen came up with a solution: He turned an old Honda 350 motor into a remote-control device that launched him and his glider into the air. Sans partner. He never marketed it. He made this unique remote-flying machine for his own enjoyment.

Every now and then, word of one of our Kansas inventions gets out and people come calling. Here are nine life-changing innovations that some-how managed to sneak out of Kansas:

The Slurpee

The time-release capsule

The bumper sticker

Mentholatum

The bulldozer

The Oh Henry! candy bar

The helicopter

The dial telephone

Autopilot

A Little Bit of Scandinavia

Scandia

Located in the small town of Scandia, you will find the Scandia Museum. P. T. Strom and his family settled in the small town that was home to Swedish, Danish, and Norwegian inhabitants. Strom's travels took him to many parts of the globe. When he died in 1947, the family donated over 200 artifacts from his travels. From there the donations grew and began to include relics of settlers who came to the area in 1868. The Scandia Museum now has a wide variety of items including buggies, farm tools, military items, and even a soda fountain. There is also a replica of the colony house where Strom and his family lived when they settled here and hand carvings by the late Allen D. Larson. Larson's "Wagon Train Attack" is housed here and has over 8,557 pieces. The museum hosts music events and has genealogy information for those interested in their own Scandinavian heritage.

The museum opens in the spring and stays open until late September. Visitors can stop by 409 Fourth St. from 1 to 4 p.m. or by appointment. For more information call (785) 335-2266.

Trivia

In the 1870s, Kansans not only drove cattle to and from Texas, they drove wild turkeys, 5,000 of them, from Mitchell County to the railhead in Waterville, 60 miles away.

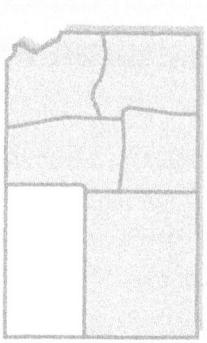

Cawker City
Portis
Smith Center
Phillipsburg
Meade's Ranch
Luray
Lucas
Wilson
Logan
Norton
Morland
Hays
Oberlin
Colby
Oakley
St. Francis
Goodland
Sharon Springs
Weskan

N. Fork Solomon R.
Beaver Creek
Smoky Hill River

281
183
70
18
183
36
9
283
283
70
83
24
70
27
27
70
40
25

Northwest

Northwest

In northwest Kansas, practically every fourth person is a grassroots artist, an artist who takes whatever material is handy—tree trunks, old refrigerator doors, broken milk of magnesia bottles—and makes it into art. Other than Vincent van Gogh, who is represented by a three-story sunflower painting in Goodland, most of the artists from northwest Kansas make what the hoity-toity art world calls "outsider art."

They paint, draw, sculpt, and put petrified shark teeth in wax because "they have to." Because they're called by God, by angels, by unremitting dreams, or by a compelling need to express themselves.

Many of these artists have never heard of Monet or Matisse or their fellow northwest Kansas artist, van Gogh. Most, in fact, have little formal art schooling of any kind. Inez Marshall, for example, was a truck driver before she started carving native Kansas limestone into motorcycles and life-size Abraham Lincolns. Lawrence Reynolds was a janitor; Leroy Wilson, a farmer.

There are also a lot of natural wonders in northwest Kansas, such as the Arikaree Breaks, a mini Grand Canyon near St. Francis, and Monument Rocks, 70-foot chalk walls near Oakley.

And when it comes to unnatural wonders, I dare anyone to try to top Cawker City's world's largest ball of twine.

Goodness, Gracious, Great Balls of Twine

Cawker City

You can't grow up in Kansas without a flicker of pride for what used to be our only nationally known tourist attraction: the world's largest ball of twine in Cawker City.

This "king of string" weighs more than 28,000 pounds—that's 28,571 to be exact and 8,635,742 feet of twine attached as of this reporting—and would wind anybody who dared to run all the way around it. It's memorialized in downtown Cawker in an open-air gazebo. I've heard as many as 300,000 people come to see it each year. One couple from Salt Lake City

Anyone got a really big package that needs tying up?
LINDA B. CLOVER/CAWKER CITY'S BALL OF TWINE

reported in the guest book that they'd driven 9 hours out of their way for a once-in-a-lifetime photo op in front of the big ball.

But here's the problem: There are contenders for the title that Cawker City so proudly displays on signs leading into the city: WELCOME TO CAWKER CITY, HOME OF THE WORLD'S LARGEST BALL OF TWINE. There's a ball of twine in Minnesota and one at Ripley's Believe It or Not! in Branson, Missouri, both of which claim to be larger.

All I know is that the Kansas ball keeps growing, thanks to Cawker City's annual Twine-a-Thon, which takes place the third Friday of every August.

The infamous tourist attraction was started by farmer Frank Stoeber, who allegedly tripped over some twine one day in 1953. In those days, hay bales were held together with twine, and the farmer had two choices: burn it or make it into a ball. Stoeber opted for the ball. Within 4 years, his ball of twine weighed 5,000 pounds and stood 8 feet tall. He continued to work on it until the state's centennial in 1961, when, feeling patriotic, he decided to donate it to the city.

If you want to be like Chevy Chase, who stopped to see the world's largest ball of twine in *National Lampoon's Vacation,* look for the open-air gazebo on the south side of Wisconsin Street (US 24) in beautiful down-town Cawker City. And if you call Linda Clover, who calls herself the Belle of the Ball, at (785) 781-4470, you can add twine at any time.

Where Is Ball-Do?
Cawker City

A little known art fact is that in the background of Leonardo da Vinci's famous *Mona Lisa* is the Rhine River. Well, if you go to Cawker City and look at its *Mona Lisa* (you can't miss it, it's right there in the old Basco Building), you'll see Waconda Lake, the nearest body of water to Cawker City. Look even closer and you'll see another Cawker City landmark, a rendition of the world's largest ball of twine. Mona herself is leaning on it.

We all scream for ice string?
LINDA B. CLOVER/CAWKER CITY'S BALL OF TWINE

In 2003, to celebrate the 50th anniversary of the great ball of twine, artist Cher Olsen painted 40 of the world's most recognizable paintings, all featuring miniature versions of the now-famous orb—Cawker City's own *"Where's Waldo?"* There's Vincent van Gogh's *Starry Night* with the ball of twine as the sun, and Andy Warhol's famous soup can with the ball of twine instead of the soup label. In Edgar Degas's *The Dancers,* the twine ball is being kicked around on the wooden floor. Olsen even did a painting of the Statue of Liberty with the twine as the torch.

Although the paintings were all hauled out for the illustrious anniversary event (and are still there in the main drag's empty storefronts), Olsen had started painting them 2 years earlier, after being transferred with her husband, Cawker City's Methodist minister, to the tiny town.

"I used to be an art teacher, but there weren't many jobs for art teachers in Cawker, so I came up with this project to keep from getting bored," Olsen said.

The community loved Olsen's paintings . . . except for one. Olsen's rendition of Michelangelo's *David,* with the twine ball covering his privates, had to be taken down after a local complained about the lack of propriety. The artist, after all, is the minister's wife.

Although you really can't miss them (they're placed in storefront windows along Cawker's Main Street), Olsen's paintings can be viewed from the "Twine Walk," a piece of twine painted on the sidewalk by a couple of high school kids.

Trapping Tourists
Cawker City

Brian Hodges, an avid road-tripper from Troy, Maine, claims there are five American landmarks that any sightseer worth their steel-belt Michelins simply must visit: Mount Rushmore, the Gateway Arch in St. Louis, Niagara Falls, the Grand Canyon, and, of course, the world's largest ball of twine.

However, in his own quest to mark these must-see attractions off his list, he was shocked to discover nary a single souvenir shop in Cawker City. How was he going to prove to the "folks back home" that he'd really been to the ball of twine if he didn't have a postcard, a key chain, a beer mug, or a shot glass from the tourist destination?

Just when he was about to despair, Linda Clover, the self-appointed groundskeeper for the great ball, came to his rescue. She told him she'd seen Lottie Herod out watering her yard. All he had to do was stop by and Lottie would gladly open her Great Plains Art Gallery, an antiques store/souvenir shop with a working hand-cranked elevator.

Turns out Lottie, besides being a gardener, an antiques collector, and a souvenir stand operator, is an accomplished potter. She crafts teakettles, coffee mugs, salt-and-pepper shakers, and utensil holders all bearing the ball of twine's likeness. She also makes handmade postcards and made a handmade shot glass just for Brian when she heard he liked to collect them. She mailed it to him a couple of years after his visit.

Lottie and her gallery have been gone for quite a few years now. Today if you want souvenirs, you can find them at Local Talent, the Wisconsin Street Trading Post, and the City of Cawker City. They are more than happy to field any questions. You can call (785) 781-4713 or stop by the city office at 804 Locust St.

> ## Trivia
>
> Cawker City won its name in a poker game. Four friends—Huchell, Ride, Kshinka, and Colonel E. H. Cawker—played a rousing game of poker to see whose name would be plastered on the town's post office. Had they known then about the future ball of twine, perhaps Huchell, Ride, and Kshinka might have cheated more.

The Great Pyramid of Colby

Colby

I think it's safe to say that Nellie Kuska of Colby wasn't fond of throwing things away. When she died in 1973, she had 17 tons of possessions.

They weren't just any possessions, mind you. They were collections—big, big collections of dolls, toys, clocks, glass, ceramics, and furniture.

Several communities in California, where she was living at the time, wanted Nellie's collections. After all, Nellie, who even had her own radio show on the art of collecting, had rare dolls from Roosevelt's WPA program, a French fashion doll with a necklace of famous Louvre paintings, and a rare mechanical doll that blew kisses and waved. But no one in California was willing to take all 17 tons.

When Kuska's three sons contacted the historical society in Colby, where she and her husband, agronomist Joseph Kuska, had lived for 50 years, they said, "Sure, bring it on down." Three moving vans later, the Prairie Museum of Art and History ended up with all 28,000 items, only 5 percent of which are on display. Even a 24-acre site has limitations.

Nellie's collection is displayed in a three-story blue pyramid designed by her son, George Kuska, a California architect. It's next to a sod house, an old church, a one-room schoolhouse, and the largest barn in Kansas. Talk about open zoning.

The Prairie Museum of Art and History is at 1905 S. Franklin St., a quarter mile off I-70, exits 53 and 54. Phone (785) 460-4590 or visit www.prairiemuseum.org.

Van Gogh Lives Large
Goodland

You can't really miss a 24-by-32-foot painting, especially when it was painted by van Gogh and sits on an eight-story easel. Actually, the painting is a giant reproduction of one of seven paintings of sunflowers that van Gogh completed in Arles, France, in 1888 and 1889. Canadian artist Cameron Cross decided to reproduce those seven famous paintings, and he chose seven sites in seven countries that had a connection either to van Gogh or to sunflowers.

In Goodland's case, it has two sunflower processing plants, one of which produces oil for Pringles potato chips.

Easel-y the largest van Gogh reproduction in the US
SHERMAN COUNTY CONVENTION AND VISITORS BUREAU

The painting's easel alone weighs 40,000 pounds and requires 30-foot-deep cement pilings just to hold it up. The painting weighs in at a mere 6,000 pounds. It took a month and a half and thousands of gallons of industrial-strength paint to create.

To go van Gogh, take I-70 to Goodland. You'll see Pioneer Park, where it's located, from the highway.

Now That's a Fish Story

Hays

In the 2000 presidential election, a fish in Barton County got 235 votes, only 15 fewer than Ralph Nader. Of course, the fish wasn't just any fish. It was an 85-million-year-old fossil fish, a 14-foot sea monster that made Kansas famous in paleontology circles. The *Xiphactinus* fish, known as the X-fish, was one of hundreds that swam the great seas of Kansas back when Kansas was a sea.

Next to Sue, the *T. rex* that spawned a huge battle among the Feds, paleontologists, and private fossil hunters, an X-fish that sits in the Sternberg Museum of Natural History in Hays is the most famous fossil in the world. It's certainly the most photographed. Ask any paleontologist about the Gillicus in *Xiphactinus* (that means fish within a fish) and you'll get a knowing smile. It seems a 14-foot X-fish got a little greedy one day and tried to swallow a 6-foot cousin. Alas, it was the greedy fish's last meal. The cousin, a *Gillicus arcuatus*, thrashed so violently that it ripped the X-fish's insides to ribbons, killing it and causing it to sink into the paleontology record books.

A bad case of indigestion FORT HAYS STATE UNIVERSITY'S STERNBERG MUSEUM OF NATURAL HISTORY

George F. Sternberg, one of three brothers from a famous fossil-hunting family, found the rare fish-within-a-fish fossil 85 million years later. He excavated it in 1952.

The photogenic fossil is one of 3.75 million artifacts in the Sternberg Museum, a 100,000-square-foot, four-story dome at 3000 Sternberg Dr. Phone (785) 628-4286 or visit www.facebook.com/sternbergmuseum/.

Full Metal Racket

Hays

You never could call Lawrence Reynolds. He didn't have a phone. Everything he ever needed to say is right there in his unique sculptures.

One of his scrap metal men trips over his tongue. The bottom reads, Man is judged by the transgressions of his lips.

In another Reynolds sculpture, the Easter bunny is being crucified, the idea being that we've unjustly turned a religious holiday into a big commercial.

A man with deep convictions, Reynolds based all his work on verses from the Bible or sayings from popular culture. He worked as a recruiter for

Reynolds's rap on life STEVE SCHULTZ

the Salvation Army before he moved to Hays, but he liked his janitor job at Fort Hays State University much better. With first dibs on the wood and old crates in the university's dumpsters, he plucked out two-by-fours and old shipping crates to carve into human figures.

Reynolds also carved several trees in Buffalo Park, across from historic Fort Hays off US 183, but the trees deteriorated and had to be removed. Today, his work can be viewed at the Grassroots Art Center in Lucas (213 S. Main St.; 785-525-6118).

May the Fort Be with You
Hays

"Old Historic Fort Hays is a big deal around here," the Fort Hays Chamber said. As well it should be. Established in 1865, moved to its current location in 1867, it was plopped down in the middle of Cheyenne and Arapahoe country. The fort's soldiers were stationed there to protect the railroad workers and travelers heading west on the Smoky Hill Trail. Many now-famous individuals were stationed at Fort Hays: General George A. Custer, Buffalo Bill Cody, and Wild Bill Hickok.

Trivia

White bison calves are extremely rare, occurring in the wild at a rate of about 1 in 10 million births. In American Indian tradition, white bison are considered sacred. They are signs that prayers are being heard and the prophecies foretold are coming true. While white bison are slightly more common with modern help, they are still an anomaly. And wouldn't you know it, Fort Hays, has one. To view the bison herd, travel on US 183, 4 miles south of I-70. They are located right across from Historic Fort Hays. Call (785) 628-7375 for information.

Visitors to the fort can take a guided or self-guided tour. Items on display include Plains Indian clothing, arrows, rifles, and revolvers; General Custer's dumbbell; and everyday objects that show what life was really like at the fort, such as washstands, ladies' dresses, and soldiers' uniforms.

There is no charge to get steeped in infantry history. You can find the site 4 miles south of Hays on I-70, exit 157. Open year-round. Call (785) 625-6812 for more information or visit www.kansashistory.gov/fort-hays.

Smithsonian West
Logan

Look at a schedule for the Smithsonian Institution Traveling Exhibitions Service (SITES) and you'll mostly see big cities, places like Miami and Chicago and Phoenix. But look again and you'll also notice the name of a little town in Kansas that you've probably never heard of, a tiny burg with a population of fewer than 600 that shows up on SITES several times most years.

Logan, Kansas, is anything but a popular travel destination. It doesn't even have a motel. But smack-dab in the middle of its 2-block downtown is the Dane G. Hansen Memorial Museum, a modern 10,000-square-foot museum that just happens to be one of the Smithsonian's best customers.

By the time it celebrated its 20 anniversary, it had already hosted 100 traveling exhibits from the venerable Washington, DC, institution.

Thanks to Dane G. Hansen, an eccentric bachelor who slept until noon every day and who left the museum's foundation $9 million when he died on his 82nd birthday, the prosperous museum has been able to show Alaska Indigenous art, drawings by da Vinci, Japanese dolls, and moon rocks from NASA that Houston wouldn't loan unless a personal representative showed up to fetch them. Logan sent its mayor.

Hansen, an oil and construction magnate who sold mules to the US Cavalry during World War I, lived in Logan his entire life. At one time his construction company employed 300, nearly half the town. He slept until noon every day because, as he said, "Nobody ever made a dollar in the morning. Mornings are for opening mail and answering phones." Instead, he worked until midnight, waking up colleagues all over the country with his late-night phone calls.

Polly Bales, former president of the museum association and wife of Dane's nephew, said that while Dane would undoubtedly be proud of the memorial to his name, he'd probably question the budget for some of the exhibits.

Admission to the museum is free. It's open daily except Thanksgiving, Christmas, and New Year's Day, and can be found in Logan on Highway 9 between Speed and Densmore. Phone (785) 689-4846 or visit www.hansen museum.org.

Concrete Evidence

Lucas

When S. P. Dinsmoor was 64, an age at which most people consider retirement, he launched an unusual career as an artist and social commentator.

Already he'd sired five children, raised two more stepchildren, served as a nurse in the Civil War, taught school, and farmed a small patch of property outside Lucas.

His real work, though, the work for which he's still remembered, began when he sold the farm and bought a half-acre plot of land in full view of the railroad tracks and only blocks from downtown Lucas.

The year was 1907. Dinsmoor, a staunch Populist, decided that just because the Populist Party had gone down the tubes didn't mean its philosophy had to.

He spent the next 21 years espousing his mostly Populist views on religion, society, and monopolistic trusts in the only medium he could afford: concrete.

He started with an unusual 11-room log cabin made out of limestone logs. Giving tours, he used the admission fees to buy more concrete—113 tons, in fact—which he used to sculpt concrete grape arbors, American flags that swiveled on flagpoles, 40-foot trees, a life-size Adam and Eve, a devil whose eyes lit up (Dinsmoor was the first in Logan to have electricity), and 100 other statues.

With 113 tons of concrete and an overactive imagination, you, too, can build your own Garden of Eden. JON BLUMB

His philosophy and humor were evident in everything he sculpted. A carved concrete octopus representing monopolistic trusts had their tentacles in bags of bonds, sacks of interest, the North Pole, and the Panama Canal. He always said he used himself as the model for Adam, a move that created quite a stir in Logan until he agreed to add an apron to cover the statue's eyebrow-raising genitalia.

After Dinsmoor's first wife died, he married again when he was 81. His wedding to 20-year-old Emilie Brozek (who subsequently had two children with Dinsmoor) scandalized Lucas and brought even more publicity for his monument to modern masonry.

Dinsmoor called it the Garden of Eden and stipulated that when he died, he wanted his body placed in a glass-enclosed concrete coffin, so he could continue to keep an eye on admission-paying customers. He also sculpted an angel and a jug above the coffin. The angel, he said, was there in case he went up, the water jug in case he went the other way.

To view the work and the dead body of an unusual self-taught sculptor, a man some called the William Blake of the Wild, Wild West, visit the Garden of Eden in Lucas at the corner of Kansas and Second Streets (785-525-6395; www.gardenofedenlucas.org).

Big Things in Small Packages
Lucas

If you send $25 to Erika Nelson, you can become an official member of her Museum of the World's Largest Collection of the World's Smallest Versions of the World's Largest Things. Erika, who lives in Lucas when she's not out rescuing small towns in her art car, is a hero. She's an artist, a visionary, and the world's foremost expert on the world's largest things. She has one of the top five coolest jobs in America.

Plus, by simply doing what she loves most, she is literally saving the world. In case you hadn't noticed, the choices in American cuisine are getting narrower by the day. So are the choices of retail establishments. These days, it's hard to tell if you're in Cleveland or Fort Lauderdale or Fremont, Nebraska, because they all have the same Walmart, Pizza Huts, and Taco Bells. And some people think this is a good thing.

That's where Erika comes in. She has dedicated her life to one simple mission: "Combatting generica." That means she celebrates the one-of-a-kind, the kooky, the things that the rest of us tend to ignore or, worse yet, detonate. Erika reported that the folks in Sac City, Iowa, had the nerve to blow up their 2,225-pound popcorn ball.

Not only does Erika visit and take painstaking notes about each world's largest attraction, she makes her own tiny version that goes on display in either the Lucas museum, a converted senior citizen bus, or in Scout, the smallest art car in her fleet.

The smallest version of the world's largest ball of rubber bands, for example, is made of those tiny rubber bands used on braces. The world's smallest version of the world's largest otter is made from a dachshund figurine and modeling clay. Other exhibits in her rolling museum are the world's smallest versions of the giant talking cow (made from an Elvis Presley

Now retired, the rolling museum hosts visitors on-site in Lucas. ERIKA NELSON

valentine box), doughnuts, bats, eight balls, and badgers. The world's largest catsup bottle (which stands tall at 170 feet) stands 3 inches in Erika's
museum.

Furthermore, after she creates the tiny knockoff, she returns to the
original and shoots a photo of the big guy and its smaller clone.

For your $25 membership, you'll receive a full-year subscription to her
newsletter, your own membership card, and a refrigerator magnet of one
of the world's largest things. If you are slightly wealthier and want to kick
in to be an Otter ($50), you would be awarded your own World's Largest
Challenger Ball Starter Kit, which means that if you are dedicated enough,
you could create your own world's largest ball of something and then Erika
herself would come out, photograph it, and make a tiny version of it. If you
want to jump all in at the Buffalo level ($1,000), you'll get more stuff than
you know what to do with . . . or maybe you do know what to do with and
that's why you want to go all in.

Decisions, decisions.

But How Do I Cut My Sirloin?

Most towns with populations of 427 are lucky to have a gas station, let alone a museum. But Lucas, an anything but sleepy town in northwest Kansas, has five major museums, attracts scads of international visitors, and is definitely in contention for most interesting town in Kansas.

Especially if you like grassroots art. Also called folk art, outsider art, primitive art, and, yes, downright bizarre by some people, grassroots art thrives in Kansas—a state with more grassroots artists per capita than any other. And the Lucas Triangle, with its three vortexes of the Grassroots Art Center (a fascinating three-building museum with art made with everything from grapefruit peels and dried chewing gum to empty milk of magnesia bottles), the Garden of Eden, and the Deeble Rock Garden, is definitely the hotbed of grassroots art. To celebrate their grassroots heritage, the wacky folks of Lucas recently borrowed on the Chicago Cow idea and created unusual versions of giant "fork art," another name for grassroots art.

Their most recent installation is Bowl Plaza, the world's largest toilet bowl. Created by several well-known Lucas artists, the big bowl has one tiny drawback. The stalls are so intricately designed (the women's side is mosaicked with female accoutrements, the men's side with masculine stuff) that people hog the bathrooms' glory while those outside in line suffer.

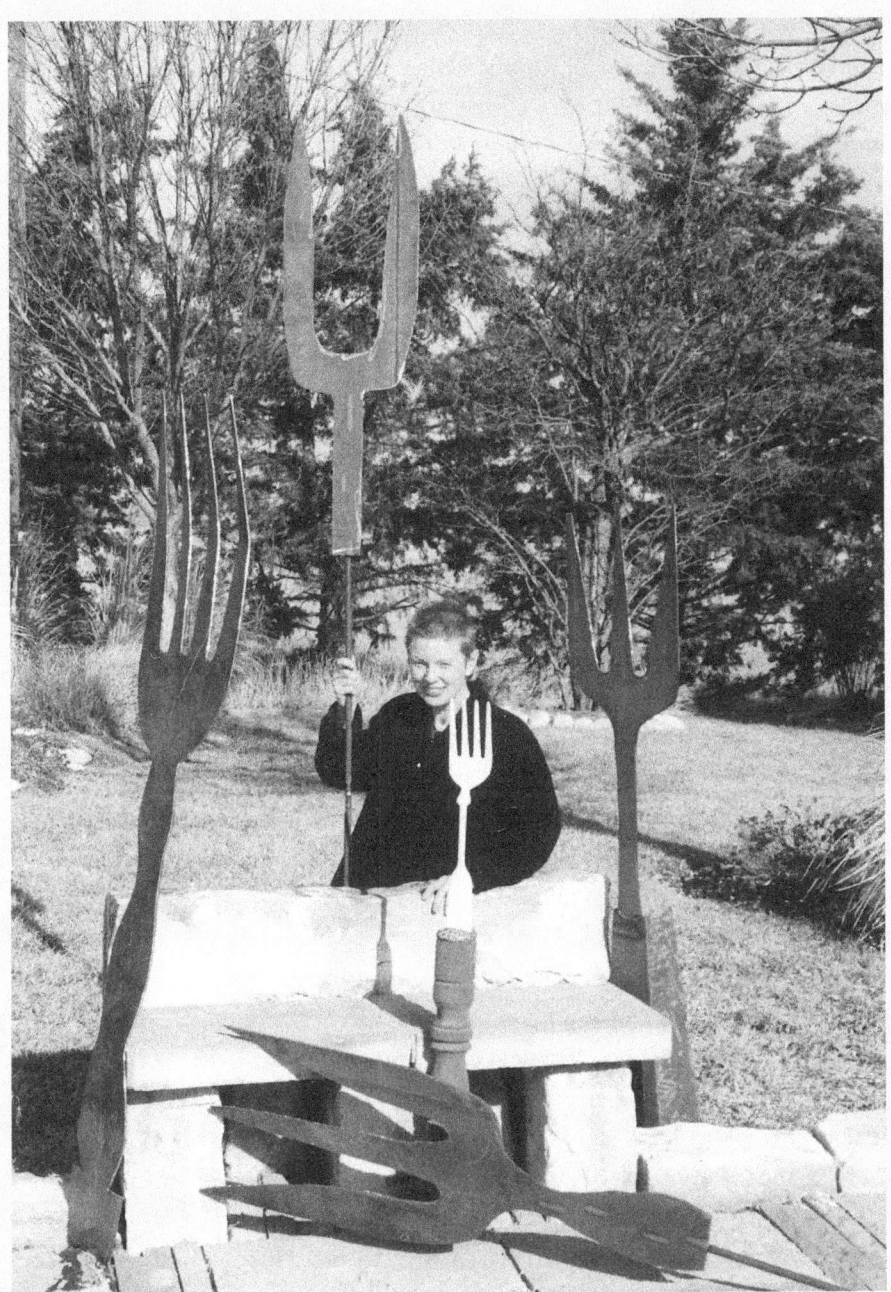

National Fork Producers Council? STEVE SCHULTZ

Before Erika became the self-appointed curator of this unique museum, she was an art instructor at Kansas University. To contact Erika or view her museum, call (785) 760-0826, check out www.worldslargestthings.com, or write her at World's Largest Things, PO Box 101, Lucas, KS 67648-0101.

Think Pig

Lucas

Internationally acclaimed porcelain artist Eric Abraham said he always wanted to have a New York City loft and studio. In 2004, he bought one. In Lucas, Kansas.

"This studio fulfills my longtime desire to have a New York City loft. It's just that it doesn't have the hassles of New York City," Abraham said about the 6,000-square-foot Chevy dealership he converted into his Flying Pig Studio and Gallery.

The space included a huge studio, a retail gallery, and a living space complete with a kitschen (yes, I spelled that right) that features 150 old radios.

Abraham had been making flying pigs since 1968, when an architecture student in his ceramics class at graduate school made 30 thrown piggy banks, much to the chagrin of the "serious art students." Abraham figured, "Well, if he can get away with it, so can I," and he concocted an unusual Mexican-style piggy bank mounted on a tall base with a Greek temple. He called it the *First National Oink*.

Abraham's ceramics (which have been featured on the *Today* show, the Discovery Channel, and HGTV) only got wilder and crazier after that. Fairy tales are a popular theme, complete with fire-breathing dragons, hat-wearing pigs, and other whimsical creatures.

Abraham, who was born smack-dab in the middle of Harlem, started making art when he was a kid, not a huge surprise since both his parents were artists who met while illustrating children's books for the public schools of New York City.

Today, his Flying Pig Studio is a private residence. Abraham passed away in 2013. However, his porcelain art lives on at Erika Nelson's Sideshow Expo on Main Street. You can give her a call at (785) 760-0826.

Welcome to Eric's world. ERIC ABRAHAM

The Art Is in the Details
Lucas

Sometimes whittlin' takes on a life of its own, and that's what happened when Kathy Ruth Neal took up carving tools. Neal lived in Kansas City working as a TWA flight attendant until she was diagnosed with breast cancer in 1994. Treatment was successful, and as she recovered in the hills of Tennessee, one day she picked up a gnarled piece of wood and started to carve. She taught herself the art, and when she picked up a twig or branch, she saw events of life or monsters with hats.

She traveled around doing shows, even stopping at the Grassroots Art Center. She was so humble that they didn't even know who she was until they received pieces from the collections of her work.

One of her particularly detailed pieces is on display at the Art Center as well as a video talking about her work. "Pass the Popcorn" is a very elaborate wooden carving of a family sitting in their living room, watching Marilyn Monroe, eating popcorn. When you study the details, you may find yourself looking for your own bag of popcorn. While visiting the Art Center, don't forget to look at her monsters and other creations. You'll be glad you did.

And You Thought Concrete Was for Bridges and Sidewalks
Lucas

Not 10 miles from Dinsmoor's Garden of Eden, another unknown artist was also busy casting concrete. This artist, Ed Root, didn't do it to make his political or religious views known. He did it because he broke his hip in a car accident and could no longer farm the family homestead or make illegal moonshine. Until the Kansas Grassroots Art Association discovered him, it's doubtful anybody but his wife and 10 kids ever saw the magnificent work he created by casting concrete and then embedding it with shards of glass and pottery, milk of magnesia bottles, plastic toys, screw-in fuses, perm rods, buttons, and anything else he could find. After his wife died, he even used the family china. When the grandkids came to visit, he'd hand them 5-gallon buckets and instruct them not to come back until they'd filled them up.

He made hundreds of concrete pieces, ranging from three-tier birdhouses and 7-foot tomb-like creations to small doorstops with rabbits, which he showcased in the family home, along with rambling collages of foil, crepe paper, and paper flowers.

When the Army Corps of Engineers decided to turn Root's property into Wilson Lake, Root went after them with a shotgun. But in 1960, when he was 94, he finally died and the corps flooded his land.

The good news is the Grassroots Art Center still has hundreds of Root's pieces on display at 213 S. Main St. Phone (785) 525-6118.

Postcards from the Edge

Lucas

Florence Deeble was just a punk kid when S. P. Dinsmoor was constructing his lavish, nationally known Garden of Eden. Although she enjoyed walking by his house, she didn't fancy herself a wannabe. Rather, she aspired to teach English and history, which she did for 42 years.

But in 1951, after a kid in nearby Osborne fell into a fish pond and drowned, her mom asked her to fill in the family's backyard fish pond with concrete. It was a moment of destiny.

First, she added a bit of color, a few rocks. Uh-oh. Florence was hooked. She soon began creating concrete postcards of all the places she visited. An avid traveler, she made postcards of Mount Rushmore; the Grand Tetons; Arizona deserts; Shiprock, New Mexico; Colorado's Long's Peak; and Estes Park, where she owned a cabin and spent her summers. When she was no longer able to travel, she concentrated her efforts on Mount Lucas with Mount Rushmore–like heads of Lucas dignitaries. The Lucas City Band was prominently featured.

Until her death in 1999 (she was 6 months away from turning 100), she led tours of her rock garden dressed in heels and turquoise jewelry.

"I like to garden—to rock garden," is how she explained it.

Deeble's Rock Garden can be viewed at 126 S. Fairview Ave. For more information, call the Grassroots Art Center at (785) 525-6118.

South Dakota? Who needs South Dakota? STEVE SCHULTZ

But Where's Ken?

Lucas

The Garden of Isis, inside the old Florence Deeble house, is not the place to plan a birthday party for 5-year-olds. At that age, partygoers still have a tendency to put Barbie (you know, that plastic doll with the 36-24-36 figure) on a pedestal. They like to dress her like a prom queen or a bride or a candy striper and hope that someday they'll grow up to be just like her.

They might not look too kindly on the fact that Mri Pilar has created a whole art installation from discarded Barbie dolls. She calls them Rebarbs and, yes, some of them have been dismembered, reassembled, and given butch haircuts.

Not that Pilar has a personal vendetta against Barbie. Well, maybe she's a tad bit put off by Barbie's role as an icon of perfect womanhood. She just likes taking things that people no longer see a use for and turning them into art. She's nothing if not democratic in her choice of art materials. Besides Rebarbs, the five-room Garden of Isis features clocks, hair

Tinfoiled again STEVE SCHULTZ

barrettes, kitchen utensils, car parts, computer motherboards, plastic dino-saurs, and anything else Pilar can scrounge from the recycle bin.

All of the walls and ceilings of this 1906 home are covered in foil and silver insulation. There's not a single square inch that hasn't been trans-formed into an art assemblage, all woven together by Slinkys. Besides the Rebarbs, Pilar's installation features lots of unclocks (that's a clock that no longer keeps time), an Isis Chapel, and an Isis Grotto.

Viewing of the Garden of Isis is included in the admission fee for the Grassroots Art Center. The Garden of Isis is located a few blocks away at 126 S. Fairview Ave. Call (785) 525-6118 for more information.

Quilted Basement

Luray

From the street, Leroy Wilson's house in Luray looked like every other house on his block—beige, middle class, relatively boring.

But, boy oh boy, open the door to the basement and you'd fall head-first into Alice in Wonderland's rabbit hole.

Leroy, who retired from farming after an unfortunate car wreck, painted every door, wall, water pipe, phone line, furnace, and gas valve in the family basement. And when that was finished, he painted over it and started again. For 12 years until his death in 1991, he did little but paint wild triangles, mosaics, and quilting patterns on every square millimeter of the family basement.

Neighbors used to drop off leftover paint. His wife, who wasn't crazy about his new hobby, refused to let him touch anything upstairs.

In fact, a former tenant of one of Wilson's rental houses reported that the insides of the kitchen cabinets were painted with Wilson's mosaics. Thankfully, his wife didn't bother to open the cabinets, so she never caught on.

Although the basement was painted over when the Wilson house was sold, a cabinet and pieces of the wall have been preserved at the Grassroots Art Center in Lucas, 213 S. Main St., (785) 525-6118.

A Pin Through the Heart of America
Meade's Ranch

In 1918, the US Coast and Geodetic Survey took a piece of cardboard, cut out the shape of the lower 48 states, and balanced it on a pinpoint. This center of the US (39.25° 50' N latitude, 98.25° 35' W longitude, to be exact) just happened to fall in the middle of a hog farm near Lebanon, Kansas. The locally run Hub Club, assuming this designation could lead to considerable tourist revenue, ceremoniously installed a pyramidal stone monument with a brass plaque on a hilltop just outside of town. Inscribed with a bold declaration—THE GEOGRAPHIC CENTER OF THE UNITED STATES—the plaque wasn't exactly correct. The farm was three quarters of a mile away, but hog farmer Johnny Grib wasn't too keen on turning his beloved farm into a tourist trap. Especially when the state government got involved, ponying up the money for a hotel and road crews to pave a 1-mile strip leading to the site.

Unfortunately, the great hordes of tourists never arrived, and the hotel was sold to Texas investors who only visit once a year during hunting season.

Center of the universe JAMES S. DICK

Forty-two miles south of Lebanon, another sign and plaque announce yet another center, THE GEODETIC CENTER OF NORTH AMERICA. This sign makes no claims at being the geodetic center itself; rather it indicates that the real geodetic center lies on private property 8 miles away at Meade's Ranch, which is also marked with a small bronze geodetic survey marker.

Every calculation of latitude or longitude anywhere in North America uses this base on Meade's Ranch as the starting point. Anytime a surveyor between Mexico and Canada checks property lines using geodetic markers, he's positioning that property in relationship to a ranch in Kansas.

Holy Guacamole, Batman, What Are We Doing in a Bank?

Morland

Would-be robbers beware! In Morland, a little town of 165, the local bank boasts its very own collection of superheroes.

Morland's Citizens State Bank doubles as a comic book museum, with 164 comic books on display.

Once belonging to local Morland boy Floyd Riggs, the collection was uncovered by Floyd's mom after he died of cancer at age 42. Carefully bundled in old lard cans, the colorful collection, which includes the Lone Ranger, Tarzan, Lassie, and other popular comics from the '40s and '50s, was carefully mounted and framed. For a while, thanks to the prompting of a local art teacher who recognized the collection's value, it toured the state as a traveling art exhibition.

To see the Floyd Riggs comic book collection, visit the bank at 511 W. Main St. The bank also has a brick mural of all the flora and fauna unearthed in the local fossil dig funded by the National Geographic Society in 1985 and 1986. Phone (785) 627-3165.

Hail to the Losers

Norton

On January 22, 2009, when the rest of the country was celebrating Barack Obama's inauguration, Lee Ann Shearer, the curator of Norton's Gallery of Also-Rans, inaugurated a 16-by-20 black-and-white photograph of John McCain.

While McCain's name is still a household word, try these on for size: Winfield Hancock, Rufus King, or DeWitt Clinton? These men, powerful and famous during their lifetimes, are victims of a well-known political rule of thumb: The winner in presidential elections gets the White House; the loser gets doomed to obscurity.

DeWitt Clinton, for example, was a mover and shaker who launched the Erie Canal and swept the Republican nomination in 1812. But thanks to James Madison, the Democrat who defeated him, his name can barely be recalled.

That's not the case in Norton, Kansas, where presidential losers get their glory at the Gallery of Also-Rans. Housed in the mezzanine of Norton's First State Bank, this little museum was even more obscure than its subjects, hosting 30 or so visitors a year, until *USA Today* got wind of it.

Sparked by the Bush-Gore election, the outcome of which held the country's attention for 37 long days after votes were cast, this museum suddenly took on a new importance.

W. W. Rouse, former president of the bank, started the museum in 1965, after one of his daughters gave him a book by Irving Stone called *They Also Ran*. A history buff who loved lively political debate, Rouse was particularly intrigued by Horace Greeley, who lost to Ulysses S. Grant in 1872. He decided the losers, too, needed a tribute, and he began collecting pictures of them. Until his death in 1981, Rouse wrote to the Library of Congress every 4 years requesting a photo. He also wrote the commentary about each candidate, and his colorful personality is apparent in every entry.

Now Shearer serves as curator, commentary writer, and tour guide for all who come to see the ones history eventually leaves behind.

The Gallery of Also-Rans is at the First State Bank at 105 W. Main St. in Norton. Call (785) 877-3341; www.theyalsoran.com.

The Show Must Go On
Oakley

In 2001, when the owners of the Palace Theatre were forced to shutter the one entertainment venue left in Oakley, "We just looked at each other and thought, 'Now what?'" said Nicole Keenan, who was in high school at the time. "We didn't have anywhere to go."

And it didn't take long to show.

"Mischief skyrocketed," Oakley chief of police Dan Shanks said. "Our kids had nothing to do."

Community leaders put their heads together and hatched an innovative plan to kill two birds with one stone. They'd reopen the theater as a nonprofit with high school kids running the show.

"The students do everything from keeping the books, writing the checks, and paying the bills to recruiting volunteers for the concession stand," Jim Keenan said, the high school business teacher who developed the yearlong entrepreneurship curriculum.

Their idea was a smashing success: Teen crime is down as crowds of 250 pack the house on weekends. The Palace prices rock: $6 tickets and $6 for snacks and a drink.

"This has been one of the best things I've seen this community do," moviegoer Barb Glover said. "It gives parents a safe place to drop off their kids. It keeps teens off the highway. But more importantly, it gives these teenagers real-life experience in running a business."

Indeed, Taylor Ellegood, one of six students who ran the theater in 2009, said, "It's not very often you find a job that gives you all this real-world experience. After a year of doing this, I could easily go out and start my own business. Plus, I've learned how not to flip out when customers get upset." To catch a flick, stop by 101 Center Ave., (785) 672-3115; www.palacetheatreoakley.com.

Teeth for Two

Oakley

One day back in 1964, Viola Fick looked down at the ground on her ranch near Monument Rock and saw 72 fossils of shark teeth. She and her husband, Earnest, borrowed what Vi called "a learner's book on fossils" from Earnie's nephew, who was attending Fort Hays State University, and began to search in earnest. Before it was all said and done, the amateur paleontologists found thousands of Cretaceous fossils, including 11,000 fossilized shark teeth, all within 50 miles of Oakley.

After a while, the shark teeth started looking the same, so Vi did what any sensible person would do—she started turning them into art. She made eagles, American flags, the presidential seal, the state seal of Kansas, and, of course, a bas-relief sculpture of a shark—all out of shark teeth. One of the eagles had a snake in its talons, but she used rattlesnake rattlers for that. Her best shark teeth were reserved for embedding in the fancy frames she made to show off her portraits of flowers, trees, and people, all made with melted wax, papier-mâché, paint, glue, and fossils.

As one of the curators at the Fick Fossil Museum said, "They didn't have cable back then."

Vi's final body of work includes hundreds of artworks from fossilized shark teeth, vertebrae, fish jaws, shells, and crinoids.

The museum is located at 700 W. Third St. Phone (785) 672-4839 or visit www.visitoakleyks.com/fick-fossil-history-museum.com.

Cinderella Story

Oberlin

In an age where fitness centers vie for the hottest new workout equipment, LandMark Inn, an historic Oberlin bank turned B&B, is an oddity. Owner Gary

Do they teach Pilates? JAMES S. DICK

Anderson bids on the oldest, out-of-date workout equipment he can find—dinosaurs, really, from the turn of the century. He uses the antique workout equipment to stock the Historic Registered inn's vintage gym. Among other things, he landed an 1866 rowing machine, an antique cedar sauna, and an 1886 stationary bicycle. The LandMark's gym is so authentic that when director Ron Howard filmed *Cinderella Man,* the period movie about boxer James Braddock's 1930s comeback, he went straight to Gary Anderson, begging to rent out most of his gym. LandMark Inn also has an old-time mercantile, Teller Restaurant, and seven suites with carved beds, ornate wallpaper, arched pine windows, Victorian sinks, and original pictures of Buffalo Bill Cody, who may or may not have worked out on the stationary bike. The LandMark Inn is at 189 S. Penn, (785) 475-2340; www.landmarkinn.com.

Who Needs a River?

Phillipsburg

At last count, there were 9,485 American towns with annual river festivals. You know, those summer festivities where antique fire trucks parade through downtown, kids smear cotton candy on their spankin' new rompers, and old-timers reminisce about "the good ole days." Most of these towns come by their river festivals honestly, which is to say, there's an actual river running through town.

Trivia

Twenty miles south of Oakley, off a dirt road on a private ranch, are 70-foot towering chalk walls and turrets. They're called Monument Rocks, and the owners don't mind people visiting the nationally designated landmark, but they don't appreciate climbers. It's 20 miles south of the junction of US 40 and US 83, then 7.5 miles east and south on Jayhawk Road.

Phillipsburg, a county seat on US 36, didn't consider the fact that its closest river is an entire county away to be a hindrance. Heck, in a move that undoubtedly ranks in the Final Four of Turning Lemons into Lemonade, Phillipsburg turned its lack of river into a cause for celebration. Every year since 1984, the Phillipsburg Area Chamber of Commerce throws an annual festival, complete with turtle races, arts and crafts booths, a car and motorcycle show, and more than 20,000 revelers who show up each year to chow down on Phillipsburgers, a local hamburger drenched in a secret sauce found only in Phillips County. And as for watering holes, Phillipsburg does have a swimming pool, admission for which is completely free during the tongue-in-cheek festival, going strong now for more than 25 years.

For more info, contact Phillipsburg Area Chamber of Commerce, 205 F St., (785) 543-2321.

From Limestone to Limelight
Portis

Back when Inez Marshall was giving personal 40-minute tours of her Continental Sculpture Hall, she used to tell her guests, "It's the only one of its kind in the world."

She was not exaggerating. For 50 years, the former truck driver, auto mechanic, and traveling evangelist sculpted Model Ts, churches, log cabins, and just about anything else you can think of out of native Kansas limestone. The Model T, which weighs 600 pounds, has a motor, a transmission, U-joints, a driveshaft, a radiator, and headlights and taillights that still work.

In the full-size dining room scene she sculpted of Abraham Lincoln and his family, Abe alone weighed 500 pounds. Even though she was partially disabled, Marshall managed to turn monstrous and very heavy pieces of limestone into the Lord's Supper, a Kennedy table (a tribute to JFK, it had dozens of Kennedy dollars embedded in it), and an 11-room Sunshine Hospital that had doctors, an operating room, a nursery, and a dining hall complete with food on the tables.

After lying in bed for a year and a half (she'd broken her back while hauling corn to Kansas from Iowa), Inez suddenly felt the urge to get up and go to the door. She immediately was drawn to a small rock. She said to her dad, "Hand me that rock."

He did.

"Now, hand me a knife."

Again, he heeded her request.

Even though she'd never shown even the slightest inclination toward carving, she immediately sculpted a cute little squirrel with its tail standing up. Within a few months, she'd made dozens of small rock sculptures.

Her dad ran an ad in the back of a magazine, and before she knew it, she was carving limestone salt and pepper shakers of hundreds of species of birds. A pair of scarlet tanagers or orange-crowned warblers, for example, sold for $1. Soon, she had so many commissions she couldn't keep up with them.

Besides, bigger projects were beckoning. In the 1960s and '70s, she opened the Continental Sculpture Hall, first in Abilene and then in an old gas station in her hometown of Portis. She gave tours wearing her signature red cap and blue sweater.

After she died in 1984, a dentist from Florida snatched up most of her work, but now it's back in Kansas. You can see 95 of her pieces at the Grassroots Art Center at 213 S. Main St. in Lucas.

Snake, Rattle, and Roll
Sharon Springs

When I see a snake, I scream bloody murder. When women in Sharon Springs see snakes, they think, "Wow! What a great idea for a festival." Or they did.

Of course, the five women who launched the Sharon Springs Rattlesnake Roundup were used to seeing snakes, big prairie rattlers that slither rampantly in this part of the state.

Snakes, in fact, are a lot more rampant than tourists, who tend to avoid this little burg that's a good 30 miles south of I-70. After the sugar beet

Custer's First Stand

Everybody knows about the Battle of Little Bighorn, the infamous battle where General Custer lost his life. But the 12-year Plains War that culminated on that famous Montana battlefield actually started in northwestern Kansas when on November 29, 1864, a tribe of Cheyenne men, women, and children were brutally massacred in their camp on Sand Creek in Colorado. Survivors made their way to Cherry Creek near St. Francis, Kansas, and began passing the war pipe. Nearly 3,000 Indians from many tribes came to declare war on the white man who was destroying their people. On New Year's Day 1865, they set out to get their revenge.

The Dog Soldier Monument at the Cherry Creek Encampment site stands as a memorial to the Cheyenne who died at Sand Creek. The monument, by Cheyenne County historian and metal sculptor Tobe Zweygardt, features a metal tepee guarded by an Indian brave astride his horse atop a nearby bluff. It is located north of St. Francis on Highway 27.

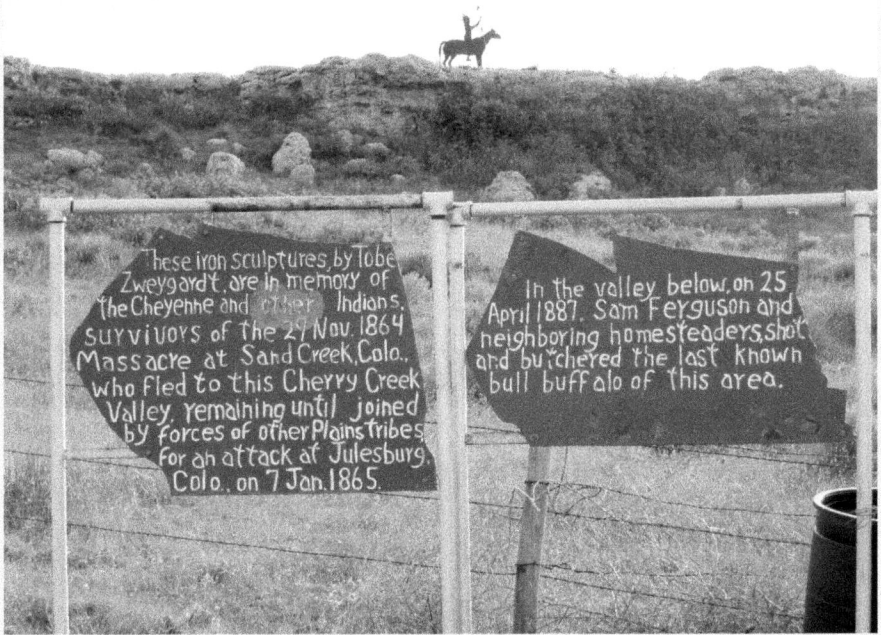

Sign, sign, everywhere a sign JAMES S. DICK

industry went belly up in the 1980s, the traffic in Sharon Springs dried up almost completely, except for the few mountain climbers who traipsed there to climb Mount Sunflower, the highest point in Kansas.

Judie Withers and four of her friends started pondering what they had to offer.

"We didn't have much except snakes. Lord, did we have snakes," Judie said.

The five women proposed a rattlesnake roundup, testified in Topeka to make it legal, and hosted the yearly event. Talk about killing two snakes with one stone.

Thousands trooped to Sharon Springs to eat rattlesnake meat, view the 12-by-24-foot rattlesnake pit, and watch Fangs and Rattlers, a touring exhibition team that performed such tricks as stuffing 12 live rattlers into a sleeping bag with a live man in it.

A $100 prize and a trophy went to the rattlesnake wrangler who brought in the biggest snake. The record was 53.5 inches. The festival was held Mother's Day weekend each year.

Into Thick Air

Weskan

Mount Sunflower, the highest point in Kansas, used to have a cow skull sitting on it. Now it has a giant sunflower made of railroad spikes, a mailbox, and a plaque that says nothing happened here in 1897.

Still, mountain climbers from around the country troop here to mark its 4,039-foot elevation off their list.

For some low-altitude mountaineering, visit Sunflower, mountain of doom, just 0.5 mile east of the Colorado border. Go 3 miles west on US 40, 11 miles north on a gravel road, then 0.9 mile west and you should see a sign at the pasture gate. Three-tenths of a mile later, after crossing the cattle guard, you'll reach the summit. Be sure to sign the register to prove you were there. It's located in the mailbox at the summit.

Grand Canyon of Kansas

Ten miles north of St. Francis, the yucca-covered high plains suddenly drop off into a breathtaking canyon sculpted out of 9,000-year-old loess hills. This 36-mile Grand Canyon of the plains that stretches into Nebraska is called the Arikaree Breaks, and if it were located anywhere else, tourists would flock and buses would be dispatched. As it is now, it's accessed by a potholed dirt road with numbered red metal disks that correspond to the Self-Guided Driving Tour. You can grab a copy of that at the St. Francis Information Kiosk at the rest area on US Highway 36 in St. Francis.

As flat as Dolly Parton JAMES S. DICK

Winning Isn't Everything, but It Sure Ain't Bad

New York Times reporter Joe Drape spent the fall of 2008 in Smith Center covering the high school football team that hadn't lost a game in eight seasons. At Hubbard Stadium, locals duct-taped their blankets to the bleachers the night before to save seats. Every morning from 8 to 9, a group of men, mostly senior citizens, hooked up at the Second Cup Café. They called themselves "As the Bladder Fills," and their shenanigans were detailed every week in the *Echo*, a four-page, typewritten newspaper that former mail carrier Ivan Burgess wrote and distributed through his Last Legs Publishing. He reported on jokes and local news and provided vital definitions of such Smith Center pastimes as bingo. (It's when one little old lady yelling "Bingo" makes 50 little old ladies say, "Damn.") And guess what? Hubbard Stadium, Second Cup Café, and bingo can still be found in Smith Center with as much news as was reported back then.

Talk About Going Round and Round
Wilson

If the prisoners in *Midnight Express*, the 1978 movie about American college kids thrown into a Turkish prison, had been captured in Wilson, they'd have no choice but to walk in circles, an activity that many of the prisoners in the movie undertook once they lost their minds. The Wilson City Jail, a tiny two-story native limestone structure with a tin roof, is round. Until 1912, it was used as the city water tower. When the newfangled water tower went in, the round stone building took on a new life. But unlike the Turkish prisons, the prisoners here couldn't stay much longer than 8 hours. It didn't have a bathroom, and the sheriff had to transfer them to Ellsworth, the county seat, the next morning.

The historic round jail is located a half block off Main Street on E Street, just past the railroad tracks.

Giving prisoners the runaround

Southwest

Southwest

Get out your facial tissue. There was no Matt Dillon. At least not in Dodge City. The famous Gunsmoke *character was a composite of many famous lawmakers who tried (most of the time unsuccessfully) to maintain order in the town that between 1872 and 1885 was called everything from "hell on the plain" to "the wickedest city in America."*

Wyatt Earp and Bat Masterson are just two of the real marshals who tried to keep an eye on all the buffalo hunters, cavalry soldiers, and cowboys who drove herds of longhorns right down the main street of Dodge. Indian territory was 10 miles west of town, and Boot Hill Cemetery (where scores of men were buried with their boots on) was right on the main drag.

For the most part, the Wild West has been tamed, but in southwest Kansas, there's still a lot of wild (and crazy) goings-on: wild animals (elephants that take baths in public swimming pools), wild museum artifacts (people riding giant locust and huge cow hairballs), and artists using wild media (Pizza Hut boxes, for starters). Desperadoes still roam the plains, like Perry Smith and Richard Hickock, who shocked the world in 1959 and even lured Truman Capote out of New York to research In Cold Blood, *and M. T. Liggett, who is doing everything he can to kill any vestige of conventionality. Well, read on. You'll see.*

Of Course Pluto's Different—It Was Discovered by a Kansan
Burdett

Back in 2006, some astronomers with a bee in their bonnet decided to create a stir. What with no new planets having been discovered in 76 years, they started getting antsy and decided the astronomy circle needed shaking up. They started arguing that Pluto, the ninth planet, should be downgraded to a dwarf planet. Pluto, they insisted, was too puny, had an eccentric orbit, was solid rather than gaseous like the rest of the planets, and hadn't knocked other stuff out of its orbital neighborhood.

Unfortunately for Burdett, Kansas, the International Astronomical Union decided to rearrange all those science teachers' charts. Technically, Pluto is still a planet, but it's only a dwarf. Still, this little town of 241 has kept the sign on the west edge of town, the sign that tells about Clyde Tombaugh, the local kid who discovered Pluto—the only planet discovered by an American—on February 18, 1930.

When Clyde was just a kid, he built a 9-inch telescope from junk farm machinery and a shaft out of his father's 1910 Buick. At age 22, he wrote to the Lowell Observatory in Arizona, figuring experts there could explain some of the questions his high school instructors couldn't answer.

Those experts were so impressed with Tombaugh that they wrote him back and offered him a job. Two years later, when he was a still-wet-behind-the-ears 24, he found Pluto.

As he once said, "It was better than pitching hay on my father's farm."

The plaque honoring Tombaugh is west of Burdett on Highway 156. If you'd rather look at some stars in his honor, call the Clyde W. Tombaugh Observatory at the University of Kansas in Lawrence at (785) 864-3166.

In Search of Gold
Dodge City

In 1540, Francisco Vasquez de Coronado and 30 of his conquistadors traveled from Mexico into present-day Kansas on an expedition in search of the City of Gold. They crossed the Arkansas River near present-day Fort Dodge June 29, 1541. The Franciscan friar Juan de Padilla who traveled with them, held the first Christian service deep within the interior of the continent.

To commemorate this occasion, the Ford County Historical Society erected a 38-foot-tall cross on June 18, 1975. It sits on a hill within a 10-acre native grass prairie park. It is 1.5 miles east of Fort Dodge on US 400, making it about 8 minutes from downtown Dodge City.

There is a large parking area but wear your walking shoes. You slip through a little gate, go across the bridge, and then hike up the unkept path to the top of the hill where the cross is. There are a few park benches to sit on and rest when you get to the top. You'll want to take some time

Coronado Cross marks the spot. DEBORAH BOUZIDEN

and look out across the country. You can see for miles, east, west, and south. To be able to stand where Coronado may have stood all those many years ago, see what he saw, where the Santa Fe Trail passed, and where the Fort Dodge soldiers kept watch for Indians is well worth the 5-minute trek.

Dance All Night to the Dodge City Cow-Boy Band
Dodge City

Matt Dillon may be fictitious, but there really was a Long Branch Saloon, owned at various times by different folks, none of whom, unfortunately, was named Miss Kitty.

Between 1878 and 1883, the Long Branch was owned by one Chalk Beeson, who was also the guy who formed the world-famous Dodge City Cow-Boy Band. This brass band, led by a conductor keeping time with a pearl-handled six-shooter, had gigs at Madison Square Garden, the Chicago World's Fair, and Benjamin Harrison's 1889 presidential inauguration.

Band members wore gray cowboy hats, flannel shirts, leather chaps, spurs, and holsters with Colt .45s. Beeson loved to say that despite some folks' claims that the band was made up of musicians and not cowboys, any one of the band members could easily throw a steer over a horse in 10 seconds flat.

After their raging success at Harrison's inauguration, the Dodge City Cow-Boy Band launched a 2-year world tour. Unfortunately, it only lasted 6 months. The band had its last hurrah in the Spanish-American War, entertaining the 2nd US Cavalry in Cuba.

To see photos of the notorious band, visit the Boot Hill Museum, which has the old cemetery, Front Street, and a nightly cancan show. It's located on US 400 (also called Wyatt Earp Boulevard) just west of downtown. Phone (620) 227-8188 or visit www.boothill.org.

No Clocks, No Problem

Dodge City

When settlers started arriving to Dodge City, it was a little confusing. Were they in Central time or Mountain time? No one knew because at the time the two time zones cut right through where the train stopped. In 1897, town folks decided to fix the problem by building two sundials—one Mountain and one Central—and letting the dividing line run right between them. That worked for a while until powers that be decided to move the darn line several hundred miles to the west.

But while the line didn't stay there, the two sundials did. Today, still located by the train station, you can figure out what time it is in either time zone and never even have to look at your watch. Now, if it's cloudy, you're on your own.

Mountain and Central time zone sundials doing their thing DEBORAH BOUZIDEN

Down Under

Ellinwood may be the world's best town for weathering a tornado. Underneath the business district is an underground city that could easily fit the town's entire population and then some.

Back in the 1880s, when the underground city was fully operating, a passenger on the Atchison, Topeka and Santa Fe could get a haircut and a bath and then travel, via the secret underground passageway beneath Main Street, to an underground saloon.

In its heyday, Ellinwood's underground, which ran the full length of the business district, had Jung's Barber Shop, John Weber's Sample Room, Petz Meat Market, Wolitz Shoe Shop, Tom Drake's Harness Shop, a bathhouse, several saloons, and quite possibly an unmentionable place where "ladies of the night" entertained.

Several theories abound as to why the underground city was built back in the late 1800s. The most likely (and this part we know) is that Ellinwood was settled by beer-loving Germans. When changes in state liquor laws forced the closing of the town's highly successful aboveground brewery, the settlers probably did what any sensible beer lover would do. They went underground.

All but three of the underground's eight entrances (you had to lift wooden sidewalks to gain entry) have been sealed off, and most of the underground stores have been filled with sand.

Adrianna Dierolf, who rediscovered the underground city in 1980 after inheriting her grandfather's building, has managed to preserve 50 feet of tunnel, the harness shop, the barbershop, and the bathhouse. The barbershop still has faded pieces of Victorian wallpaper, wainscoting of cypress, a beaded ceiling, an old barber's chair, and a poker table. The bathhouse, with its stone walls and wooden floors, has graffiti left by a fastidious cowpoke who figured his wages right on the wall.

Until she sold it in 1992, Dierolf led tours by flashlight. It's still open for tours, but you have to call and make an appointment. Tours begin with check-in inside the Ellinwood Emporium, which is located at 2 N. Main St. You can call (620) 564-2400 or visit www.historicwolfhotel.com/underground-tours for more information.

Ellinwood's underground city PHYLLIS MILLER

Back when a shave an' a haircut was two bits PHYLLIS MILLER

Dodge City Flicks

Gunsmoke, a popular TV show set in this notorious cowboy town, ran for 20 years and 635 episodes before it bit the trail dust in 1975. But did you know the TV series was not an original idea? Not only was there a radio show also called *Gunsmoke*, which aired 413 episodes, but dozens of Dodge City movies came first. To name just a few:

- *Dodge City Trail*, 1936
- *Dodge City*, 1939, starring Errol Flynn
- *The King of Dodge City*, 1941
- *Vigilantes of Dodge City*, 1944
- *West of Dodge City*, 1947
- *Desperadoes of Dodge City*, 1948
- *Gunfight at Dodge City*, 1958 (before *Gunfight at the OK Corral*)

Trivia

It was July 1884. Gunfights had been outlawed, and the rabble-rousing Dodge City was looking for a new adrenaline rush.

A. B. Webster, a former mayor, decided to host America's first official bullfight.

Within 24 hours of his brainstorm, Webster had raised $10,000, hired five matadors from Mexico, and corralled a pen of 12 snorting bulls.

Despite warnings from the American Society for the Prevention of Cruelty to Animals, Webster and his Dodge City Driving Park and Fair Association built a grandstand for 4,000 and a 100-foot bullring, and attracted reporters from all over the US.

Water-Ski Kansas
Garden City

The public swimming pool in Garden City is big. Put enough adjectives in front of it and it's the world's largest. But rather than convince you that it's the largest free concrete outdoor municipal pool in the entire known universe, I'd rather tell you that it's big enough for a motorboat with two skiers. The Jaycees used to host bathtub races in it, and the city council considered closing it down for leaks. The elephants from the Lee Richardson Zoo (right across the street) used to take baths in it. However, since it was such a community draw, they put together a community pool committee to figure out how their pool could be saved. And saved it was, by breaking the repairs and upgrades down into bite-size pieces. The swimming pool holds 2.5 million gallons of water, it takes up half a city block, and its dimensions are 337 feet by 218 feet. It is divided into north and south halves and has multiple slides with a plunge pool.

With all those upgrades they have to charge a small fee these days, but when you've got the hot Kansas sun cooking you, there's no better place to be. To cool off and get your swim on, visit the pool in Finnup Park (620-276-1255) at 504 E. Maple St., right across from the zoo.

Elvis Spotted in Pizza Hut Delivery Box
Garden City

Give Jessie Montes a stack of Pizza Hut boxes and he's likely to find Elvis Presley. Give him a few refrigerator boxes and he might find Wyatt Earp, Tiger Woods, Jay Leno, or even Antonio Banderas. Using tweezers, razor blades, glue, and corrugated cardboard that he cuts into quarter-inch strips, Montes makes 3-D cardboard-inlay portraits and 3-D sculptures that look like they've been carved from wood. His rendition of Frank Sinatra sold for $2,250 at a New York City art gallery, and a more recent sculpture sold for 10 grand.

A former janitor for Dodge City High School, Montes had thrown away plenty of boxes before he recognized their potential as an art medium. In 1990, when his daughter was sent to the Gulf War, he needed something to

Dream Catcher, *a 3-D sculpture made from recycled cardboard*

calm his nerves, so he began cutting up boxes and gluing them together. In 1994, he showed a portrait he'd made of William Shakespeare to the high school art teacher.

The teacher was blown away. Her encouragement sparked Montes on.

In 1998, Duane West, a Garden City attorney, saw a show of Montes's unique artwork at the Garden City Community College. Not only did he buy the entire show of 25 pieces, he signed on to be his agent.

"This guy's a genius," West said. "He deserves all the recognition I can get him."

Although Jessie's work is available at galleries around the country, the biggest gallery was located in Duane West's Garden City basement until 2017 when West donated his collection to the Boy Scout Santa Fe Trail Council. West died in 2023, but his devotion to the artist and contribution to humanity lives on at the Boy Scouts of America Jessie Montes Art Gallery located at 402 Fulton St. Admission is free. Call (620) 275-5162 or visit Garden City's website at www.visitgck.com/things-to-do/boy-scouts -of-america-jessie-montes-art-gallery/.

The Great Plague of Grasshopper Postcards
Garden City

In the Dust Bowl days of the 1930s, Kansas swarmed with grasshoppers. Lots of people packed up and moved west, but Frank "Pop" Conard, a Garden City photographer and owner of a local radio station, decided to make the best of the disaster.

Yeehaw!!! FINNEY COUNTY HISTORICAL MUSEUM

One morning at 3:00, while thinking about the grasshoppers, he came up with the idea of turning them into a joke. Later that day, with the help of his trusty camera, he began making funny montages of people and giant grasshoppers.

Calling them "hopper whoppers," he made postcards of grasshoppers holding up trains, grasshoppers fighting men with sticks, and grasshoppers sprawled out on giant flatbed trucks. They sold like wildfire at cabin camps, service stations, and tourist spots.

By the time he retired in 1963, Conard had sold some 3 million hopper whoppers.

Replicas of the postcards are still for sale at the Finney County Historical Museum, 403 S. Fourth St. in Garden City, (620) 272-3664.

Hairballs R Us
Garden City

While calling around to find Pop Conard postcards, I discovered that I'd nearly overlooked another of Garden City's premier tourist attractions.

The Finney County Historical Museum is the proud owner of the world's largest hairball. It was found inside the stomach of a cow at Iowa Beef Processors in nearby Holcomb. When wet, it weighs 55 pounds. It's dry in the display case, so the weight dips to a mere 20 pounds, but even then it measures 37 inches in circumference. I probably don't need to tell you that that's bigger than a basketball.

Another meatpacking plant recently offered the historical society a second large hairball, but they turned it down. Probably a wise decision. Put two hairballs of that magnitude in one place and crowd control becomes a problem. Not to mention the fact that there's a rumor going around that you can actually touch the original one. Better stand back, that news will cause a stampede for sure, with there only being one to see and touch.

Finney County Historical Museum is at 403 S. Fourth St., near the entrance to the zoo. Phone (620) 272-3664.

Hairball today, hairball tomorrow FINNEY COUNTY HISTORICAL MUSEUM

All the Whos Down in Mixville Liked Scrap Metal a Lot

Great Bend

If you've looked everywhere for a Reel Supersonic Espresso-Powered Bug Sucker and still come up empty handed, consider a trip to Great Bend. Bob Mix, a metal fabricator by day and a mad scientist/da Vinci by night, has at least one he could loan you. He also has a pint-size pool shark welded from scrap metal, a 5-foot *Hesperornis regalis* with a spine made from a drilling rig gear chain, and a miniature castle he welded for his wife, Beverly, when it became obvious his promise to "build her a castle" wasn't coming true as quickly as he'd hoped.

Mix, who works and lives in Mixville, a trailer park near Great Bend where several family members live, can make anything. Tell him what you want, wait while it percolates in his creative mind, and before long he'll have made it out of something he either found or concocted from scrap metal. Mix has made miniature motorcycles, alien fishermen, German war

Bob Mix and his talking junk STEVE SCHULTZ

machines, English mastiffs, a family tree out of old car tires, and a Chariot of the Gods cycle that his grandson pedals proudly through Mixville.

Mix's biggest thrill is taking things that nobody else wants and giving them new life.

"Junk talks to me," he said. "I walk by it and it tells me what it wants me to do."

Mix's work can be seen at the Grassroots Art Center at 213 S. Main St. in Lucas.

Well, Well, Well
Greensburg

I'm happy to report that Greensburg's world's largest hand-dug well, long a standout tourist attraction, was one of the few things that survived the tornado of 2007 with flying colors. Unfortunately, the gift shop behind the big well flew off with Dorothy, and for legal reasons, no one was allowed down the four flights of metal steps for a few years.

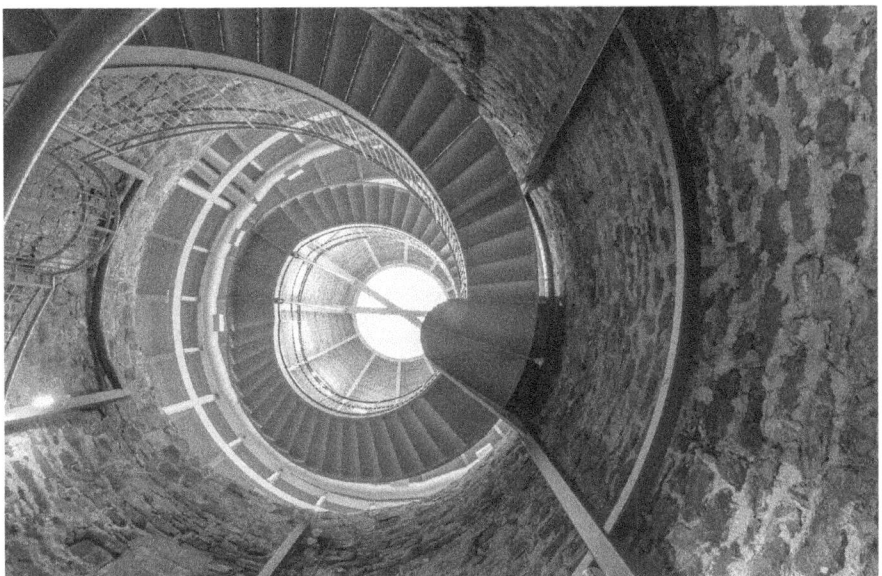

Way down to the bottom of the well CITY OF GREENSBURG

Thankfully, the 109-foot well, which was excavated in 1887 with shovels, picks, pulleys, and ropes, reopened in 2010 when the new gift shop was rebuilt. Needless to say, Greensburg had a few other priorities with the rebuilding after the twister.

The humongous well was built by the big cheeses at Santa Fe Railroad, who were racing the Rock Island Line across the country. They figured a well to power the steam locomotives would give the company a leg up. For more than a year, crews of 12 to 15 farmers, cowboys, and itinerants were hired each morning at sunup and paid $1 a day to dig.

Despite their hard work, the Rock Island Line won the race, the Santa Fe tracks were dismantled, and the giant well was left to provide the railroad-less town with water. It did a good job for 50 years, but in 1937 the City of Greensburg came up with an alternative water source and the well was turned into a tourist attraction.

Guests can descend the steps into the gigantic man-made hole. The big well is located at 315 S. Sycamore St. in Greensburg, or you can call (620) 723-4102 or check them out at www.bigwell.org.

Visitors going down CITY OF GREENSBURG

It Came from Outer Space

Greensburg

Before you go traipsing down those stairs, you'll want to stop a minute and take a look at "The Space Wanderer." That's what locals call the 1,000-pound pallasite meteorite. According to accounts, H. O. Stockwell found the space rock at the Peck Farm not far from Greensburg in 1949, using a metal detector. Now, they had to dig deep—6 feet down—to get the rock freed, so no one knows how long it had been resting there when it was found or where exactly it came from, except "out there."

When it was identified as one of the largest ever found, locals wanted to keep the meteorite in the area. After all, it was found on Kansas land and residents didn't see any reason why it should be carried off to a museum in the East. So, with the urging of residents and the Greensburg Chamber of Commerce behind them, they made an offer and got themselves a meteorite.

Stockwell getting the rock out of the ground
CITY OF GREENSBURG

Surface of the meteorite CITY OF GREENSBURG

It was placed in the Greensburg Big Well Museum and sits there under glass where visitors can go see—and thousands do each year. The Smithsonian in Washington, DC, has a specimen weighing 740 pounds from the same shower, but "The Space Wanderer" is bigger.

You will find the world's largest pallasite meteorite in the gift shop of the world's largest hand-dug well.

In Cold Blood
Holcomb

Before Charles Manson, Son of Sam, and Jeffrey Dahmer, there were Perry Smith and Richard Hickock, two ex-cons who met in a Lansing prison. On November 14, 1959, they drove to Holcomb and murdered Herbert Clutter, his wife, Bonnie, and two of their four kids.

The crime was all the more shocking considering that Holcomb, a town of fewer than 200 people, was a quiet, unassuming little community that no one would have ever heard of had Truman Capote not spent 5 years and 343 pages on it in his best-selling true crime novel, *In Cold Blood*. Smith and Hickock got a bad tip from a fellow con who had once worked for Herb Clutter, the prosperous owner of River Valley Farm. Mistakenly believing he left thousands of dollars in the family safe, Smith and Hickock left the scene of the crime with nothing but $50, a transistor radio, and binoculars. They were executed for the four murders in 1965.

All these years later, the Clutters' murder site, a five-bedroom, two-story brick and clapboard house, still attracts interested folks who drive 8 miles west of Garden City to see it. The four murdered victims were laid to rest at Valley View Cemetery in Garden City.

What a Gas!
Hugoton

Kansas has a gas field that's five times bigger than the state of Rhode Island. It's the largest gas field in North America.

Millions of years ago, when the earth's crust was rumbling and roaring and pushing up the Rocky Mountains, Kansas got left with an abundance of natural gas and oil. Not a bad geological trade-off when you think about it. Colorado got Marla Maples in Bogner designer ski wear. We get enough natural gas to heat every home in the state until 2350.

Natural gas, which forms between layers of chalk, shale, limestone, and sandstone, is often accompanied by helium. Sure enough, the Hugoton Gas Field also contains the world's largest reserve of helium.

To learn more about the Hugoton Gas Field, stop by the Stevens County Gas and Historical Museum in Hugoton. It's open 1 to 5 p.m. Monday through Friday and 2 to 4 p.m. Saturday and Sunday at 905 S. Adams St., (620) 544-8751; www.stevenscountyks.com/museum/.

Better Than Colt .45s and Dedicated US Marshals

LaCrosse

For years, nothing could put a crimp in the Wild West's crazy gunslingers and cattle rustlers. But then barbed wire was invented in 1874 and strung across the prairies. Cattle rustlers and cowboys had little choice but to calm down. No wonder its inventor claimed it was "cheaper than dirt and stronger than steel."

LaCrosse, which holds the title of Barbed Wire Capital of the World, has a museum dedicated to the formidable fencing, and hosts an annual Swap and Sell, where barbed wire collectors from around the country converge. The museum features some 2,100 types and styles of devil's rope (that's what they called it back then), a 72-pound crow's nest made of barbed wire, and a collection of barbed wire liniments, potions that were sold to cure cuts and injuries incurred by man or beast.

At the Swap and Sell, held the first weekend in May, there's a riveting splicing contest in which splicers armed with nothing but leather gloves are required to put a barbed wire fence back together, strong enough to suspend a 75-pound weight.

The Museum of Barbed Wire is located at 120 W. First St. and can be contacted at (785) 222-9900 or www.rushcounty.org/BarbedWireMuseum/.

Diplomatic Relations in Pancake Flipping
Liberal

In 1949, R. J. Leete, president of the Liberal Jaycees, heard about a unique pancake-flipping race in Olney, England. He wrote to the vicar of Olney's St. Peter's and Paul's Church, the sponsor of the centuries-old race, and challenged him to an international match. The housewives of Liberal, he proposed, would race against the housewives of Olney.

Olney, of course, had a leg up. They'd been flipping pancakes and racing with skillets since 1445, when one of the church members got so caught up in her pancake making that she almost missed the Shrove Tuesday church service. Because lard was forbidden during Lent, the women of the village fried stacks and stacks of pancakes in order to use up their remaining fat stashes. Still clad in her apron, with a skillet in her hand, the tardy woman raced to church, flipping the last of her pancakes as she ran. The next year, her neighbors decided to get in on the act, challenging her to a race with skillets, aprons, and pancakes. Running from the town pump to the church steps every year, the winner of the race is presented with a "kiss of peace" by the bell ringer.

The Olney vicar liked Leete's suggestion, and on February 21, 1950, the first International Pancake Race was staged. It has been held every year since, attracting thousands of visitors and loads of media attention. So much, in fact, that the 1980 race was declared a tie because a television news truck inadvertently blocked the finish line in Olney.

To watch the Liberal race, which runs from Sixth and Kansas Streets to Third and Lincoln Streets, be on hand about quarter till noon any Shrove Tuesday. You can visit the International Pancake Day Hall of Fame any day. To get a copy of the pancake recipe (it serves 100 and uses 280 pounds of pancake mix, 10 dozen eggs, and 35 gallons of water), check out www.pancakeday.net or call (620) 620-6423.

There's No Place Like Dorothy's House

Liberal

What do Salman Rushdie, Carl Sagan, and Gloria Estefan have in common? At one time or another, all of them were members of IWOC. Never heard of it? It's the International Wizard of Oz Club, and the above mentioned are just three of the club's 3,000 members. Founded in 1957, the club tracks all things having to do with L. Frank Baum and *The Wizard of Oz*, which means they're certainly up on Liberal, Kansas. Not only does Liberal have Dorothy's house—a 1907 farmhouse that looks just like the house she couldn't wait to return to—it also has a 5,000-square-foot animated *Wizard of Oz* complex and 20 Dorothy tour guides, all of whom have gone through an intensive two-week Dorothy training.

That's right, if you fork over the $12.50 admission fee, you'll be led by one of the Dorothys (of course she'll be wearing a blue-checked gingham dress and ruby-red slippers) down the yellow brick road. You'll see animated Munchkins, good and bad witches, talking trees, and winged monkeys. At the end of the tour, if you can still stand more, you can hurry to the gift shop in the Coronado Museum (it's on the same grounds), where the movie is shown from the moment the museum opens until it closes.

Every second weekend in October, the museum hosts a 2-day Oz Fest. Visit the museum at 567 Yellow Brick Rd. (aka Cedar) or call (620) 624-7624 or go to www.dorothyshouse.com.

There's a What? Where? Who Knew?

Coldwater

When my grandfather said we were going fishing, I thought he was talking about to a pond. When he said he was going to take his boat, I asked him if we were going to be gone all day. I wasn't aware of any pond big enough for a boat. He said no and after a few more inquiries, he told me to just wait and see. So I did.

Imagine my surprise when just a couple of miles south of Coldwater, nestled among the landscape like a turtle in its shell, sits Coldwater Lake.

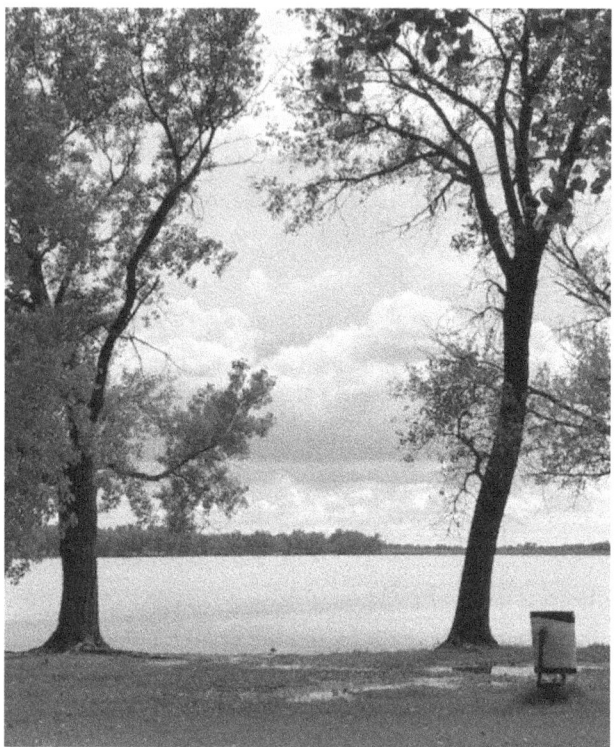

Coldwater Lake, the place to go relax DEBORAH BOUZIDEN

The lake sits on a 930-acre park with 109 camping spots that have water, electric, and sewer hookups. The lake itself covers 250 acres. Now, I don't know about a yacht, but you can put a fishing boat, ski boat, or even jet skis on it.

It's open year-round and even though full accommodation sites close down in September, 17 rough camping sites are still available. Reservations are required for all the sites. According to the caretaker, the 17 sites are usually filled with hunters, so make your reservations early. The lake is city owned, and there are some special events planned here like the Fourth of July.

We put the boat on the water and caught some crappie and catfish—only two of the types of fish Kansas Fish and Game stocks the lake with, along with wipers and largemouth bass. Most people are like me, have no idea there is a lake, a little jewel sitting out in the middle of nowhere in southwestern Kansas. To see for yourself, travel 2.5 miles south of Coldwater on Highway 183 and make a right turn at the Coldwater Lake sign.

Little Town That Can and Does

Wilmore

About 75 miles southeast of Dodge City sits a little town no one seems to know about unless you've been there. Wilmore used to be a bustling town with a train station, churches, a grocery store, and even an elementary school. Today, there's the post office and a hardware-type store, opened on request, where you might be able to purchase a hammer or a candy bar. But don't let that stop you from visiting because there are a few things you might want to check out.

First is the grain elevator, which is still operational. When I first visited Wilmore, I remember I was captivated by a huge mural painted on the side of it. It was painted by Stan Herd in celebration of Wilmore's Centennial in 1987. It depicts the legendary "coin toss" between rancher C. C. Peppard

A mural almost bigger than the town DEBORAH BOUZIDEN

and his foreman, Thomas Wilmore. The coin toss was over what to name the town. Peppard won the coin toss but named the town after Wilmore. The mural shows the town in its busier days. You can still get up close and personal to the mural, and if you've never been near a grain elevator, this is your chance.

Second is the Wilmore Carousel. It is located right off Main Street, just about 2 blocks from the grain elevator. Ernie Griffin had always wanted a carousel, and in 2013 he had his chance. He and his wife, Christy, bought it to Wilmore. It had been built in Venice, Italy, about 10 years earlier, had been used in shopping malls and then stored in a warehouse. Beautifully restored, the bright yellow, orange, and red colors plus the many carousel

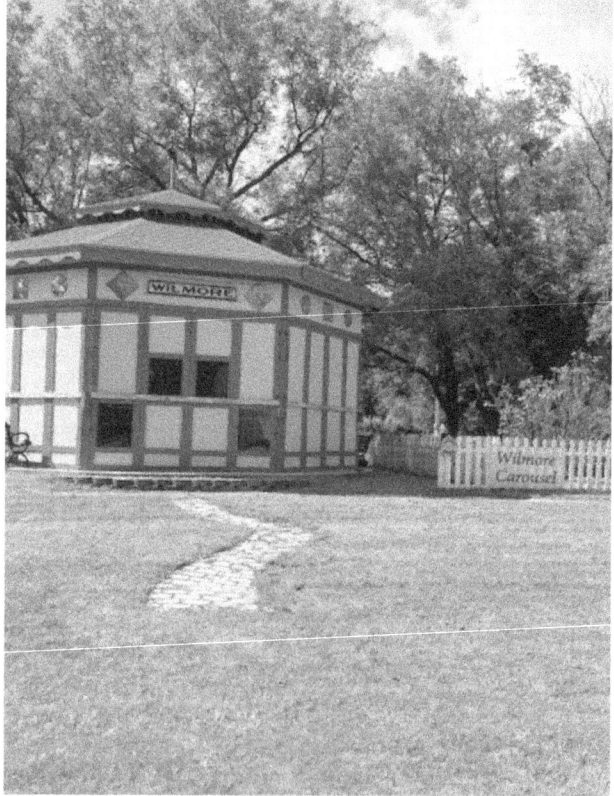

Round and round on the Wilmore Carousel

DEBORAH BOUZIDEN

Sears home built to stand the test of time and tornadoes DEBORAH BOUZIDEN

lights brighten up that end of town. And yes, you can ride one of the 13 horses. There is no charge. To ride, you just pull up and honk. If the Griffins or a neighbor are available, they'll come out and turn it on.

Third is the 1913 Sears Catalog home. It is located right next to the carousel and owned by none other than the Griffins. Sears sold between 70,000 and 75,000 homes between 1908 and 1940. This home cost $823 when it was purchased in 1913. It was sold as a kit and came with millwork, flooring, ceiling, siding, finishing lumber, gutter, sash weights, hardware, paint, lumber, lath, and shingles. All you had to supply was the elbow grease.

My parents lived in the home for 3 or 4 years before they moved to the other side of town. My dad loved to take people through and show them the unique doorways and the parlor. My mom would share some of the history. (She was hesitant to share how Mrs. Alcana Ferrin, one of the former owners, was laid out in her casket right there in the parlor for a few days while mourners came and paid their respects.)

Today, sharing all that information is left up to the Griffins. I know they'll be more than happy to tell you the home's history if they're there. They don't spend all their time in Wilmore, so call (620) 738-4420 to see if they're in town.

So, if you're traveling down Highway 160 and want to visit a town with a big history and a big heart, turn on Road 19. You can see the grain elevators when you turn and they'll lead you straight to Main Street.

Birth of a (Hatchet-Wielding) Nation
Medicine Lodge

If only Al-Anon had existed back in 1899, Carry A. Nation, the infamous hatchet-wielding teetotaler from Medicine Lodge, Kansas, could have saved herself a lot of jail time.

Until that fateful day in 1899 when Carry and Mrs. Wesley Cain, fellow chair of the Medicine Lodge Women's Christian Temperance Union, put on their best dresses and bonnets and headed to Mort Strong's Saloon, Nation lived a relatively quiet life.

She was a preacher's wife, a mom, and a devout Christian, thanks to 6 years of a youthful illness that required bed rest and study of the Bible. Sure, she fought with her second husband, David Nation, tried to write his sermons and coach him on proper elocution, but overall, she was just an everyday common citizen.

But once the fervor of the temperance movement began boiling in her veins, there was no stopping her. Not only did she successfully close down all seven saloons in Medicine Lodge, she went on a national rampage, chopping up saloons with rocks, clubs, and hatchets. Eventually, her infamy prompted speaking engagements at Carnegie Hall, lecture tours of Europe (where she tried to convince England of the evils of tea), and a nationally distributed newsletter called *The Smasher's Mail*.

As for the Al-Anon . . . Carry's hatred of demon rum had less to do with Kansas being the first state to make liquor illegal and more to do with her first husband, Dr. Charles Gloyd, who drank himself to death before Carry was 24, leaving her with an infant daughter.

To buy a miniature hatchet, a silver or gold version of the one Carry often sold to raise jail bond, visit the brick home that Carry and her second husband, David Nation, bought for $2,500 in 1880 when they moved to Kansas from Texas. On the National Register of Historic Places, the home is now a museum at 209–211 W. Fowler St., (620) 886-3553, www.kansas travel.org/carrynation.htm.

Crossed Smoke Signals

Medicine Lodge

In 1867, before Carry Nation came along, Medicine Lodge hosted Dog Fat, Iron Mountain, Black Kettle, Ten Bears, Kicking Eagle, Gap in the Wood, Standing Feather, and 15,000 other Kiowa, Comanche, Cheyenne, Arapaho, and Apache Indians who made the mistake of believing government commissioners who promised to quit killing buffalo in return for the right to build railroads across their lands.

The Medicine Lodge Peace Treaty, a historic treaty that basically marked the beginning of the end for Native ways, was signed October 21, 1867, on the banks of the Medicine River and Elm Creek. The 15,000 Indians from the five Great Plains tribes set up camp near this sacred Native spot, and 500 cavalry soldiers, federal bigwigs, and reporters from around the world showed up.

In case you're wondering the outcome of the treaty, just look around. The trains, of course, zoom by at the rate of hundreds a day. The buffalo? Let's just say the herds that once covered the plains are long gone.

Every 3 years, the city of Medicine Lodge reenacts the famous peace treaty. It's no small feat. The show alone employs 1,200 actors. Thousands show up at the Native rock amphitheater for the 3-day celebration, which has been going on since 1927. For more info, call the Peace Treaty Office at (620) 886-9815, or visit www.peacetreaty.org.

Claude, Claude, Claude of the Jungle

Montezuma

Ever been to Angkor, Cambodia, or Trondheim, Norway? Claude Stauth and his wife, Donnie, sure have. In fact, the longtime residents of Montezuma (population 879) traveled to 95 countries on six continents before they died and left their entire collection of "travel souvenirs" to their "family," the citizens of Montezuma.

Their extensive collection of rare Indigenous art, tribal instruments, weapons, costumes, and statues is housed in a striking earth-colored copper-roofed structure worthy of any large city.

In addition to Berber daggers, thumb pianos from Cameroon, and carved lion leg bones, the Stauth Memorial Museum showcases bookends, lamps, and ashtrays made from parts of big game animals.

They're not from countries you can't pronounce. They were made right here in Kansas by Ralph Fry, a hunter and the Stauths' neighbor, who owned a hardware store in town but was so avid in his conservation practices that he was made an honorary game warden. The weird lamps and bookends were the result of Fry's belief in using all parts of the animals he shot. There are also lots of big moose heads and exotic game animals in the Fry collection.

The Stauths, generous folks that they were, wanted the museum to go beyond their personal travels, so a large portion of the museum is dedicated to traveling exhibits from such sources as the Smithsonian Institution and the London Museum of Natural History. Donnie also designated one room of the building for her bridge club.

To see lip disks from Bunia, carved lion leg bones from Goma, and ivory from Nepal, visit the Stauth Memorial Museum at 111 N. Aztec St. in Montezuma, (620) 846-2527, www.stauthmemorialmuseum.org.

Political Cartoons on Highway 400

Mullinville

M. T. Liggett would never have called himself an artist. He had enough of that in grade school, when his art teacher told the class to paint a dinosaur, then frowned on the fact that Liggett painted his purple and gave it wings.

No, he had a good career in the air force, didn't take up art—or what some people like to think of as art—until he retired to the family farm in Mullinville. With tousled silver hair, a red bandanna, overalls, and black cowboy hat, Liggett could have easily passed for a typical Kansas farmer.

Until you see his totems—wild political statements mounted on poles, standing side by side, many moving in the wind. Working from an old house he painted and called the "wacky shack," Liggett took the junk farmers left down by the barn and welded it into his controversial interpretations of the world.

Political lampoonery at its best STEVE SCHULTZ

> **Trivia**
>
> Just outside Montezuma is 20 square miles of windmills. Gray County Wind Energy, owner of the windmill farm, erected 170 windmills, each of which weighs 147,000 pounds and generates massive BPUs (Basic Power Units) of electricity.

Hundreds of totems lampooning everything from Monica Lewinsky's blue dress and Roller Derby queens to what Liggett called "Doctor Lorena Bobbitt" and Archimedes line a half-mile stretch on US 400.

For a while, the powers that be tried to outlaw them, tried to impose a roadside ban, said they caused too much of a disturbance. Luckily, the ban didn't stick, and Liggett continued to caricature politicians and their bureaucratic nonsense.

To learn more about the visitor center and Liggett's art, you can www .mtliggettartenvironment.org or call (620) 723-2600. To view Liggett's political lampoonery, drive west on US 400 from Mullinville. You can't miss them.

Spiker and the Gang
Scott City

To say the Keystone Gallery is in Scott City is a bit misleading. This unique art gallery/curio shop/fossil-hunting headquarters is actually in the middle of the Kansas Niobrara Chalk formation, 18 miles north of Scott City. A herd of 200 buffalo roam nearby. The closest structure over two stories is Monument Rocks. But since Scott City is where Chuck Bonner and his wife, Barbara Shelton, get their mail, that's where they claim to be from. Their gallery has at least two distinctions separating it from other art gallery/ curio shop/fossil-hunting headquarters. First, the limestone building used to be a Pilgrim Holiness Church, built in 1916 by locals hankering for a little religion. Second, it meets all its electricity needs from the sun and the wind.

When Bonner and Shelton decided to renovate the little church in 1981, they figured the last thing they needed to do was depend on the mainstream electric grid. They went in with shovels, cleared out the debris

Trivia

Plains has the widest main street in America. Grand Avenue, the main drag through this tiny town in Meade County, measures 155 feet, 5 inches across, inspiring Ripley's Believe It or Not! to give it the record-breaking nod. All we know is it takes 69 hand-holding fourth graders to reach storefront to storefront, and if you want to holler at your neighbor across the street, you'd better take a megaphone.

(the church had been abandoned since 1950), and added solar panels and a wind charger.

Show up at the gallery and you never know what Bonner, a painter and fossil hunter, might be up to. He could be leading fossil hunters on an expedition to the Smoky Hill River Valley in Spiker, his 1949 Chevy Suburban, or he could be painting in the back room. If he's around, he'll be happy to tell you everything he knows about the museum's (yes, it's a museum

Mugging for the camera KEYSTONE GALLERY

too) late-Cretaceous study collection. Bonner and Shelton themselves have found 100 significant fossils, many of which now reside at universities and natural history museums around the country. They're particularly proud of a 4-foot skull of a *Pteranodon*, a flying reptile, that's on display at the Natural History Museum of Los Angeles County.

To see Bonner's unique collection or buy everything from black-and-white mosasaur T-shirts to onyx fiber-optic spheres, visit the Keystone Gallery, 18 miles north of Scott City on US 83 (620-872-2762; www.key stonegallery.com).

That's One Way to Beat the Tax Man
Ulysses

During western migration, towns all over newly settled lands fought rigorous battles over who would get the county seat, who would get the railroad. Ulysses, which did outwit Appomattox in the struggle for Grant County seat, ended up going so far into debt to do it that the whole town was in danger of foreclosure.

A few months before government tax men came to foreclose, however, a contingent of folks led by George Washington Earp (Wyatt's cousin and the mayor of the town) loaded the town's 12 restaurants, four hotels, and 12 saloons onto rollers and moved them 3 miles west. When the foreclosure agents showed up, the only thing left was a masonry school.

You can hear all about the town that outwitted the tax man at the Historic Adobe Museum and Hotel Edwards, a restored frontier hotel, located at 300 E. Oklahoma St. (620-356-3009; www.grantcoks.org/552 /Visit-Our-Museum).

Shoo, Fly, Don't Bother Me

The flyswatter was invented in Kansas. It all started with the *Mosquito Gazette,* a weekly newsletter published in 1906 by Dr. Samuel Crumbine, the state's first secretary of health. Believing that flies were the main source of typhoid fever, Crumbine headlined a summer issue of his state medical bulletin with the words "Swat the Fly."

Frank Rose, a Weir City teacher and local Boy Scout leader, saw that issue of the *Gazette* and wanted his troop to be involved. He bought wire mesh, which his Scouts cut into squares and attached to wooden yard-sticks given away by the local drugstore.

Crumbine, who often dressed in a Prince Albert coat with a six-shooter strapped to his hip, was also partially responsible for the invention of Dixie cups. One of his first goals as executive secretary of the brand-new state board of health was to outlaw public drinking cups. Hugh Moore, an ex-Kansan living in New England, showed Crumbine samples of a throw-away cup he'd made from paper. Crumbine suggested he sell his invention in penny vending machines on railroad cars. This cup was the first product Moore manufactured in his new business, the Dixie Cup Company.

Acknowledgments

A project of this magnitude is never done alone. I spoke to many people who shared their life experiences in their beloved state, and for that I am truly grateful. I would like to thank all the people who had a hand in making this book a success, but especially to Jeannie Stramel, who took the time to read through the book and advise me on some deletions and point me in the direction for some additions; Erika Nelson; Marci Penner; Linda Clover; and Marilyn Helmer. Also, all those at businesses, historical societies, and museums who helped me love Kansas a little bit more with each new discovery.

Index

About the Author

Pam Grout has written more books than she can count on both hands. Despite her literary agent's advice to build a platform (which means pick a genre and stick with it), she has written books about breathing, God, creativity, the environment, the mind-boggling power of one person to make a difference, and Colorado, to name but a few topics. She lives in Lawrence, Kansas, with her amazingly cool daughter, Tasman.

About the Reviser

Deborah Bouziden has been writing and publishing books and articles since 1983. She writes in different genres, dipping into fiction and poetry, but mainly sticking to nonfiction. Over the years, she has had hundreds of articles published and over 20 books at last count. She loves research, doing interviews, and learning about new places to visit across the country. In her other life, she works as a medical assistant at a clinic in Estes Park, Colorado.

Explore More

GLOBE PEQUOT IS YOUR GUIDE to special places, focusing on local pride close to home and helping you discover new destinations to explore from coast to coast. We publish books about iconic people and places, tapping into regional interest, history, cooking and food culture, folklore and the paranormal – all the things that make each region unique. With more than 75 years in publishing, we strive to give you the most up-to-date, regional information by local experts.

Globe Pequot

Available wherever books are sold.
Orders can also be placed at www.GlobePequot.com,
by phone at (800) 223-2336,
or by email at Purchaseorders@simonandschuster.com.